Nadia Murad is a human rights activist. She is the recipient of the Vaclav Havel Human Rights Prize and the Sakharov Prize, and is the UN's first Goodwill Ambassador for the Dignity of Survivors of Human Trafficking. Together with Yazda, a Yazidi rights organisation, she is currently working to bring the Islamic State before the International Criminal Court on charges of genocide and crimes against humanity. She is also the founder of Nadia's Initiative, a programme dedicated to helping survivors of genocide and human trafficking to heal and rebuild their communities.

Jenna Krajeski is a journalist based in New York. Her work from Turkey, Egypt, Iraq and Syria has been published in print and online in the *New Yorker*, *Slate*, *The Nation*, *Virginia Quarterly Review* and elsewhere. She was a 2016 Knight-Wallace Fellow at the University of Michigan.

nadiamurad.org

'*The Last Girl* offers powerful insight into the barbarity the Yazidi suffered alongside glimpses into their mystical culture . . . this is an important book by a brave woman, fresh testament to humankind's potential for chilling and inexplicable evil'   Ian Birrell, *The Times*

'Courageous . . . Anyone who wants to understand the so called Islamic State should read *The Last Girl*'   *The Economist*

'This devastating memoir unflinchingly recounts her experiences and questions the complicity of witnesses who acquiesced in the suffering of others'   *New Yorker*

'Nadia Murad has put a human face on one of the world's most complicated and intractable conflicts'   *Sunday Business Post*

THE LAST GIRL

MY STORY OF CAPTIVITY
AND MY FIGHT
AGAINST THE ISLAMIC STATE

NADIA MURAD

with Jenna Krajeski

virago

VIRAGO

First published in the United States in 2017 by Tim Duggan Books
First published in Great Britain in 2017 by Virago Press
This paperback edition published in 2018 by Virago Press

16

A CIP catalogue record for this book
is available from the British Library.

ISBN 978-0-349-00977-3

Printed and bound in Great Britain by
Clays Ltd, Elcograf S.p.A.

Papers used by Virago are from well-managed forests
and other responsible sources.

Virago Press
An imprint of
Little, Brown Book Group
Carmelite House
50 Victoria Embankment
London EC4Y 0DZ

An Hachette UK Company
www.hachette.co.uk

www.virago.co.uk

This book is written for every Yazidi.

TURKEY

PKK Concentration

Rojava
(Syrian Kurdistan)

YPG Concentration

Zakho

Duhok

Lalish

Mosul Dam
Lake

SYRIA

Mount Sinjar

Sinjar City
Solagh

Tal
Afar

Bahzani

Bashiqa

Siba
Sheikh
Khider

Tel
Ezeir

Kocho

Mosul

Hamdaniya
District

Tigris River

IRAQ

IRAQ AND THE MIDDLE EAST

TURKEY

Raqqa
SYRIA

Mosul

IRAN

Baghdad

JORDAN

IRAQ

KUWAIT

SAUDI
ARABIA

N
W E
S

0 miles   25   50
0 km   25   50

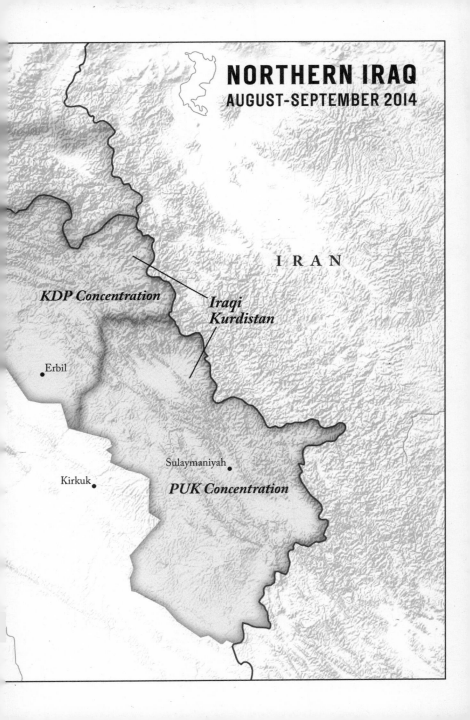

NORTHERN IRAQ
AUGUST–SEPTEMBER 2014

IRAN

KDP Concentration

Iraqi Kurdistan

Erbil

Sulaymaniyah

PUK Concentration

Kirkuk

Foreword

NADIA MURAD IS NOT JUST MY CLIENT, SHE IS MY FRIEND. When we were introduced in London, she asked if I would act as her lawyer. She explained that she would not be able to provide funds, that the case would likely be long and unsuccessful. But before you decide, she had said, hear my story.

In 2014, ISIS attacked Nadia's village in Iraq, and her life as a twenty-one-year-old student was shattered. She was forced to watch her mother and brothers be marched off to their deaths. And Nadia herself was traded from one ISIS fighter to another. She was forced to pray, forced to dress up and put makeup on in preparation for rape, and one night was brutally abused by a group of men until she was unconscious. She showed me her scars from cigarette burns and beatings. And she told me that throughout her ordeal ISIS militants would call her a "dirty unbeliever" and brag about conquering Yazidi women and wiping their religion from the earth.

Nadia was one of thousands of Yazidis taken by ISIS to be sold in markets and on Facebook, sometimes for as little as twenty dollars. Nadia's mother was one of eighty older women who were executed and buried in an unmarked grave. Six of her brothers were among the hundreds of men who were murdered in a single day.

What Nadia was telling me about is genocide. And genocide

doesn't happen by accident. You have to plan it. Before the genocide began, the ISIS "Research and Fatwa Department" studied
the Yazidis and concluded that, as a Kurdish-speaking group that
did not have a holy book, Yazidis were nonbelievers whose enslavement was a "firmly established aspect of the Shariah." This is
why, according to ISIS's warped morality, Yazidis—unlike Christians, Shias, and others—can be systematically raped. Indeed,
this was to be one of the most effective ways to destroy them.

What followed was the establishment of a bureaucracy of evil
on an industrial scale. ISIS even released a pamphlet entitled
Questions and Answers on Taking Captives and Slaves to provide
more guidelines. "Question: Is it permissible to have intercourse
with a female slave who has not reached puberty? Answer: It is
permissible to have intercourse with the female slave who hasn't
reached puberty if she is fit for intercourse. Question: Is it permissible to sell a female captive? Answer: It is permissible to buy, sell,
or gift female captives and slaves, for they are merely property."

When Nadia told me her story in London, it had been almost
two years since ISIS's genocide against the Yazidis had begun.
Thousands of Yazidi women and children were still held captive
by ISIS, but no member of ISIS had been prosecuted in a court
anywhere in the world for these crimes. Evidence was being lost
or destroyed. And prospects for justice looked bleak.

Of course, I took the case. And Nadia and I spent more than
a year campaigning together for justice. We met repeatedly with
the Iraqi government, United Nations representatives, members
of the UN Security Council, and ISIS victims. I prepared reports,
provided drafts and legal analysis, and gave speeches imploring
the UN to act. Most of our interlocutors told us it would be impossible: the Security Council had not taken action on international justice in years.

But just as I write this foreword, the UN Security Council has
adopted a landmark resolution creating an investigation team that

will collect evidence of the crimes committed by ISIS in Iraq. This is a major victory for Nadia and all the victims of ISIS, because it means that evidence will be preserved and that individual ISIS members can be put on trial. I sat next to Nadia in the Security Council when the resolution was adopted unanimously. And as we watched fifteen hands go up, Nadia and I looked at each other and smiled.

As a human-rights lawyer, my job is often to be the voice of those who have been silenced: the journalist behind bars or the victims of war crimes fighting for their day in court. There is no doubt ISIS tried to silence Nadia when they kidnapped and enslaved her, raped and tortured her, and killed seven members of her family in a single day.

But Nadia refused to be silenced. She has defied all the labels that life has given her: Orphan. Rape victim. Slave. Refugee. She has instead created new ones: Survivor. Yazidi leader. Women's advocate. Nobel Peace Prize nominee. United Nations Goodwill Ambassador. And now author.

Over the time I have known her, Nadia has not only found her voice, she has become the voice of every Yazidi who is a victim of genocide, every woman who has been abused, every refugee who has been left behind.

Those who thought that by their cruelty they could silence her were wrong. Nadia Murad's spirit is not broken, and her voice will not be muted. Instead, through this book, her voice is louder than ever.

AMAL CLOONEY
Barrister
September 2017

PART I

Chapter 1

EARLY IN THE SUMMER OF 2014, WHILE I WAS BUSY PREPAR-ing for my last year of high school, two farmers disappeared from their fields just outside Kocho, the small Yazidi village in northern Iraq where I was born and where, until recently, I thought I would live for the rest of my life. One moment the men were lounging peacefully in the shade of scratchy homemade tarps, and the next they were captive in a small room in a nearby village, home mostly to Sunni Arabs. Along with the farmers, the kidnappers took a hen and a handful of her chicks, which confused us. "Maybe they were just hungry," we said to one another, although that did nothing to calm us down.

Kocho, for as long as I have been alive, has been a Yazidi village, settled by the nomadic farmers and shepherds who first arrived in the middle of nowhere and decided to build homes to protect their wives from the desert-like heat while they walked their sheep to better grass. They chose land that would be good for farming, but it was a risky location, on the southern edge of Iraq's Sinjar region, where most of the country's Yazidis live, and very close to non-Yazidi Iraq. When the first Yazidi families arrived in the mid-1950s, Kocho was inhabited by Sunni Arab farmers working for landlords in Mosul. But those Yazidi families had hired a lawyer to buy the land—the lawyer, himself a Muslim, is still considered a hero—and by the time I was born, Kocho had grown to about two hundred families, all of them Yazidi and as close as if we were one big family, which we nearly were.

The land that made us special also made us vulnerable. Yazidis have been persecuted for centuries because of our religious beliefs, and, compared to most Yazidi towns and villages, Kocho is far from Mount Sinjar, the high, narrow mountain that has sheltered us for generations. For a long time we had been pulled between the competing forces of Iraq's Sunni Arabs and Sunni Kurds, asked to deny our Yazidi heritage and conform to Kurdish or Arab identities. Until 2013, when the road between Kocho and the mountain was finally paved, it would take us almost an hour to drive our white Datsun pickup across the dusty roads through Sinjar City to the base of the mountain. I grew up closer to Syria than to our holiest temples, closer to strangers than to safety.

A drive in the direction of the mountain was joyful. In Sinjar City we could find candy and a particular kind of lamb sandwich we didn't have in Kocho, and my father almost always stopped to let us buy what we wanted. Our truck kicked up clouds of dust as we moved, but I still preferred to ride in the open air, lying flat in the truck bed until we were outside the village and away from our curious neighbors, then popping up to feel the wind whip through my hair and watch the blur of livestock feeding along the road. I easily got carried away, standing more and more upright in the back of the truck until my father or my eldest brother, Elias, shouted at me that if I wasn't careful, I would go flying over the side.

In the opposite direction, away from those lamb sandwiches and the comfort of the mountain, was the rest of Iraq. In peacetime, and if he wasn't in a hurry, it might take a Yazidi merchant fifteen minutes to drive from Kocho to the nearest Sunni village to sell his grain or milk. We had friends in those villages—girls I met at weddings, teachers who spent the term sleeping in Kocho's school, men who were invited to hold our baby boys during their ritual circumcision—and from then on bonded to that Yazidi family as a *kiriv*, something like a god-parent. Muslim doctors traveled to Kocho or to Sinjar City to treat us when we were sick, and Muslim merchants drove through town selling dresses and candies, things you couldn't find in Kocho's few shops, which carried mostly necessities. Growing up, my brothers often traveled to non-Yazidi villages to make a little money doing odd jobs. The relationships were burdened by centuries of distrust—it was hard not to feel bad when a Muslim wedding guest refused to eat our food, no matter how politely—but still, there was genuine friendship. These connections went back generations, lasting through Ottoman control, British colonization, Saddam Hussein, and the American occupation. In Kocho, we were particularly known for our close relationships with Sunni villages.

But when there was fighting in Iraq, and there always seemed to be fighting in Iraq, those villages loomed over us, their smaller Yazidi neighbor, and old prejudice hardened easily into hatred. Often, from that hatred, came violence. For at least the past ten years, since Iraqis had been thrust into a war with the Americans that began in 2003, then spiraled into more vicious local fights and eventually into full-fledged terrorism, the distance between our homes had grown enormous. Neighboring villages began to shelter extremists who denounced Christians and non-Sunni Muslims and, even worse, who considered Yazidis to be *kuffar*, unbelievers worthy of killing (*kafir* is singular). In 2007 a few of those extremists drove a fuel tanker and three cars into the busy centers of two Yazidi towns about ten miles northwest of Kocho, then blew up the vehicles, killing the hundreds of people who had rushed to them, many thinking they were bringing goods to sell at the market.

Yazidism is an ancient monotheistic religion, spread orally by holy men entrusted with our stories. Although it has elements in common with the many religions of the Middle East, from Mithraism and Zoroastrianism to Islam and Judaism, it is truly unique and can be difficult even for the holy men who memorize our stories to explain. I think of my religion as being an ancient tree with thousands of rings, each telling a story in the long history of Yazidis. Many of those stories, sadly, are tragedies.

Today there are only about one million Yazidis in the world. For as long as I have been alive—and, I know, for a long time before I was born—our religion has been what defined us and held us together as a community. But it also made us targets of persecution by larger groups, from the Ottomans to Saddam's Baathists, who attacked us or tried to coerce us into pledging our loyalty to them. They degraded our religion, saying that we worshipped the devil or that we were dirty, and demanded that we renounce our faith. Yazidis survived generations of attacks that were intended to wipe us out, whether by killing us, forcing us to convert, or simply pushing us from our land and taking everything we owned. Before 2014, outside powers had tried to destroy us seventy-three times. We used to call the attacks against Yazidis *firman*, an Ottoman word, before we learned the word *genocide*.

When we heard about the ransom demands for the two farmers, the whole village went into a panic. "Forty thousand dollars," the kidnappers told the farmers' wives over the phone. "Or come here with your children so you can convert to Islam as families." Otherwise, they said, the men would be killed. It wasn't the money that made their wives collapse in tears in front of our *mukhtar*, or village leader, Ahmed Jasso; forty thousand dollars was an otherworldly sum, but it was just money. We all knew that the farmers would sooner die than convert, so the villagers wept in relief when, late one night, the men escaped through a broken window, ran through the barley fields, and showed up at home, alive, dust up to their knees and panting with fear. But the kidnappings didn't stop.

Soon afterward Dishan, a man employed by my family, the Tahas, was abducted from a field near Mount Sinjar where he watched our sheep. It had taken my mother and brothers years to buy and breed our sheep, and each one was a victory. We were proud of our animals, keeping them in our courtyard when they weren't roaming outside the village, treating them almost like pets. The annual shearing was a celebration in itself. I loved the ritual of it, the way the soft wool fell to the ground in cloudlike piles, the musky smell that took over our house, how the sheep bleated quietly, passively. I loved sleeping beneath the thick comforters my mother, Shami, would make from the wool, stuffing it between colorful pieces of fabric. Sometimes I got so attached to a lamb that I had to leave the house when it came time to slaughter it. By the time Dishan was kidnapped, we had over a hundred sheep—for us, a small fortune.

Remembering the hen and chicks that had been taken along with the farmers, my brother Saeed raced in our family's pickup truck to the base of Mount Sinjar, about twenty minutes away now that the road was paved, to check on our sheep. "Surely, they took them," we groaned. "Those sheep are all we have."

Later, when Saeed called my mother, he sounded confused. "Only two were taken," he reported—an old, slow-moving ram and a young female lamb. The rest were grazing contentedly on the brownish-green grass and would follow my brother home. We laughed, we were so relieved. But Elias, my eldest brother, was worried. "I don't get it," he said. "Those villagers aren't rich. Why did they leave the sheep behind?" He thought it had to mean something.

The day after Dishan was taken, Kocho was in chaos. Villagers huddled in front of their doors, and along with men who took turns manning a new checkpoint just beyond our village walls, they watched for any unfamiliar cars coming through Kocho. Hezni, one of my brothers, came home from his job as a policeman in Sinjar City and joined the other village men who loudly argued about what to do. Dishan's uncle wanted to get revenge and decided to lead a mission to a village east of Kocho that was headed by a conservative Sunni tribe. "We'll take two of their shepherds," he declared, in a rage. "Then they'll have to give Dishan back!"

It was a risky plan, and not everyone supported Dishan's uncle. Even my brothers, who had all inherited bravery and a quickness to fight from our father, were split on what to do. Saeed, who was only a couple of years older than me, spent a lot of his time fantasizing about the day he would finally prove his heroism. He was in favor of revenge, while Hezni, who was over a decade older and the most empathetic of us all, thought it was too dangerous. Still, Dishan's uncle took what allies he could find and snatched two Sunni Arab shepherds, then drove them back to Kocho, where he locked them in his house and waited.

———

MOST VILLAGE DISPUTES were solved by Ahmed Jasso, our practical and diplomatic mukhtar, and he sided with Hezni. "Our relationship with our Sunni neighbors is already strained," he said. "Who knows what they will do if we try to fight with them." Besides, he warned, the situation outside Kocho was far worse and more complicated than we imagined. A group calling itself the Islamic State, or ISIS, which had largely been born here in Iraq, then grown in Syria over the past few years, had taken over villages so close to us, we could count the black-clad figures in their trucks when they drove by. They were holding our shepherd, our mukhtar told us. "You'll only make things worse," Ahmed Jasso said to Dishan's uncle, and barely half a day after the Sunni shepherds had been kidnapped, they were set free. Dishan, however, remained a captive.

Ahmed Jasso was a smart man, and the Jasso family had decades of experience negotiating with the Sunni Arab tribes. Everyone in the village turned to them with their problems, and outside Kocho they were known for being skilled diplomats. Still, some of us wondered if this time he was being too cooperative, sending the message to the terrorists that Yazidis would not protect themselves. As it was, all that stood between us and ISIS were Iraqi Kurdish fighters, called *peshmerga*, who had been sent from the Kurdish autonomous region to guard Kocho when Mosul fell almost two months earlier. We treated the peshmerga like honored guests. They slept on pallets in our school, and each week a different family slaughtered a lamb to feed them, a huge sacrifice for the poor villagers. I also looked up to the fighters. I had heard about female Kurds from Syria and Turkey who fought against terrorists and carried weapons, and the thought made me feel brave.

Some people, including a few of my brothers, thought we should be allowed to protect ourselves. They wanted to man the checkpoints, and Ahmed Jasso's brother Naif tried to convince Kurdish authorities to let him form a Yazidi peshmerga unit, but he was ignored. No one offered to train the Yazidi men or encourage them to join the fight against the terrorists. The peshmerga assured us that as long as they were there, we had nothing to worry about, and that they were as determined to protect Yazidis as they were the capital of Iraqi Kurdistan. "We will sooner let Erbil fall than Sinjar," they said. We were told to trust them, and so we did.

Still, most families in Kocho kept weapons at home—clunky Kalashnikov rifles, a big knife or two usually used to slaughter animals on holidays. Many Yazidi men, including those of my brothers who were old enough, had taken jobs in the border patrol or police force after 2003, when those jobs became available, and we felt sure that as long as the professionals watched Kocho's borders, our men could protect their families. After all, it was those men, not the peshmerga, who built a dirt barrier with their own hands around the village after the 2007 attacks, and it was Kocho's men who patrolled that barrier day and night for a full year, stopping cars at makeshift checkpoints and watching for strangers, until we felt safe enough to go back to a normal life.

Dishan's kidnapping made us all panic. But the peshmerga didn't do anything to help. Maybe they thought it was just a petty squabble between villages, not the reason Masoud Barzani, the president of the Kurdistan Regional Government, had sent them out of the safety of Kurdistan and into the unprotected areas of Iraq. Maybe they were frightened like we were. A few of the soldiers looked like they couldn't be that much older than Saeed, my mother's youngest son. But war changed people, especially men. It wasn't that long ago that Saeed would play with me and our niece, Kathrine, in our courtyard, not yet old enough to know that boys were not supposed to like dolls. Lately, though, Saeed had become obsessed with the violence sweeping through Iraq and Syria. The other day I had caught him watching videos of Islamic State beheadings on his cell phone, the images shaking in his hand, and was surprised that he held up the phone so I could watch, too. When our older brother Massoud walked into the room, he was furious. "How could you let Nadia watch!" he yelled at Saeed, who cowered. He was sorry, but I understood. It was hard to turn away from the gruesome scenes unfolding so close to our home.

The image from the video popped back into my head when I thought about our poor shepherd being held captive. *If the peshmerga won't help us get Dishan back, I will have to do something,* I thought, and ran into our house. I was the baby of the family, the youngest of eleven, and a girl. Still, I was outspoken and used to being heard, and I felt giant in my anger.

Our house was close to the northern edge of the village, a one-story row of mud brick rooms lined up like beads on a necklace and connected by doorways with no doors, all leading out to a large courtyard with a vegetable garden, a bread oven called a tandoor, and, often, sheep and chickens. I lived there with my mother, six of my eight brothers and my two sisters, plus two sisters-in-law and the children they had between them, and within walking distance of my other brothers, half brothers, and half sisters and most of my aunts, uncles, and cousins. The roof leaked in the winter when it rained, and the inside could feel like an oven in the Iraqi summertime, pushing us up a staircase onto the roof to sleep. When one part of the roof caved in, we patched it with pieces of metal we scavenged from Massoud's mechanic shop, and when we needed more space, we built it. We were saving money for a new home, a more permanent one made of cement blocks, and we were getting closer every day.

I entered our house through the front door and ran to a room I shared with the other girls, where there was a mirror. Wrapping a pale scarf around my head, one I normally wore to keep my hair from getting in my eyes when bending over rows of vegetables, I tried to imagine what a fighter might do to prepare for battle. Years of labor on the farm made me stronger than my appearance let on. Still, I had no idea what I would do if I saw the kidnappers or people from their village drive through Kocho. What would I say to them? "Terrorists took our shepherd and went to your village," I practiced in the mirror, scowling. "You could have stopped them. At least you can tell us where he was taken." From the corner of our courtyard, I grabbed a wooden stick, like the ones used by a shepherd, and made for the front door again, where a few of my brothers stood with my mother, deep in conversation. They barely noticed when I joined them.

A few minutes later a white pickup truck from the kidnappers' village came down the main road, two men in the front and two in the back. They were Arabs I vaguely recognized from the Sunni tribe that had taken Dishan. We watched as their truck crept down the main dirt road that snaked through the village, slowly, as though totally without fear. They had no reason to drive through Kocho—roads around the village connected cities like Sinjar and Mosul—and their presence seemed like a taunt. Breaking away from my family, I ran into the middle of the road and stood in the path of the truck. "Stop!" I shouted, waving the stick over my head, trying to make myself look bigger. "Tell us where Dishan is!"

It took half my family to restrain me. "What did you think you were going to do?" Elias scolded. "Attack them? Break their windshield?" He and a few of my other siblings had just come from the fields and were exhausted and stinking from the onions they were harvesting. To them, my attempt to avenge Dishan seemed like nothing more than a child's outburst. My mother was also furious with me for running into the road. Under normal circumstances she tolerated my temper and was even amused by it, but in those days everyone was on edge. It seemed dangerous to draw attention to yourself, particularly if you were a young, unmarried woman. "Come here and sit," she said sternly. "It's shameful for you to do that, Nadia, it's not your business. The men will take care of it."

Life went on. Iraqis, particularly Yazidis and other minorities, are good at adjusting to new threats. You have to be if you want to try to live something close to a normal life in a country that seemed to be coming apart. Sometimes the adjustments were relatively small. We scaled down our dreams—of finishing school, of giving up farmwork for something less backbreaking, of a wedding taking place on time—and it wasn't hard to convince ourselves that those dreams had been unreachable in the first place. Sometimes the adjustments would happen gradually, without anyone noticing. We would stop talking to the Muslim students at school, or be drawn inside in fear if a stranger came through the village. We watched news of attacks on TV and started to worry more about politics. Or we shut out politics completely, feeling it was safest to stay silent. After each attack, men added to the dirt barrier outside Kocho, beginning on the western side, facing Syria, until one day we woke up to see that it surrounded us completely. Then, because we still felt unsafe, the men dug a ditch around the village as well.

We would, over generations, get used to a small pain or injustice until it became normal enough to ignore. I imagine this must be why we had come to accept certain insults, like our food being refused, that probably felt like a crime to whoever first noticed it. Even the threat of another firman was something Yazidis had gotten used to, although that adjustment was more like a contortion. It hurt.

With Dishan still captive, I returned with my siblings to the onion fields. There nothing had changed. The vegetables we planted months before were now grown; if we didn't pick them, no one would. If we didn't sell them, we wouldn't have money. So we all knelt in a line beside the tangles of green sprouts, tugging bulbs out of the soil a few at a time, collecting them in woven plastic bags where they would be left to ripen until it was time to take them to market. *Will we take them to the Muslim villages this year?* we wondered but could not answer. When one of us pulled up the black, poisonous-smelling sludge of a rotten onion, we groaned, plugged our noses, and kept going.

Because it was what we normally did, we gossiped and teased one another, telling stories each had heard a million times before. Adkee, my sister and the joker of the family, recalled the image of me that day trying to chase the car, a skinny farm girl, my scarf falling in front of my eyes, waving the stick over my head, and we all nearly tipped over into the dirt laughing. We made a game of the work, racing to see who could pick the most onions just as, months before, we had raced to see who could plant the most seeds. When the sun started to go down, we joined my mother at home for dinner in our courtyard and then slept shoulder to shoulder on mattresses on the roof of our house, watching the moon and whispering until exhaustion brought the whole family to complete silence.

We wouldn't find out why the kidnappers stole the animals—the hen, the chicks, and our two sheep—until almost two weeks later, after ISIS had taken over Kocho and most of Sinjar. A militant, who had helped round up all of Kocho's residents into the village's secondary school, later explained the kidnappings to a few of the village's women. "You say we came out of nowhere, but we sent you messages," he said, his rifle swinging at his side. "When we took the hen and the chicks, it was to tell you we were going to take your women and children. When we took the ram, it was like taking your tribal leaders, and when we killed the ram, it meant we planned on killing those leaders. And the young lamb, she was your girls."

Chapter 2

M Y MOTHER LOVED ME, BUT SHE DIDN'T WANT TO HAVE me. For months before I was conceived, she saved money whenever she could—a spare dinar here and there, change from a trip to the market or a pound of tomatoes sold on the sly—to spend on the birth control she didn't dare ask my father for. Yazidis don't marry outside the religion or allow conversion into Yazidism, and large families were the best way to guarantee that we didn't die out completely. Plus, the more children you had, the more help you had on the farm. My mother managed to buy the pills for three months until she ran out of money, and then, almost immediately, she was pregnant with me, her eleventh and last child.

She was my father's second wife. His first had died young, leaving him with four children who needed a woman to help raise them. My mother was beautiful, born to a poor and deeply religious family in Kocho, and her father happily gave her to my father as a wife. He already had some land and animals and, compared to the rest of Kocho, was well-off. So before her twentieth birthday, before she had even learned how to cook, my mother became a wife and stepmother to four children, and then quickly she became pregnant herself. She never went to school and didn't know how to read or write. Like many Yazidis, whose mother tongue is Kurdish, she didn't speak much Arabic and could barely communicate with Arab villagers who came to town for weddings or as merchants. Even our religious stories were a mystery to her. But she worked hard, taking on the many tasks that came with being a farmer's wife. It wasn't enough to give birth eleven times— each time, except for the dangerous labor with my twin brothers, Saoud and Massoud, at home—a pregnant Yazidi woman was also expected to lug firewood, plant crops, and drive tractors until the moment she went into labor and afterward to carry the baby with her while she worked.

My father was known around Kocho for being a very traditional, devout Yazidi man. He wore his hair in long braids and covered his head with a white cloth. When the *qawwals*, traveling religious teachers who play the flute and drums and recite hymns, visited Kocho, my father was among the men who would greet them. He was a prominent voice in the *jevat*, or meeting house, where male villagers could gather to discuss issues facing the community with our mukhtar.

Injustice hurt my father more than any physical injury, and his pride fed his strength. The villagers who were close to him loved to tell stories of his heroism, like the time he rescued Ahmed Jasso from a neighboring tribe who were determined to kill our mukhtar, or the time the expensive Arabian horses belonging to a Sunni Arab tribal leader escaped from their stables and my father used his pistol to defend Khalaf, a poor farmer from Kocho, when he was discovered riding one in nearby fields.

"Your father always wanted to do what was right," his friends would tell us after he passed away. "Once he let a Kurdish rebel who was running away from the Iraqi Army sleep in his house, even though the rebel led the police right to his doorstep." The story goes, when the rebel was discovered, the police wanted to imprison both men, but my father talked his way out of it. "I didn't help him because of politics," he told the police. "I helped him because he is a man and I am a man," and they let him go.

"And that rebel turned out to be a friend of Masoud Barzani!" his friends recall, still amazed all these years later.

My father wasn't a bully, but he fought if he had to. He had lost an eye in a farm accident, and what was left in the socket—a small milky ball that looked like the marbles I played with as a kid— could make him look menacing. I've often thought since then that if my father had been alive when ISIS came to Kocho, he would have led an armed uprising against the terrorists.

By 1993, the year I was born, my parents' relationship was falling apart, and my mother was suffering. The eldest son born to my father's first wife had died a few years earlier in the Iran-Iraq War, and after that, my mother told me, nothing was ever good again. My father had also brought home another woman, Sara, whom he married and who now lived with their children on one end of the house my mother had long considered her own. Polygamy isn't outlawed in Yazidism, but not everyone in Kocho would have gotten away with it. No one questioned my father, though. By the time he married Sara, he owned a great deal of land and sheep and, in a time when sanctions and war with Iran made it hard for anyone to survive in Iraq, he needed a big family to help him, bigger than my mother could provide.

I still find it hard to criticize my father for marrying Sara. Anyone whose survival is directly linked to the number of to-matoes grown in one year or the amount of time spent walking their sheep to better grass can understand why he wanted another wife and more children. These things weren't personal. Later on, though, when he officially left my mother and sent us all to live in a small building behind our house with barely any money and land, I understood that his taking a second wife hadn't been com-pletely practical. He loved Sara more than he loved my mother. I accepted that, just as I accepted that my mother's heart must have been broken when he first brought home a new wife. After he left us, she would say to me and my two sisters, Dimal and

Adkee, "God willing, what happened to me won't happen to you." I wanted to be like her in every way, except I didn't want to be abandoned.

My brothers weren't all as understanding. "God will make you pay for this!" Massoud shouted at our father once, in a rage. But even they admitted that life got a little easier when my mother and Sara weren't living together and competing for my father's attention, and after a few years we learned how to coexist. Kocho was small, and we often saw him and Sara. I passed by their house, the house I was born in, every day on my way to elementary school; theirs was the only dog along that walk that knew me well enough not to bark. We spent holidays together, and my father would sometimes drive us to Sinjar City or to the mountain. In 2003 he had a heart attack, and we all watched as my strong father instantly became an ill, elderly man, confined to a wheelchair in the hospital. When he died a few days later, it seemed just as likely that it was out of shame over his frailty as it was because of his bad heart. Massoud regretted having yelled at him. He had assumed his father was strong enough to take anything.

My mother was a deeply religious woman, believing in the signs and dreams that many Yazidis use to interpret the present or predict the future. When the moon first appeared in the sky as a crescent, I would find her in the courtyard, lighting candles. "This is the time when children are most vulnerable to illness and accidents," she explained. "I am praying that nothing happens to any of you."

I often got sick to my stomach, and when I did, my mother took me to Yazidi healers who gave me herbs and teas, which she urged me to drink even though I hated the taste, and when someone died, she visited a *kochek*, a Yazidi mystic, who would help confirm that the deceased had made it into the afterlife. Many Yazidi pilgrims take a bit of soil before they leave Lalish, a valley in northern Iraq where our holiest temples are, and wrap it up in a small cloth folded into a triangle, which they keep in their pocket or wallet as a talisman. My mother was never without some of that holy soil, particularly after my brothers started leaving home to work with the army. "They need all the protection they can get, Nadia," she would say. "It's dangerous, what they are doing."

She was also practical and hardworking, trying against great odds to make our lives better. Yazidis are among the poorest communities in Iraq, and my family was poor even by Kocho's standards, particularly after my parents separated. For years, my brothers dug wells by hand, lowering themselves delicately into the wet, sulfurous ground inch by inch, careful not to break a bone. They also, along with my mother and sisters, farmed other people's land, taking only a small percentage of the profit for the tomatoes and onions they harvested. The first ten years of my life, we rarely had meat for dinner, living on boiled greens, and my brothers used to say they bought new pants only when they could see their legs through the old ones.

Gradually, thanks to my mother's hard work and the economic growth in northern Iraq after 2003, our situation, and that of most Yazidis, improved. My brothers took jobs as border guards and policemen when the central and Kurdish governments opened up positions to Yazidis. It was dangerous work—my brother Jalo joined a police unit guarding Tal Afar airport that lost a lot of its men in combat in the first year—but it paid well. Eventually we were able to move from my father's land into our own house.

People who knew my mother only for her deep religious beliefs and work ethic were surprised by how funny she could be, and how she turned her hardship into humor. She had a teasing way of joking, and nothing, not even the reality that she would almost certainly never marry again, was off-limits. One day, a few years after she and my father separated, a man visited Kocho hopeful for my mother's attention. When she heard he was at the door, she grabbed a stick and ran after him, telling him to go away, that she would never marry again. When she came back inside, she was laughing. "You should have seen how scared he was!" she told us, imitating him until we were all laughing too. "If I was going to marry, it wouldn't be to a man who ran away from an old lady with a stick!"

She joked about everything—about being abandoned by my father, about my fascination with hair and makeup, about her own failures. She had been going to adult literacy classes since before I was born, and when I became old enough, I started tutoring her. She was a fast learner, in part, I thought, because she was able to laugh off her mistakes.

When she talked about that scramble for birth control before I was conceived, it was as if she were telling a story from a book she had read long ago and liked only for its punch lines. Her reluctance to get pregnant with me was funny because now she couldn't imagine life without me. She laughed because of how she had loved me the moment I was born, and because I would spend each morning warming myself by our clay oven while she baked bread, talking to her. We laughed because I would get jealous whenever she doted on my sisters or nieces instead of me, because I vowed never to leave home, and because we slept in the same bed from the day I was born until ISIS came to Kocho and tore us all apart. She was our mother and our father at the same time, and we loved her even more when we became old enough to understand how much she must have suffered.

———

I GREW UP attached to my home and never imagined living anywhere else. To outsiders, Kocho may seem too poor to be happy, and too isolated and barren to ever be anything but desperately poor. American soldiers must have gotten that impression, given the way kids would swarm them when they came to visit, begging for pens and candy. I was one of those kids, asking for things.

Kurdish politicians occasionally came to Kocho, although only in recent years and mostly before elections. One of the Kurdish parties, Barzani's Kurdistan Democratic Party (KDP), opened a small two-room office in Kocho after 2003, but it seemed to exist mostly as a clubhouse for the village men who belonged to the party. A lot of people complained privately that the KDP pressured them into supporting the party and into saying Yazidis were Kurds and Sinjar was part of Kurdistan. Iraqi politicians ignored us, and Saddam had tried to force us to say we were Arab, as though we could all be threatened into giving up our identities and that once we did we would never rebel.

Just living in Kocho was, in a way, defiant. In the mid-1970s Saddam began forcibly moving minorities, including Kurds and Yazidis, from their villages and towns into cinder-block houses in planned communities, where they could be more easily controlled, a campaign people call the "Arabization" of the north. But Kocho was far enough away from the mountain that we were spared. Yazidi traditions that became old-fashioned in these new communities thrived in my village. Women wore the gauzy white dresses and headscarves of their grandmothers; elaborate weddings featured classic Yazidi music and dance; and we fasted in atonement for our sins when many Yazidis had given up that custom. It was safe and close-knit, and even fights over land or marriage ended up feeling minor. At least none of it had an impact on how much we loved one another. Villagers went to one another's houses late into the night and walked the streets without fear. I heard visitors say that at night, from afar, Kocho glowed in the darkness. Adkee swore she once heard someone describe it as "the Paris of Sinjar."

Kocho was a young village, full of children. There were few people living there who were old enough to have witnessed firmans first hand, and so a lot of us lived thinking those days were in the past, that the world was too modern and too civilized to be the kind of place where an entire group could be killed just because of their religion. I know that I felt that way. We grew up hearing about past massacres like folktales that helped bond us together. In one story, a friend of my mother's described fleeing oppression in Turkey, where many Yazidis once lived, with her mother and her sister. Trapped for days in a cave with nothing to eat, her mother boiled leather to keep them alive. I heard this story many times, and it made my stomach turn. I didn't think I could eat leather, even if I were starving. But it was just a story.

Admittedly, life in Kocho could be very hard. All those children, no matter how much they were loved, were a burden on their parents, who had to work day and night to feed their families. When we were sick, and the sickness couldn't be healed with herbs, we would have to be taken to Sinjar City or to Mosul to see a doctor. When we needed clothes, those clothes were sewn by hand by my mother or, after we got a little wealthier, purchased once a year in a city market. During the years of United Nations sanctions on Iraq, intended to force Saddam from power, we cried when it became impossible to find sugar. When schools were finally built in the village, first a primary school and then, many years later, a secondary school, parents had to weigh the benefits of their kids getting an education against keeping them at home to work. Average Yazidis had long been denied an education— not just by the Iraqi government but also by religious leaders who worried that a state education would encourage intermarriage and, therefore, conversion and loss of Yazidi identity—but for the parents, giving up the free labor was a great sacrifice. And for what kind of future, the parents wondered, for what jobs, and where? There was no work in Kocho, and a permanent life outside the village, away from other Yazidis, attracted only the very desperate or the very ambitious.

A parent's love could easily become a source of pain. Life on the farm was dangerous, and accidents happened. My mother pinpoints the moment she grew from a girl into an adult to when her older sister was killed, thrown from a speeding tractor and then run over right there in the middle of the family wheat field. Illnesses were sometimes too expensive to treat. My brother Jalo and his wife Jenan lost baby after baby to a disease that was inherited from Jenan's side of the family. They were too poor to buy medication or take the babies to a doctor, and out of eight births, four children died.

Divorce took my sister Dimal's children away. In Yazidi society, as in the rest of Iraq, women have few rights when a marriage ends, no matter what happened to end it. Other children died in wars. I was born just two years after the first Gulf War and five years after the end of the Iran-Iraq War, a pointless eight-year conflict that seemed to fulfill Saddam's desire to torture his people more than anything else. The memories of these children, who we would never see again, lived like ghosts in our house. My father cut off his braids when his eldest son was killed, and although one of my brothers was named after this son, my father could only bear to call him by a nickname, Hezni, which means "sadness."

We measured our lives by harvests and by Yazidi holidays. Seasons could be brutal. In the wintertime Kocho's alleyways filled with a cement-like mud that sucked the shoes off your feet, and in the summertime the heat was so intense, we had to drag ourselves to the farm at night rather than risk collapsing under the sun during the day. Sometimes harvests would disappoint, and when that happened, the gloom would stretch on for months, at least until we planted the next round of seeds. Other times, no matter how much we harvested, we didn't make enough money. We learned the hard way—by lugging bags of produce to market and then having customers turn the vegetables over in their hands and walk away—what sold and what didn't. Wheat and barley were the most profitable. Onions sold, but not for much. Many years we fed overripe tomatoes to our livestock, just to get rid of the excess.

Still, no matter the hardship, I never wanted to live anywhere other than Kocho. The alleyways may have filled with mud in the winter, but no one had to go far to see the people they loved most. In the summer, the heat was stifling, but that meant we all slept on the roof, side by side, talking and laughing with neighbors on their own roofs. Working on the farm was hard, but we made enough money to live a happy, simple life. I loved my village so much that when I was a child, my favorite game involved creating a miniature Kocho out of discarded boxes and bits of trash. Kathrine and I filled those model homes with handmade wooden dolls and then married the dolls to one another. Of course, before every wedding, the girl dolls would visit the elaborate house I made out of a plastic tomato crate, where I ran a hair salon.

Most importantly, I would never have left Kocho because my family was there. We were a little village ourselves. I had my eight brothers: Elias, the eldest, was like a father. Khairy was the first to risk his life as a border guard to help feed us. Pise was stubborn and loyal and would never let anything happen to us. There was Massoud, who grew up to be the best mechanic (and one of the best soccer players) in Kocho, and his twin Saoud, who ran a small convenience store in the village. Jalo opened his heart to everyone, even strangers. Saeed was full of life and mischief and longed to be a hero, and it was Hezni, the dreamer, whose affection we all competed for. My two sisters—the mothering, quiet Dimal, and Adkee, who one day would fight with our brothers to let her, a woman, drive our pickup truck and the next weep over a lamb who collapsed dead in the courtyard—still lived at home, and my half brothers, Khaled, Walid, Hajji, and Nawaf, and my half sisters, Halam and Haiam, were all nearby.

Kocho was where my mother, Shami, like good mothers everywhere, devoted her life to making sure we were fed and hopeful. It's not the last place I saw her, but it's where she is when I think about her, which I do every day. Even during the worst years of the sanctions, she made sure we had what we needed. When there was no money for treats, she gave us barley to trade for gum at the local store. When a merchant came through Kocho selling a dress we couldn't afford, she badgered him into taking credit. "At least now our house is the first one they visit when they come to Kocho!" she joked if one of my brothers complained about the debt.

She had grown up poor, and she never wanted us to appear needy, but villagers wanted to help us and gave us small amounts of flour or couscous when they could. Once when I was very young, my mother was walking home from the mill with only a little flour in her bag and was stopped by her uncle Sulaiman. "I know you need help. Why don't you ever come to me?" he asked.

At first, she shook her head. "We're fine, uncle," she said. "We have everything we need." But Sulaiman insisted, "I have so much extra wheat, you have to take some," and the next thing we knew, four big oilcans full of wheat had been delivered to our house, enough for us to make bread for two months. My mother was so ashamed that she needed help that when she told us what happened, her eyes filled with tears, and she vowed that she would make our lives better. Day by day she did. Her presence was a reassurance even with terrorists nearby. "God will protect the Yazidis," she told us every day.

There are so many things that remind me of my mother. The color white. A good and perhaps inappropriate joke. A peacock, which Yazidis consider a holy symbol, and the short prayers I say in my head when I see a picture of the bird. For twenty-one years, my mother was at the center of each day. Every morning she woke up early to make bread, sitting on a low stool in front of the tandoor oven we kept in the courtyard, flattening balls of dough and slapping them against the sides of the oven until they were puffy and blistered, ready to be dipped into bowls of golden melted sheep's butter.

Every morning for twenty-one years I woke up to the slow *slap, slap, slap* of the dough against the oven walls and the grassy smell of the butter, letting me know my mother was close by. Half asleep, I would join her in front of the tandoor, in the winter warming my hands by the fire, and talk to her about everything— school, weddings, fights with siblings. For years, I was convinced that snakes were hatching babies on the tin roof of our outdoor shower. "I heard them!" I insisted to her, making slithering sounds. But she just smiled at me, her youngest child. "Nadia is too scared to shower alone!" my siblings mocked me, and even when a baby snake fell on my head, prompting us to finally rebuild the shower, I had to admit they were sort of right. I never wanted to be alone.

I would pick burned edges off the fresh bread, updating my life plan for her. No longer would I simply do hair in the salon I planned to open in our house. We had enough money now to afford the kohl and eye shadow popular in cities outside Kocho, so I would also do makeup after I got home from a day teaching history at the secondary school. My mother nodded her approval. "Just as long as you never leave me, Nadia," she would say, wrapping the hot bread in fabric. "Of course," I always replied. "I will never leave you."

Chapter 3

YAZIDIS BELIEVE THAT BEFORE GOD MADE MAN, HE CRE-
ated seven divine beings, often called angels, who were mani-
festations of himself. After forming the universe from the pieces
of a broken pearl-like sphere, God sent his chief Angel, Tawusi
Melek, to earth, where he took the form of a peacock and painted
the world the bright colors of his feathers. The story goes that on
earth, Tawusi Melek sees Adam, the first man, whom God has
made immortal and perfect, and the Angel challenges God's decision. If Adam is to reproduce, Tawusi Melek suggests, he can't
be immortal, and he can't be perfect. He has to eat wheat, which
God has forbidden him to do. God tells his Angel that the decision is his, putting the fate of the world in Tawusi Melek's hands.
Adam eats wheat, is expelled from paradise, and the second generation of Yazidis are born into the world.

Proving his worthiness to God, the Peacock Angel became
God's connection to earth and man's link to the heavens. When
we pray, we often pray to Tawusi Melek, and our New Year celebrates the day he descended to earth. Colorful images of the
peacock decorate many Yazidi houses, to remind us that it is because of his divine wisdom that we exist at all. Yazidis love Tawusi
Melek for his unending devotion to God and because he connects
us to our one God. But Muslim Iraqis, for reasons that have no

real roots in our stories, scorn the Peacock Angel and slander us for praying to him.

It hurts to say it, and Yazidis aren't even supposed to utter the words, but many people in Iraq hear the story of the Peacock Angel and call us devil worshippers. Tawusi Melek, they say, is God's chief Angel, like Iblis, the devil figure of the Koran. They claim that our Angel defied Adam and therefore God. Some cite texts—usually written by outside scholars in the early twentieth century who were unfamiliar with the Yazidi oral tradition—that say that Tawusi Melek was sent to Hell for refusing to bow to Adam, which is not true. This is a misinterpretation, and it has had terrible consequences. The story we use to explain the core of our faith and everything we think of as good about the Yazidi religion is the same story others use to justify genocide against us.

This is the worst lie told about Yazidis, but it is not the only one. People say that Yazidism isn't a "real" religion because we have no official book like the Bible or the Koran. Because some of us don't shower on Wednesdays—the day that Tawusi Melek first came to earth, and our day of rest and prayer—they say we are dirty. Because we pray toward the sun, we are called pagans. Our belief in reincarnation, which helps us cope with death and keep our community together, is rejected by Muslims because none of the Abrahamic faiths believe in it. Some Yazidis avoid certain foods, like lettuce, and are mocked for their strange habits. Others don't wear blue because they see it as the color of Tawusi Melek and too holy for a human, and even that choice is ridiculed.

Growing up in Kocho, I didn't know a lot about my own religion. Only a small part of the Yazidi population are born into the religious castes, the sheikhs and elders who teach all other Yazidis about the religion. I was a teenager before my family had enough money to take me to Lalish to be baptized, and it was not possible for me to make that trip regularly enough to learn from the sheikhs who lived there. Attacks and persecution scattered us and decreased our numbers, making it even harder for our stories to be spread orally, as they are supposed to be. Still, we were happy that our religious leaders guarded Yazidism—it was clear that in the wrong hands, our religion could be easily used against us.

There are certain things all Yazidis are taught at a young age. I knew about the Yazidi holidays, although more about how we celebrate them than about the theology behind them. I knew that on Yazidi New Year, we color eggs, visit the graves of family, and light candles in our temples. I knew that October was the best month to go to Lalish, a holy valley in the Sheikhan district where the Baba Sheikh, our most important spiritual leader, and Baba Chawish, the custodian of the shrines there, greet pilgrims. In December we fast for three days to atone for our sins. Marriage outside the faith is not allowed; nor is conversion. We were taught about the seventy-three past firmans against Yazidis, and these stories of persecution were so intertwined with who we were that they might as well have been holy stories. I knew that the religion lived in the men and women who had been born to preserve it, and that I was one of them.

My mother taught us how to pray—toward the sun in the morning, Lalish during the day, and the moon at night. There are rules, but most are flexible. Prayer is meant to be a personal expression, not a chore or an empty ritual. You can pray silently by yourself or out loud, and you can pray alone or in a group, as long as everyone in that group is also Yazidi. Prayers are accompanied by a few gestures, like kissing the red and white bracelet that many Yazidi women and men wear around their wrist or, for a man, kissing the collar of his traditional white undershirt.

Most Yazidis I grew up with prayed three times a day, and prayers can be made anywhere. More often than I've prayed in temples, I've prayed in the fields, on our rooftop, even in the kitchen, helping my mother cook. After reciting a few standard lines in praise of God and Tawusi Melek, you can say anything you want. "Tell Tawusi Melek what is bothering you," my mother told us, demonstrating the gestures. "If you are worried about someone you love, tell him that, or if you are scared of something. These are the things that Tawusi Melek can help you with." I used to pray for my own future—to finish school and open my salon— and the futures of my siblings and my mother. Now I pray for the survival of my religion and my people.

Yazidis lived like this for a long time, proud of our religion and content to be removed from other communities. We had no ambition for more land or power, and nothing in the religion commands us to conquer non-Yazidis and spread our faith. No one can convert to Yazidism anyway. But during my childhood, our community was changing. Villagers bought televisions, first settling for state-run TV before satellite dishes allowed us to watch Turkish soap operas and Kurdish news. We bought our first electric clothes washer, which seemed almost like magic, although my mother still hand-washed her traditional white veils and dresses. Many Yazidis emigrated to the United States, Germany, or Canada, creating connections to the West. And of course, my generation was able to do something our parents hadn't even dreamed of. We went to school.

Kocho's first school was built in the 1970s, under Saddam. It went only through the fifth grade, and the lessons were in Arabic, not Kurdish, and were deeply nationalistic. State curriculum was clear about who was important in Iraq and what religion they followed. Yazidis didn't exist in the Iraqi history books I read in school, and Kurds were depicted as threats against the state. I read the history of Iraq as it unfolded in a sequence of battles, pitting Arab Iraqi soldiers against people who would take their country away from them. It was a bloody history, meant to make us proud of our country and the strong leaders who had kicked out the British colonists and overthrown the king, but it had the opposite effect on me. I later thought that those books must be one reason why our neighbors joined ISIS or did nothing while the terrorists attacked Yazidis. No one who had been through an Iraqi school would think that we deserved to have our religion protected, or that there was anything bad or even strange about endless war. We had been taught about violence since our very first day of school.

As a child, my country bewildered me. It could seem like its own planet, made up of many different lands, where decades of sanctions, war, bad politics, and occupation pulled neighbors apart. In the far north of Iraq were Kurds, who longed for independence. The south was home mostly to Shiite Muslims, the country's religious and now political majority. And lodged in the middle were Sunni Arabs, who, with Saddam Hussein as president, once dominated the state they now fight against.

That's the simple map, one with three solid color-coded stripes painted more or less horizontally across the country. It leaves out Yazidis or labels them as "other." The reality of Iraq is harder to illustrate and can be overwhelming even for people who were born here. When I was growing up, the villagers in Kocho didn't talk a lot about politics. We were concerned with the cycle of the crops, who was getting married, whether a sheep was producing milk—the kind of things that anyone from a small rural town will understand. The central government, apart from campaigns to recruit Yazidis to fight in their wars and to join the Baath Party, seemed just as uninterested in us. But we did think a lot about what it meant to be a minority in Iraq, among all the other groups in that "other" category with Yazidis that, if included on the map, would swirl those three horizontal stripes into colorful marble.

To the northeast of Kocho, a line of dots near the southern edge of Iraqi Kurdistan shows the places where Turkmens, both Shiite and Sunni Muslim, live. Christians—among them Assyrians, Chaldeans, and Armenians—have many communities scattered throughout the country, especially in the Nineveh Plain. Elsewhere, flecks indicate the homes of small groups like Kaka'i, Shabak, Roma, and Mandaeans, not to mention Africans and Marsh Arabs. I have heard that somewhere near Baghdad there is still a tiny community of Iraqi Jews. Religion blends into ethnicity. Most Kurds, for instance, are Sunni Muslim, but for them, their Kurdish identity comes first. Many Yazidis consider Yazidism both an ethnic and a religious identity. Most Iraqi Arabs are Shiite or Sunni Muslims, and that division has caused a lot of fighting over the years. Few of these details appeared in our Iraqi history books.

To get from my house to the school, I had to walk along the dusty road that ringed the edge of the town, past Bashar's house, whose father was killed by Al Qaeda; past the house I was born in, where my father and Sara still lived; and finally past my friend Walaa's house. Walaa was beautiful, with a pale, round face, and her quiet demeanor balanced my rowdiness. Every morning she would run out to join me on my walk to the school. It was worse to walk alone. Many of the families kept sheepdogs in their yards, and the enormous animals would stand in the gardens, barking and snarling at whoever passed by. If the gate was open, the dogs lunged after us, snapping their jaws. They weren't pets; they were big and dangerous, and Walaa and I would sprint away from them, arriving at school panting and sweating. Only my father's dog, who knew me, left us alone.

Our school was a dull structure made of sand-colored concrete, decorated with faded posters and surrounded by a low wall and a small, dry schoolyard garden. No matter what it looked like, it felt like a miracle to be able to go and study and meet friends. In the school garden, Walaa, Kathrine, and I would play a game with a few of the other girls called *bin akhy*, which in Kurdish means "in the dirt." All at once we would each hide something—a marble, a coin, even just a soda cap—in the ground, then we would run around like crazy people, digging holes in the garden until the teacher yelled at us, caking our fingernails with dirt that was sure to upset our mothers. You kept whatever you found, which almost always ended with tears. It was an old game; even my mother remembered playing it.

History, in spite of all the gaps and injustices in the lessons, was my favorite subject and the one I excelled at. English was my worst. I tried hard to be a good student, knowing that while I studied, my siblings worked on our farm. My mother was too poor to buy me a backpack like most of the other students carried, but I wouldn't complain. I didn't like to ask her for things. When she couldn't pay the taxi fee to send me to a secondary school a few villages away while ours was being built, I started working on the farm again, and waited and prayed for the school to be finished soon. There was no point in complaining, the money wouldn't just appear, and I was far from the only kid in Kocho whose parents couldn't afford to send them away.

After Saddam invaded Kuwait in 1991, the United Nations put sanctions on Iraq, hoping that it would limit the president's power. While I was growing up, I didn't know why the sanctions existed. The only people who talked about Saddam in my house were my brothers Massoud and Hezni, and that was just to shush anyone who complained during televised speeches or rolled their eyes at the propaganda on state TV. Saddam had tried to get loyalty from Yazidis so that they would side with him against the Kurds and fight in his wars, but he did so by demanding that we join his Baath Party and call ourselves Arab, not Yazidi.

Sometimes all that was on TV was Saddam himself, seated behind a desk smoking and telling stories about Iran, with a mustached guard beside him, going on about battles and his own brilliance. "What is he talking about?" we would ask one another, and everyone shrugged. There was no mention of Yazidis in the constitution, and any sign of rebellion was quickly punished.

Sometimes I felt like laughing at what I saw on TV—the dictator in his funny hat—but my brothers cautioned me not to. "They are watching us," Massoud said. "Be careful what you say." Saddam's enormous intelligence ministry had eyes and ears everywhere.

All I knew during that time was that it was ordinary Iraqis, not the political elite and certainly not Saddam himself, who suffered the most under the sanctions. Our hospitals and markets collapsed. Medicine became more expensive, and flour was cut with gypsum, which is more often used to make cement. The deterioration was most clear to me in the schools. Once Iraq's education system had attracted students from all over the Middle East, but under the sanctions it crumbled. Teachers' salaries were reduced to nothing, and so teachers became hard to find, even though nearly 50 percent of Iraqi men were unemployed. The few teachers who came to Kocho when I started—Arab Muslims who lived in the school, joining the Yazidi teachers—were heroes as far as I was concerned, and I worked hard to impress them.

When Saddam was in power, school had one obvious purpose: by offering us a state education, he hoped to take away our identity as Yazidis. This was clear in every lesson and every textbook that made no mention of us, our families, our religion, or the firmans against us. Although most Yazidis grew up speaking Kurdish, our lessons were in Arabic. Kurdish was the language of rebellion, and Kurdish spoken by Yazidis could be seen as even more threatening to the State. Still, I eagerly went to school every day that I could, and I learned Arabic quickly. I didn't feel like I was submitting to Saddam or betraying Yazidis by learning Arabic or studying the incomplete Iraqi history; I felt empowered and smart. I would still speak Kurdish at home and pray in Kurdish. When I wrote notes to Walaa or Kathrine, my two best friends, they would be in Kurdish, and I would never call myself anything other than Yazidi. I could tell that no matter what we were learning, going to school was important. With all the children in Kocho getting an education, our connections to our country and the outside world were already changing, and our society was opening up. Young Yazidis loved our religion but also wanted to be part of the world, and when we grew up into adults, I was sure we would become teachers ourselves, writing Yazidis into the history lessons or even running for parliament and fighting for Yazidi rights in Baghdad. I had a feeling back then that Saddam's plan to make us disappear would backfire.

Chapter 4

I N 2003, A FEW MONTHS AFTER MY FATHER DIED, THE AMER- icans invaded Baghdad. We didn't have a satellite television to watch the battle unfold, or cell phones connecting us to the rest of the country, and so we learned slowly, over time, how quickly Saddam fell. Coalition forces flew noisily over Kocho on the way to the capital, jerking us from sleep; it was the first time I had ever seen an airplane. We had no idea at the time just how long the war would go on and how much of an impact it would have on Iraq, but in the simplest terms, we hoped that after Saddam, it would be easier to buy cooking gas.

What I remember most from those early months after the invasion was the loss of my father and little else. In Yazidi culture, when someone dies—particularly if that death is sudden and comes too soon—mourning lasts for a long time and sweeps up the entire village. Neighbors retreat from normal life along with the family and friends of the dead. Grief takes over every house and shop and spreads through the streets, as though everyone has been made sick on the same batch of sour milk. Weddings are canceled, holiday celebrations are moved indoors, and women switch out their white clothes for black. We treat happiness like a thief we have to guard against, knowing how easily it could wipe away the memory of our lost loved ones or leave us exposed in a moment of joy when we should be sad, so we limit our distractions. Televisions and radios are kept off, no matter what might be happening in Baghdad.

A few years before he died, my father took Kathrine and me to Mount Sinjar to celebrate the Yazidi New Year. It was my last time with him at the mountain. Our New Year is in April, just as the hills in northern Iraq glow with a light green fuzz and the sharp cold eases into a pleasant cool, but before the summer heat sneaks up on you like a speeding bus. April is the month that holds the promise of a big profitable harvest and leads us into months spent outdoors, sleeping on rooftops, freed from our cold, overcrowded houses. Yazidis are connected to nature. It feeds us and shelters us, and when we die, our bodies become the earth. Our New Year reminds us of this.

On the New Year we visited whomever in the family had been working as shepherds that year, driving our sheep closer to the mountain and walking them from field to field in order to keep them fed. Parts of the job were fun. Shepherds slept outside underneath handwoven blankets and lived simply, with lots of time to think and little to worry about. But it was also grueling work, far from home and family, and while they grew homesick, we missed them back in Kocho. The year my mother left to take care of the sheep, I was in middle school, and I was so distraught that I failed every one of my classes. "I am blind without you," I told her when she returned.

That last New Year with my father, Kathrine and I rode in the back of the truck while my father and Elias sat in front, watching us in the rearview mirror to make sure we didn't do anything reckless. The landscape whipped by, a blur of wet spring grass and yellow wheat. We held hands and gossiped, concocting overblown versions of the day's events that we would later use to taunt the kids who had to wait at home. As far as they were concerned, it would be the most fun we ever had, away from the fields and school and work. Kathrine and I would nearly bounce over the side of the truck as it raced down the road, and the lamb tied up in the back near us was the biggest lamb we had ever seen. "We ate so much candy," we would tell them back home, watching for the envy in their faces. "We danced all night, it was light outside by the time we went to sleep. You should have seen it."

The true story was only slightly less exciting. My father could hardly say no to the candy we longed for, and, at the base of the mountain, the reunion with the shepherds was always joyful. The lamb, which had in fact ridden in the back of the truck along with us and was then slaughtered by my father and cooked by the women, was tender and delicious, and we all danced Yazidi dances, holding hands and spinning in a wide circle. After the best parts of the lamb were eaten and the music turned off, we slept in tents surrounded by low fences made of reeds to keep out the wind. When the weather was mild, we took down those fences and slept in the open air. It was a simple, hidden life. All you had to worry about were the things and the people around you, and they were close enough to touch.

I don't know how my father would have felt about the Americans invading Iraq and taking Saddam out of power, but I wished he had lived long enough to see Iraq change. Kurds welcomed the U.S. soldiers, helping them enter Iraq, and they were ecstatic at the idea of Saddam being deposed. The dictator had targeted Kurds for decades, and in the late 1980s his air force had tried to exterminate them with chemical weapons in what he called the Anfal campaign. That genocide shaped the Kurds, who wanted to protect themselves from the government in Baghdad in any way they could. Because of Anfal, the Americans, British, and French established a no-fly zone over the Kurdish north, as well as the Shia areas in the south, and Kurds had been their willing allies ever since. To this day, Kurds call the 2003 U.S. invasion a "liberation," and they consider it the beginning of their transformation from small vulnerable villages into big modern towns full of hotels and the offices of oil companies.

In general, Yazidis welcomed the Americans but were less certain than Kurds about what our lives would be like after Saddam. Sanctions had made our life hard, as they had for other Iraqis, and we knew that Saddam was a dictator who ruled Iraq with fear. We were poor, cut off from education, and made to do the most difficult, dangerous, and lowest-paying jobs in Iraq. But at the same time, with the Baathists in power, we in Kocho had been able to practice our religion, farm our land, and start families. We had close ties with Sunni Arab families, particularly the kiriv, whom we considered bonded to our families, and our isolation taught us to treasure these connections while our poverty told us to be practical above all else. Baghdad and the Kurdish capital, Erbil, seemed worlds away from Kocho. The only decision the rich, connected Kurds and Arabs made that mattered to us was the decision to leave us alone.

Still, the promises Americans made—about work, freedom, and security—quickly brought Yazidis fully to their side. The Americans trusted us because we didn't have any reason to be loyal to anyone they considered an enemy, and many of our men became translators or took jobs with the Iraqi or American armies. Saddam was pushed into hiding, then found and hanged, and his Baathist institutions dismantled. Sunni Arabs, including those close to Kocho, lost authority in the country, and in the Yazidi parts of Sinjar, Sunni Arab policemen and politicians were replaced with Kurdish ones.

Sinjar is a disputed territory—claimed by both Baghdad and Kurdistan—strategically close to Mosul and Syria and potentially rich with natural gas. Like Kirkuk, another disputed territory in eastern Iraq, Kurdish political parties consider Sinjar to be part of their greater Kurdish homeland. According to them, without

Sinjar, the Kurdish nation, if there ever is one, would be born incomplete. After 2003, with American support, and with the Sunni Arabs steadily losing wealth and power, Kurds who were aligned with the KDP happily came to fill the void in Sinjar. They established political offices and staffed those offices with party members. With the Sunni insurgency mounting, they manned checkpoints along our roads. They told us that Saddam was wrong to call us Arabs; we had always been Kurds.

In Kocho the changes after 2003 were huge. Within a couple of years, the Kurds started building a cell phone tower, and after school I would go with friends just outside the village to watch the giant, metal structure grow out of our farmland like a skyscraper. "Finally Kocho will be connected to the rest of the world!" my brothers said, delighted, and soon enough, most of the men and some of the women had cell phones. Satellite dishes installed on the roofs of houses meant we were no longer limited to Syrian films and Iraqi state TV, and Saddam's marches and speeches disappeared from our living room. My uncle was among the first to get a satellite dish, and as soon as he did, we all crowded into his sitting room to see what was on. My brothers looked for the news, particularly on Kurdish channels, and I became addicted to a Turkish soap opera where the characters constantly fell in and out of love.

We had resisted calling ourselves Arab, but being told that we were Kurdish was easier for some to accept. Many Yazidis feel close to a Kurdish identity—we share a language and ethnic heritage—and it was impossible to ignore the improvements in Sinjar after the Kurds came in, even if it had more to do with the United States than with Barzani. Jobs in the military and security forces were suddenly open to Yazidis, and some of my brothers and cousins traveled to Erbil to work in the hotels and restaurants; a new one seemed to be built every day. They quickly filled with oil workers or tourists from other parts of Iraq looking for a cooler climate, reliable electricity, or a break from the violence plaguing the rest of the country. My brother Saoud worked construction jobs near Duhok, in the west of Kurdistan, operating a cement mixer. He would come home with stories of Kurds who, like Arabs, looked down on Yazidis. Still, we needed the money.

Khairy began working as a border guard, and soon afterward Hezni became a policeman in Sinjar City. Their salaries gave our family our first steady income, and we started to live what felt like real lives, thinking about the future and not just the next day. We bought our own land to farm and our own sheep to herd and didn't have to work for landlords anymore. The paved roads outside Kocho made it much quicker to drive to the mountain. We picnicked in the fields near the village, eating plates of meat and chopped vegetables, the men drinking Turkish beer and then tea so sweet it made my lips pucker. Our weddings grew even more elaborate; women sometimes made two trips to Sinjar City for clothes, and men slaughtered more lambs—and if they were very well-off, a cow—to share with the guests.

Some Yazidis envisioned a future Sinjar with a strong local government that was still in Iraq, but others thought we would eventually be part of an independent Kurdistan. With the KDP office in Kocho and the peshmerga in Sinjar, I grew up thinking that was our destiny. We became more distant from our Sunni Arab neighbors. While travel to Kurdistan got easier, it became harder to get to the Sunni villages where insurgents, and the extremist theology that guided them, were gaining ground. Sunni Arabs, meanwhile, didn't like the Kurdish presence in Sinjar. It reminded them of the power they had lost, and they said that with the Kurds in control, they didn't feel welcome in Sinjar and could no longer visit Yazidi villages, even the ones where their kiriv lived. Kurdish peshmerga interrogated them at checkpoints that were once manned by Baathists, and many lost their salaries and jobs when the Americans came and dismantled Saddam's institutions. Only recently they had been the richest and best-connected people in the country, but with a Shiite government supported by the occupying Americans in power, Sunni Arabs suddenly lost their power. Isolated in their villages, they would soon decide to fight back. Within years that fight became fueled by a religious intolerance that made Yazidis, even though we had never had any power in Iraq, their target.

I didn't know then that the Kurdish government was content to distance Yazidis from our Arab neighbors because it helped them in their campaign to take over Sinjar, or how disruptive the American occupation was for ordinary Sunnis. I was unaware that, while I went to school, an unnamed insurgency was paving the way for Al Qaeda, and eventually ISIS, to flourish in our neighboring villages. Sunni tribes across Iraq tried, and mostly failed, to rebel against the Shiite authority in Baghdad and the Americans. They became accustomed to violence and harsh rule, which went on for so long that many Sunnis my age and younger grew up knowing nothing but war and the fundamentalist interpretation of Islam that became part of that war.

ISIS built up slowly in those villages just beyond our borders, a spark that I didn't notice until it became a bonfire. For a young Yazidi girl, life only got better after the Americans and the Kurds took over. Kocho was expanding, I was going to school, and we were gradually lifting ourselves out of poverty. A new constitution gave more power to the Kurds and demanded that minorities be part of the government. I knew that my country was at war, but it didn't seem like it was our fight.

———

IN THE BEGINNING, American soldiers visited Kocho almost once a week to hand out food and supplies and talk to the village leaders. Did we need schools? Paved roads? Running water so that we no longer had to buy tanks off of trucks? The answer to all of it, of course, was yes. Ahmed Jasso invited the soldiers over for large, elaborate meals, and our men glowed with pride when the Americans said they felt so safe in Kocho they could lean their weapons against the walls and relax. "They know the Yazidis will protect them," Ahmed Jasso said.

Kids ran to the American soldiers when they pulled into Kocho, their armored cars kicking up dust and drowning out the village noises with their loud motors. They gave us gum and candy and took photos of us smiling with the presents. We marveled at their crisp uniforms and the friendly, conversational way they approached us, so unlike the Iraqi soldiers before them. They raved to our parents about Kocho hospitality, how comfortable and clean our village was, and how well we understood that America had liberated us from Saddam. "Americans love the Yazidis," they told us. "And Kocho especially. We feel at home here." Even when their visits slowed to a trickle and then stopped completely, we held on to the American praise like a badge of honor.

In 2006, when I was thirteen, one of the American soldiers gave me a ring as a present. It was a simple band with a small red stone, the first piece of jewelry I'd ever owned. It instantly became my most valued possession. I wore it everywhere—to school, digging on the farm, at home watching my mother bake bread, even to sleep at night. After a year, it had become too small for my ring finger, and I moved it onto my pinky so I wouldn't have to leave it at home. But it slid up and down on that finger, barely catching on my knuckle, and I worried about losing it. I glanced at it constantly to make sure it was still there, curling my hand into a fist to feel it pressing against my finger.

Then one day I was out with my siblings planting rows of onion seedlings when I looked down and noticed that the ring was gone. I already hated planting the onions—each one had to be laid carefully into the cold dirt, and even the seedlings made your fingers and hands stink—and now I was furious at the tiny plants, digging frantically through them, trying to find my present. My siblings, noticing my panic, asked me what had happened. "I lost the ring!" I told them, and they stopped working to help look. They knew how important it was to me.

We walked our entire field, searching in the dark dirt for a little glimpse of gold and red, but no matter how hard we looked and how much I cried, we couldn't find the ring. When the sun started to set, we had no choice but to give up and go home for dinner. "Nadia, it's no big deal," Elias said as we walked home. "It's just a little thing. You'll have more jewelry in your life." But I cried for days. I was sure that I would never have anything as nice again and I worried that the American soldier, if he ever came back, would be angry with me for losing his present.

A year later a miracle happened. Picking the new onions that had sprouted from those seedlings, Khairy saw a small gold band poking out of the dirt. "Nadia, your ring!" My brother beamed, presenting it to me, and I ran to him, grabbing it out of his hand and hugging him, my hero. When I tried to slip it on, though, I found that, no matter how hard I tried, the ring was now too small even for my pinky. Later my mother saw it lying on my dresser and urged me to sell it. "It doesn't fit you anymore, Nadia," she said. "There's no point in keeping it if you can't wear it." For her, poverty was just one wrong move away. Because I always did what she said, I went to a jewelry seller in the Sinjar City bazaar, who bought the ring from me.

Afterward I felt heavy with guilt. The ring had been a gift, and it didn't seem right for me to sell it. I worried what the soldier would say if he returned and asked about his present. Would he think that I had betrayed him? That I didn't love the ring? The armored cars were already pulling up to Kocho much less frequently—fighting had grown worse in the rest of the country, and the Americans were stretched thin—and I hadn't seen that particular soldier in months. Some of my neighbors complained that the Americans had forgotten about us, and they worried that without contact with them, Yazidis would be unprotected. But I was relieved that I wouldn't have to explain what happened to the ring. Maybe the soldier who gave it to me, even though he was kind, would be upset that I had sold his present to the jewelry merchant in Sinjar City. Coming from America, he might not understand what even that small amount of money meant to us.

Chapter 5

WHEN THINGS WERE REALLY BAD IN IRAQ, YAZIDIS IN Kocho usually felt the impact of the violence like the aftershocks of an earthquake. We were removed from the worst of it—the battles between insurgents and American marines in Anbar Province, the rise of Shiite authoritarianism in Baghdad, and the strengthening of Al Qaeda. We watched on TV and worried about the men in our village who were working for the police and the army, but Kocho was spared the suicide bombings and roadside IEDs that seemed to happen every day in the rest of the country. Iraq today is so fractured that it may be impossible to repair: we watched it break from afar.

Khairy, Hezni, and Jalo would return home after long posts with stories of the battles outside. Sometimes they went to Kurdistan, where terrorist attacks were almost unheard of. Other times they were sent outside peshmerga-protected areas into the unknown parts of Iraq, which scared those of us they left behind. Those jobs could be extremely dangerous. Even if you didn't encounter fighting or terrorism, working with the Americans as a translator made you a target. Many Yazidi men sought asylum in the United States because their lives had been threatened after insurgents discovered they had worked for the Americans.

The war dragged on for much longer than anyone expected it to. People quickly forgot about those exhilarating first few months just after Saddam had been ousted, when his statue fell in Baghdad's Firdos Square and American soldiers fanned out across the country shaking hands with villagers, promising to build schools, free political prisoners, and make life easier for average Iraqis. By 2007, just a few years after the fall of Saddam, Iraq was plagued with violence, and the United States sent in more than twenty thousand additional soldiers—calling it a "surge"—mostly as a response to increased violence in Anbar and Baghdad. For a while, the surge seemed to work. Attacks decreased, and marines took over the cities, going door-to-door looking for insurgents. But for Yazidis, the year of the surge was the year the war arrived on our doorstep.

In August 2007, the worst terrorist attack of the entire Iraq War—and the second deadliest terrorist attack in history—took place in Siba Sheikh Khider and Tel Ezeir (also known by their Baathist names Qahtaniya and Jazeera), two Yazidi towns slightly west of Kocho. Around dinnertime on August 14, a fuel tanker and three cars, which some people heard were carrying supplies and food to the Yazidis living there, parked in the centers of the towns and blew themselves up. Eight hundred people died, ripped apart by the bombs or trapped under collapsed buildings, and over a thousand were injured. The explosions were so enormous, we could see the flames and smoke all the way over in Kocho. We began to scan the roads leading to our village, frightened by any cars we didn't recognize.

As horrible as the attacks were, it had only been a matter of time. Tension had been rising between Yazidis and Sunni Arabs for years, most recently because of Kurdish influence in Sinjar and ongoing radicalization in the Sunni areas. Then earlier that year, just a few months into the American surge, Sunnis vowed to avenge the death of a young Yazidi woman named Du'a Khalil Aswad, who had been gruesomely stoned to death by her relatives after they suspected she wanted to convert to Islam and marry a

Muslim man. It didn't matter that Yazidis were equally horrified by Du'a's death; outsiders called us savage and anti-Muslim.

Honor killings happen in Yazidi society, as they do in all of Iraq, and conversion out of the faith is seen as a betrayal of the family and community, in part because over the centuries Yazidis have been forced to convert in order to save their lives. Still, we do not kill women and men who leave Yazidism, and we were ashamed by what Du'a's family did to her. Not only was she stoned to death while people watched, horrified but unable or unwilling to stop it, but a video of her murder was then broadcast online, picked up by news stations, and used as an excuse to attack us, no matter how strongly we condemned it.

As soon as the story of Du'a began to spread, propaganda calling us infidels and worthy of death—language similar to what ISIS uses today—began circulating around Mosul. Kurds, who are mostly Sunni, also turned against us. We lived in shame and fear. Yazidi university students dropped out of schools in Kurdistan and Mosul, and Yazidis living abroad suddenly found themselves having to defend themselves to people who might never have even heard of Yazidism before and who now thought we were a religion of murderers.

Since Yazidis had no real representatives in the media and no strong voice in politics to explain what had really happened, the hatred against us in Sunni communities grew. Maybe it had always been there, just beneath the surface. Now it was all out in the open, and it spread quickly. Two weeks after Du'a was killed, Sunni gunmen stopped a bus carrying Yazidis and executed twenty-three of the passengers, saying they were avenging Du'a's death. We braced ourselves for more attacks, but we could never have imagined something on the scale of what happened in Siba Sheikh Khider and Tel Ezeir.

As soon as they saw the explosions, my brothers piled into cars and drove toward the destruction, joining hundreds of Yazidis who carried food, mattresses, and medicine to the villages. They returned home later that night, their heads hung with sadness and exhaustion. "It was worse than anything you could imagine," Elias said. "The towns are destroyed, and the dead are everywhere."

My mother sat them down and made tea while they cleaned the filth off their hands. "I saw a body torn in half," Hezni said, shaking. "It looks like the whole town is covered in blood." The explosions ripped bodies apart with such force that hair and pieces of clothing clung to the power lines high above the streets. Hospitals and clinics quickly ran out of space and medication. Shawkat, a friend of my brother's, was so distraught at seeing a body being dragged by the feet that he grabbed it out of the medic's hands and carried it to the morgue himself. "It was someone's father or son," he said. "Just being dragged like that, through the dust."

Family members circled the destruction in a daze, pushing silently through air thick with smoke and dust. Or they screamed for their loved ones, some of whom would die long before their families stopped looking for them. Eventually, after the village had been cleaned up and as many bodies as possible identified, those family members would have to mourn at mass graves. "Maybe it is worse to survive," Hezni said.

After that attack, we took some precautions. Men guarded Kocho in shifts, two stationed on the east side and two on the west, armed with Kalashnikovs and pistols. They questioned anyone riding in unfamiliar cars—mostly Sunni Arabs and Kurds whom we didn't recognize—and were on constant lookout for anyone who seemed threatening. Other Yazidis made dirt barricades around their towns and dug trenches so that car bombs couldn't drive in. Even though in Kocho we were very close to the Sunni Arab villages, we didn't pile dirt or dig a trench until years later. I don't know why—maybe we still had hope that our relationships with our neighbors were strong enough to protect us. Maybe we didn't want to feel trapped and isolated. After a year went by without another attack, the men left their guard posts.

————

HEZNI WAS THE only one in my family who tried to leave Iraq. This was in 2009, two years after the attack. He had fallen in love with Jilan, our neighbor's daughter, but Jilan's parents disapproved of the match because we had so little money compared to them. This didn't stop Hezni from trying. When Jilan's parents wouldn't let my brother come into their home to visit with her, the two climbed onto the rooftops and talked across the narrow alley that separated our homes. When Jilan's parents built a wall around the perimeter of their roof to hide their daughter, Hezni piled up bricks until, standing on them, he was tall enough to see over the wall. "Nothing can stop me," Hezni said. He was naturally shy, but he had fallen so much in love that he seemed willing to do anything to be with Jilan.

Hezni sent cousins or brothers to Jilan's house, where tradition obligated her family to offer visitors tea and food, and while they were distracted, Jilan would leave and meet Hezni. She loved him as much as he loved her and told her parents that she wanted to marry him, but still they objected. I fumed over their rejection—Jilan would be lucky to have Hezni, who was so loving—but my mother, as always, laughed it off. "At least the only reason they don't like us is because we are poor," she said. "And there is nothing wrong with being poor."

Hezni knew that Jilan's parents would never approve of the marriage unless he made some money, and back then he was having no luck getting a job in Iraq. He grew depressed. Other than Jilan, he felt like there was nothing for him at home, and since he couldn't have her, he didn't see the point of staying. When a few other men in the village decided they would try to make their way to Germany, where a small number of Yazidis already lived, Hezni decided to join them. We all cried while he packed his bag. I felt terrible about him leaving; I couldn't imagine home without any of my brothers.

Before he left, Hezni invited Jilan to a wedding outside Kocho, where they could talk without the locals whispering. She arrived and separated herself from the crowd, finding him. He still remembers that she wore white. "I'll be back in two or three years," he told her. "We'll have enough money to start a life." Then, a few days before we were to start one of our two yearly fasts, Hezni and the other men left Kocho.

First, they crossed the northern Iraqi border on foot into Turkey, where they slowly made their way to Istanbul. Once there, they paid a smuggler to take them in the back of a tractor trailer into Greece. The smuggler told them to tell the border guards that they were Palestinian. "If they know you're Iraqi, they will arrest you," he said, and then he closed the doors to the truck and drove across the border.

When Hezni called us a few days later, it was from prison. We had just sat down to break our fast when my mother's cell phone rang. One of the Iraqis with Hezni had been too scared to lie about where he was from, and so they had all been discovered. The prison was horrible, Hezni said, cramped and with only concrete slabs covered with thin mattresses to sleep on. No one would tell them when they would be released or whether they would be charged with a crime. Once, to get the guard's attention, some prisoners set fire to their mattresses, and Hezni worried they would all suffocate from the smoke. He asked us how our fasts were going. "I'm also hungry," he said, and from then on whenever Hezni called, my mother cried so hard that my brothers rushed to pick up the phone before she could answer.

Three and a half months later Hezni was back in Kocho. He was gaunt and embarrassed, and I thought, seeing him, that I was glad I didn't have any desire to go to Germany. I still think that being forced to leave your home out of fear is one of the worst injustices a human being can face. Everything you love is stolen, and you risk your life to live in a place that means nothing to you and where, because you come from a country now known for war and terrorism, you are not really wanted. So you spend the rest of your years longing for what you left behind while praying not to be deported. Hezni's story made me think that the path of the Iraqi refugee always leads backward, to prison or to where you came from.

There was an upside to Hezni's failure. He came home more determined than ever to marry Jilan, and during their time apart, she had made up her mind as well. Her family still disapproved, but the couple had Yazidi custom on their side. According to our culture, if two people are in love and want to marry, they can elope no matter what their families think. This proves that they value each other more than anything, and after that it's up to the families to reconcile themselves to the match. It can sound old-fashioned, even backward, the way the custom is sometimes described—a woman "running away"—but it is actually liberating, taking power away from the parents and giving it to the young couple and specifically to the girl, who has to agree to the plan.

So one evening, without whispering a word to anyone, Jilan sneaked out her back door and met Hezni, who was waiting in Jalo's car. They left for a nearby village, taking Al Qaeda–controlled roads to avoid running into Jilan's father on the main highway. (Hezni joked that he was more scared of him than any terrorist.) A few days later they were married, and some months after that, following negotiations, mostly over money, between our families that were sometimes happy and sometimes tense, they had a real wedding in Kocho. Ever since then Hezni would look back on his failed attempt to emigrate and laugh, saying, "Thank God I got arrested in Greece!" and pulling his wife close.

After that, we all resigned ourselves to staying in Kocho, even as the threats outside continued to grow. When the Americans left a few months after the 2010 parliamentary elections, groups all over the country began a chaotic struggle for power. Every day bombs exploded across Iraq, killing Shiite pilgrims or children in Baghdad and tearing apart whatever hope we had for peace in a post-America Iraq. Yazidis who owned liquor stores in Baghdad were targeted by extremists, and we retreated further into the relative safety of our Yazidi towns and villages.

Shortly afterward antigovernment protests that started in Tunisia spread into Syria, where President Bashar al-Assad quickly and brutally suppressed them. By 2012, Syria had dissolved into civil war, and in 2013, a new extremist group calling itself the Islamic State of Iraq and al-Sham, which had previously gained traction in postwar Iraq, began to flourish in the chaos of Syria. Soon it took over large parts of Syria and set its sights on crossing the border back into Iraq, where sympathizers waited for it in Sunni areas. Two years later, ISIS completely overwhelmed the Iraqi Army in the north, which abandoned its posts to an enemy they had expected to be much weaker than they turned out to be. In June 2014, before we knew it, ISIS took over Mosul, Iraq's second-biggest city, about eighty miles east of Kocho.

———

AFTER MOSUL FELL, the Kurdistan Regional Government (KRG) sent additional peshmerga into Sinjar to guard Yazidi towns. The soldiers arrived by the truckload, assuring us they would keep us safe. Some of us, scared by ISIS and feeling that Iraqi Kurdistan was far more secure, wanted to leave Sinjar for the Kurdish camps that were already filling with displaced Christian, Shiite, and Sunni as well as Syrian refugees. But the Kurdish authorities urged us not to. Yazidis trying to leave Sinjar for Iraqi Kurdistan were turned back by Kurds stationed at checkpoints around their villages and told not to worry.

Some families thought it was suicide to stay in Kocho. "We are surrounded on three sides by *Daesh!*" they protested, using the Arabic term for ISIS, and they were right: only one road connecting us to Syria didn't lead directly to the enemy. But Kocho was a proud village. We didn't want to abandon everything we had worked for—the concrete homes families had spent their entire lives saving for, the schools, the massive flocks of sheep, the rooms where our babies were born. Other Iraqis questioned the Yazidis' claim to Sinjar, and we thought that if we left, we would be proving them right; if we weren't willing to stay in Sinjar, maybe we didn't love it as much as we said we did. Ahmed Jasso called a meeting at the jevat and it was decided. "We stay as a village," he said, believing until the end that our relationships with the Sunni Arab villages were strong enough to keep us safe. And so we stayed.

My mother tried to keep life at home as normal as she could, but still we were on alert for strange visitors or threatening noises. One night in July, around eleven, Adkee, Kathrine, Khairy, Hezni, and I walked the short distance to our farm to grind hay for the animals. In the summertime it was far too hot to spend the day on the farm, so we usually went after dinner, when the moon was big enough to help illuminate our chores and the air was a little cooler. We walked slowly. Grinding hay was strenuous and messy, and none of us were looking forward to the job. No matter how careful we were, we always went home with hay dust in our hair and under our clothes, itching and stinging our skin, and our arms sore from heaving the hay into the grinder.

We worked for a while, Kathrine and I in the trailer stacking the hay that the others tossed up to us from the ground. We talked and joked, but the conversation was more strained than usual. In the open field, we had a view of the land beyond Kocho, and we couldn't help but wonder and worry about what was going on out there in the dark. Suddenly the road connecting us to the south lit up with cars, and we stopped what we were doing to watch as the headlights grew brighter and the silhouettes of the vehicles came into focus. It was a line of big armored trucks, the kind the military might use.

"We should leave," Kathrine muttered. She and I were the most frightened. But Adkee refused to run. "We need to keep working," she said, heaving armfuls of hay into the baler. "We can't be so scared all the time."

Khairy was home on leave from his job as a border patrolman, which he had held for nine years, and he knew better than all of us what was happening outside Kocho. He had an investigative eye for these kinds of things. Looking toward the headlights, he put down his armful of hay and used his hand like a visor to protect his eyes from the headlights. "Those are Islamic State convoys," he said. "They look like they are heading toward the border into Syria." It was unusual, he told us, for them to be this close.

Chapter 6

ISIS ARRIVED ON THE OUTSKIRTS OF KOCHO EARLY IN THE morning of August 3, 2014, before the sun came up. I was lying on a mattress between Adkee and Dimal on our roof when the first trucks came. The Iraqi summer air is hot and glutted with dust, but I always preferred to sleep outside, just as I preferred to ride in the back of a truck rather than being trapped inside. We sectioned off parts of the roof to give privacy to the married couples and their small families, but we could whisper through the dividers and talk across rooftops. Normally I fell asleep easily to the sound of my neighbors discussing their days or praying quietly, and lately, as violence swept through Iraq, staying on the rooftops where we could see who was coming made us feel less vulnerable.

No one had slept that night. A few hours before, ISIS had launched surprise attacks on several nearby villages, driving thousands of Yazidis out of their homes and toward Mount Sinjar in a dizzying, panicked mass that soon thinned to a frail march. Behind them, the militants killed anyone who refused to convert to Islam or who was too stubborn or confused to flee, and they chased down those who were slow on their feet, shooting them or cutting their throats. The trucks, when they got close to Kocho, sounded like grenades in the quiet rural air. We flinched in fear and moved closer to one another.

ISIS conquered Sinjar easily, encountering resistance only from the hundreds of Yazidi men who fought to defend their villages with their own weapons but quickly ran out of ammunition. We soon learned that many of our Sunni Arab neighbors welcomed the militants and even joined them, blocking roads to stop Yazidis from reaching safety, allowing the terrorists to capture all non-Sunnis who failed to escape from the villages closest to Kocho, then looting the vacant Yazidi villages alongside the terrorists. We were even more shocked, though, by the Kurds who had sworn to protect us. Late at night, without any warning and after months of assuring us that they would fight for us until the end, the peshmerga had fled Sinjar, piling into their trucks and driving back to safety before the Islamic State militants could reach them.

It was, the Kurdish government later said, a "tactical withdrawal." There were not enough of the soldiers to hold the region, they told us, and their commanders thought that to stay would be suicide; their fight would be more useful in other parts of Iraq, where they stood a chance. We tried to focus our anger on the leaders in Kurdistan making the decision rather than on the individual soldiers. What we couldn't understand, though, was why they left without warning us or taking us with them or helping us to get to safety. Had we known they were leaving, we would have gone to Kurdistan. I am almost certain that Kocho would have been empty by the time ISIS arrived.

Villagers called it treason. Those with houses near their posts saw the peshmerga leave and begged them, with no success, to at least leave their weapons behind for the villagers to use. The news quickly spread to the rest of the village, but it took a while for reality to sink in. The peshmerga had been so revered, and many of us were so certain that they would come back and fulfill their duty, that the first time we heard the rounds of Islamic State gunfire in Kocho, some of the women whispered to one another, *"Maybe the peshmerga have come to save us."*

With the peshmerga gone, militants swiftly filled the abandoned military posts and checkpoints, trapping us in our village. We had no escape plan, and ISIS quickly blocked the road connecting southern Sinjar villages, like Kocho, to the mountain, which was already filling up with families trying to hide. The few families who tried to escape were captured as they fled and were killed or kidnapped. My mother's nephew tried to leave with his family, and when ISIS stopped them in their car, they killed the men on the spot. "I don't know what happened to the women," my mother told us after she got the phone call, and so we were left to imagine the worst. Stories like this began to fill our homes with fear.

Hezni and Saoud were both outside Kocho for work when ISIS came—Hezni in Sinjar City and Saoud in Kurdistan—and they called all night, in agony because they were so far away and because they were safe. They told us all they could about what was happening in Sinjar. Fleeing Yazidis, tens of thousands, walked with their livestock along the single-lane road to the mountain. The lucky had packed into cars or hung off the sides of trucks, traveling as quickly as they could through the crowds. Some pushed the elderly in wheelbarrows or carried them on their backs, hunched over with the weight. The midday sun was dangerously hot, and a few of the very old or sick died on the side of the road, their thin bodies collapsed into the sand like fallen branches. People who passed them were so intent on making it to the mountain, and so scared of being caught by terrorists, that they barely seemed to notice.

As the Yazidis walked toward the mountain, they dropped much of what they carried. A stroller, a coat, a cooking pot—when they first ran from their homes, it must have seemed impossible that they would leave those things. How could they eat without a pot to cook in? What would happen when their arms started to ache from carrying a baby? Would they make it home before winter? Eventually, though, as the walk became more strenuous and the distance to the mountain seemed longer with each step they took, all of that stuff became dead weight and was left by the side of the road like trash. Children dragged their feet until their shoes split apart beneath them. When they reached the mountain, some people scrambled straight up the craggy sides while others hid in caves, temples, or mountain villages. Cars sped along the winding roads, some tumbling over the sides when the drivers, in their haste, lost control. The mountain's plateaus became crowded with the displaced.

On top of the mountain, there was hardly any relief. Some Yazidis immediately went searching for food and water or for missing relatives, begging those living in the villages for help. Others sat frozen where they were. Maybe they were tired. Or maybe in the first calm moment since ISIS came to Sinjar, in relative safety, they were starting to think about what had happened to them. Their villages were occupied, and everything they had now belonged to someone else. As they swept through the region, ISIS militants destroyed the small temples that stood near the bottom of the mountain. One graveyard near the mountain that was normally reserved for children was now packed with bodies of all ages, people who had been killed by ISIS or who had died trying to reach the mountain. Hundreds of men had been slaughtered. Boys and young women were kidnapped and later taken to Mosul or to Syria. Older women, women my mother's age, were rounded up and executed, filling mass graves.

The Yazidis on the mountain thought about the decisions they had made as they fled. Maybe they cut off another car heading to the mountain so they could get there first, or didn't stop to pick up someone who was walking. Could they have managed to take their animals with them, or waited just a moment longer to save someone else? My mother's nephew had been born with a disability that made it hard for him to walk, and when ISIS came, he insisted his loved ones go to the mountain ahead of him, knowing he could not get there on foot. Would he make it at all? Now the survivors were trapped in the grueling heat on the mountaintop, with ISIS swarming below and no sign of rescue.

We received this news feeling that we were getting word of our own future, and we prayed. We called everyone we knew in the Sunni Arab villages and in Kurdistan, but no one had anything hopeful to say. ISIS didn't attack Kocho that night or that morning, but they made it known that if we tried to escape, they would kill us. Those who lived close to the edge of the village told us what they looked like. Some had scarves pulled up to their eyes. Most had beards. They carried American weapons, given to the Iraqi Army when the Americans left and then taken from the posts the army had abandoned. The militants looked exactly like they had on TV and in propaganda videos online. I couldn't see them as people. Like the guns they carried and the tanks they drove, the men themselves were just weapons to me, and they were aimed at my village.

————

THE FIRST DAY, August 3, an Islamic State commander came to Kocho, and Ahmed Jasso called the men to the jevat. Because Elias was the eldest, he went to find out what was happening. We waited for him in our courtyard, sitting in the small bits of shade beside our sheep, which we had moved there for safekeeping. They bleated softly, oblivious to what was happening.

Sitting beside me, Kathrine looked young and frightened. Although we were a few years apart in age, we were in the same grade at school, and we were inseparable. In our teens, we had both become obsessed with makeup and hair, and we practiced on each other, debuting our new styles and techniques at village weddings. The brides inspired us; they would never spend more money and time on their appearance than they did that day, and they all looked like pictures out of a magazine. I studied them closely. *How did she get her hair to do that? What shade of lipstick is she wearing?* Then I would ask the bride for a photograph, which I added to a collection I kept in a thick green photo album. I imagined that, when I opened my salon, women would flip through that album, looking for the perfect hairstyle. By the time ISIS came, I had over two hundred photographs. My favorite was one of a young brunette, her hair curled loosely on top of her head and studded with small white flowers.

Usually Kathrine and I labored over our long hair, conditioning it with palmfuls of olive oil and coloring it with henna, but today we hadn't even bothered to comb it. My niece was pale and silent, and I suddenly felt much, much older than her. I wanted to make her feel better. "Don't worry," I told her, taking her hand. "Everything is going to be all right." It was what my mother told me, and even though I hadn't believed her, it had been her job to stay hopeful for her children just as it was now my job to stay hopeful for Kathrine.

Elias came into the courtyard, and everyone turned toward him. He was breathing quickly, as though he had raced home from the jevat, and he tried to calm himself before he started talking. "Daesh has surrounded Kocho," he said. "It's not possible to leave."

The Islamic State commander had warned the men at the jevat that if they tried to escape, they would be punished. "He said that four families have already tried," Elias told us. "They stopped them. The men refused to convert. They killed them. The women held on to their children. They separated them. They took their cars and their daughters."

"Surely the peshmerga will come back," my mother whispered from where she sat. "We have to pray. God will save us."

"Someone will come to help us," Massoud said. He was angry. "They can't just leave us here."

"The commander said we should call our relatives on Mount Sinjar and tell them to come back down and turn themselves in," Elias continued. "They said to tell them that if they leave the mountain, they will be spared."

We were silent, absorbing this news. In spite of all the hardships on top of the mountain, at least the Yazidis who had made it there were away from ISIS. We trusted the mountain to protect us from persecution. Over generations Yazidis had fled to the safety of its caves, drunk from its streams, and survived on figs and pomegranates picked from its trees. Our temples and sheikhs surrounded it, and we thought God must be watching it especially closely. Hezni had made it from Sinjar City to the mountain, and when he called, he would chastise us for worrying about him. "You are crying for us, but we are crying for you," he said. "We are already saved."

We would do what the militants told us to do. When they came door-to-door to collect the villagers' weapons, we handed over all but one gun, which we buried on our farm late one night when we thought they wouldn't be able to see. We wouldn't try to escape. Every day Elias or another brother would go to the jevat to get orders from the Islamic State commander, and then he would come home to give us the news. We stayed indoors and were quiet. That buried gun would, in the end, stay buried. But no matter what promises ISIS made, we would sooner die than tell Hezni or anyone else to leave Mount Sinjar. Everyone knew what would happen to the Yazidis if they came down from the mountain.

Chapter 7

THE SIEGE OF KOCHO LASTED FOR CLOSE TO TWO WEEKS.
Some days passed by in one big blur, every moment just like
the next, while other days I felt every second like a sting. In the
morning the Islamic call to prayer echoed from the Islamic State
checkpoints, a sound that, although unusual for Kocho, I knew
well from studying Islam in school and traveling to Sinjar City.
There older Yazidis would complain about hearing the call to
prayer. "Sinjar is no longer a Yazidi city," they would sigh, convinced that we all would soon be confined in our little villages
and towns while the more desirable parts of the Yazidi areas were
left to the richer and better-connected Arabs and Kurds. Still, I
was never really bothered by the call to prayer until ISIS came to
Sinjar. With them surrounding us, the sound became menacing.

One by one relatives began pouring into our house. Jilan,
Hezni's wife, abandoned their nearly completed house just outside town to join us, and cousins and half siblings came from all
over the village, carrying small suitcases or food and formula for
the babies. Shireen, Saoud's wife, had just given birth, and when
she brought her squalling pink newborn to us, the women surrounded the baby, which was like an image of hope. Our few
rooms filled quickly with clothes and blankets, photographs and
valuables, anything they could carry. During the day we huddled
around the television, looking for stories about the massacre of

Yazidis in Sinjar. It was like something out of a nightmare. Airplanes couldn't fly low enough to properly distribute aid, and the enormous mountain seemed to swallow the packages of food and water as they fell.

Yazidis frantically tried to board Iraqi Army helicopters that landed on the roads cutting across the mountaintop, pushing babies and the elderly on board while the soldiers pushed back, shouting that there wasn't enough room. "The helicopter can't take off with this many people!" they yelled, a logic that didn't matter to the frenzied people on the mountaintop. We heard that one woman, determined to leave on a helicopter, dangled for a moment from the landing skid as it lifted off before she lost her grip and fell. Someone said that when her body hit the rocks below, it looked like an exploding watermelon.

Hezni had only narrowly made it to the mountain before ISIS took over Sinjar City. After his police station was evacuated, he took off walking with another policeman toward the mountain. Not wanting to leave any weapons behind for the terrorists heading to the city, each of the men in his unit left holding a rifle, with pistols tucked into their pants. It was hot and dusty on the way, and they were scared, unsure where the militants might be hiding or where they would be coming from. About half a mile outside Zainab, they watched as an Islamic State truck drove up to the town's Shiite mosque and then as the mosque crumbled in an explosion. Switching direction along the highway, they narrowly missed being discovered by three trucks full of Islamic State militants who would, only a few minutes later, execute the men walking behind Hezni and his colleague. "I was saved by a miracle," my brother would later tell me.

On top of the mountain, the days were brutally hot and the nights freezing. They had no food, and people were dying of dehydration. On the first day, displaced Yazidis slaughtered the sheep they had herded up the sides of the mountain, and everyone ate a small ration of meat. On the second day, Hezni and some others crept down the eastern side of the mountain on foot and went to a small village that ISIS had not yet reached. There they filled a tractor with raw wheat, which they boiled back on top of the mountain, giving everyone a cup, just enough to fill their stomachs. One day some militants from the YPG—the Syrian branch of the PKK, or Kurdistan Workers Party, a Turkey-based Kurdish guerrilla army—brought bread and food from Syria.

Eventually the YPG, with help from U.S. air strikes, cleared a path for the Yazidis from Sinjar into the Kurdish parts of Syria, which had been kept relatively safe since the beginning of the Syrian civil war. There Kurds aligned with the PKK had been trying to establish an autonomous region. ISIS shot at the Yazidis as they fled, but tens of thousands were able to make it off the mountain and into relative safety. Hezni fled the mountain to our aunt's house near Zakho. As Yazidis made their way through Kurdish Syria and into Iraqi Kurdistan, the Kurds living there, most of whom are Sunni, drove to meet them, delivering food, water, and clothing. Others opened their homes, stores, and schools to the fleeing Yazidis. It was a show of compassion that still moves us today.

Before the massacres, I hadn't given the PKK much thought. They didn't have a large presence in Sinjar, and even though I would sometimes see images of them on Kurdish television—men and women in baggy gray uniforms kneeling beside their Kalashnikovs somewhere in the Qandil Mountains, on the border with Iran—they didn't seem connected to my life, and neither did their fight against the Turkish government. But after they saved the Yazidis stranded on the mountain, the PKK became heroes in Sinjar, replacing the peshmerga in the minds of many as the protectors of Yazidis. Their involvement would end up inflaming tensions between them and Barzani's party, the KDP, which still wanted to have the most influence in Sinjar, making our home vulnerable to a different kind of war, one that began unfolding over the next few years. But at the time we were just grateful to the PKK for helping Yazidis off the mountain and for sending hundreds of soldiers to fight on the front lines against ISIS in Sinjar.

There was no sign, however, of help coming to Kocho. Each day one of my brothers would go to the jevat and come home with news, and none of it was hopeful. Kocho's men were trying to figure out a plan, they said, but no one outside the village was willing to help. "Maybe the Americans will use their planes to free us, like they did at the mountain," my mother said. The only time the Islamic State militants who surrounded Kocho seemed scared was when they heard the sound of planes or helicopters. "Or maybe the PKK will come here next," she continued. But my brothers, who were in touch with Yazidi translators who had worked with the U.S. Army and were now in America, quickly lost hope that either of those things would happen.

Airplanes and helicopters flew over us, but they were heading to the mountain, not to Kocho, and we knew it was unlikely that the PKK would make it to us. The PKK militants were brave and had been training for a long time—they had been fighting the Turkish Army for almost half a century—but they were mountain fighters and wouldn't be able to overtake ISIS on the flat plains that connected us to Mount Sinjar. Plus, Kocho was now in enemy territory, far enough south to be out of reach. We were nowhere.

For a long time, though, we held out hope that the Americans would come to break the siege of Kocho. My brother Jalo, the one who had been stationed at Tal Afar airport after the U.S. invasion, had a friend in the United States named Haider Elias, a Yazidi who had been granted asylum in Houston because he worked as a translator for the Americans. They spoke every day, usually more than once, although Haider cautioned Jalo not to call him—he was worried that if ISIS checked Jalo's phone and saw a U.S. number, they would kill him on the spot.

Haider and a group of expat Yazidis, were scrambling to help Yazidis in Iraq, petitioning the governments in Washington, Erbil, and Baghdad from a hotel room they had rented in Washington, D.C., but they were making no progress in Kocho. Jalo answered every phone call from Haider immediately, and his hope was quickly replaced with exasperation. My brother had been with the Americans when they had raided houses looking for insurgents and knew what they were capable of when they were on the ground. Jalo was sure that if the United States sent soldiers to attack Islamic State checkpoints around Kocho, they could break the siege. Sometimes Islamic State members would complain at the jevat about the American operations in Sinjar to save the Yazidis, calling Obama a "crusader." When this happened, Jalo told Haider, "I think they're losing control. They'll probably let us go." A few days earlier some Islamic State militants had taken Ahmed Jasso, who felt sick, to a nearby town for treatment. "Why would they do that unless they planned to keep us alive?" Jalo asked.

Jalo loved America. Before the siege, he would call Haider in Texas to ask him about his new life outside Iraq. He was jealous that Haider was going to college in America while Jalo had not even been able to start high school. "Find me an American wife!" Jalo joked. "Someone ugly and older, who will marry me no matter what."

Haider had less faith in the Americans coming to help us in Kocho. He thought that if anything, ISIS might retaliate against Kocho because of the air strikes. "Be careful," he told Jalo. "They might be fooling you into thinking they are weaker. They won't let you go." Everyone involved seemed overwhelmed by what was happening all over Iraq. The media weren't even reporting on the siege of Kocho. "They are changing the prime minister in Baghdad," Elias said. "They don't have time to think about us."

So we waited. The village was quiet and the streets empty. Everyone stayed inside. We stopped eating, and I watched my brothers grow thin, their faces pale. I assumed that the same thing was happening to me, but I didn't want to look in the mirror to check. We didn't bathe, and soon the stench of all our bodies filled the house. Each night we climbed up to the roof—after dark, so that militants wouldn't see us—where we slept shoulder to shoulder. We crouched low to the ground while we were up there, trying to hide behind the roof's short wall, and we whispered quietly so they wouldn't hear us. Our bodies tensed when Shireen's baby, unaware of what was happening, began to cry. None of that mattered, of course. ISIS knew we were there. That was the point.

———

ISIS HELD US prisoners in our homes while they carried out the genocide elsewhere in Sinjar. They didn't have time, yet, to take care of us. They were busy confiscating Yazidi homes and filling bags with their jewelry, car keys, and cell phones; busy rounding up the Yazidis' cows and sheep to keep as their own. They were distributing young women among militants in Iraq and Syria to be used as sex slaves and murdering the men who might be old enough to defend themselves. Thousands of Yazidis had already been killed, their bodies swept into mass graves that ISIS would try—and fail—to keep hidden.

Our last hope for outside help was with the neighboring villages, where our Sunni Arab friends and kiriv lived. We heard stories of Arabs sheltering Yazidis or driving them to safety. But we heard many more stories of them turning on Yazidis, handing them over to ISIS and then joining the militants. Some were only rumors, and some came from people close to us whom we trusted, and so we knew them to be true. One morning one of my cousins took his family to his kiriv's house, desperate for help. The family welcomed them and made them feel safe. "You can wait here," they said. "We will help you." Then they reported my cousin to the Islamic State commander, who sent militants to capture him and his family.

My brothers called everyone they could think of in these villages, climbing to the roof where there was better cell reception, and most of the people they reached sounded genuinely worried about us. None, though, had any answers or could think of ways to help. They told us to stay where we were. "Be patient," they said. Some of our Muslim neighbors came to visit us while we were under siege, bringing food to the village and telling us that our pain was their pain. They laid their palms on their hearts and promised, "We won't abandon you." But day by day, they all did.

Our Sunni neighbors could have come to us and tried to help. If they knew what was going to happen to the women, they could have dressed us all in black and taken us with them. They could have just come and told us, matter-of-factly, "This is what will happen to you," so we could stop fantasizing about being rescued. But they didn't. They made the decision to do nothing, and their betrayals were like bullets before the real bullets came.

One day I went with Dimal, Khairy, Elias, and Khaled—one of my half brothers—to our farm to get a lamb to slaughter for dinner. Unlike the adults, who had no appetite, the kids cried for something real to eat, and without any food coming into Kocho, we had to sacrifice one of our lambs.

There was good cell phone service at the farm, and Elias brought his phone so the men could continue to call for help while we got the lamb. We had just heard that my niece, Baso, was captured by ISIS trying to escape to the mountain from Tal Kassab, where she had been tending to a sick cousin, and then taken to a school in Tal Afar. The school, we were told, was painted red and was full of Yazidi girls and women. I remembered that one of my teachers, a Sunni man called Mr. Mohammed, was from Tal Afar, and I thought he might be able to help us find Baso.

Many of our teachers were Sunni Arabs from outside Kocho, mostly from Mosul. We respected them and treated them as part of our village. With ISIS now in their hometowns, I thought about what they were going through. None of them had called to see what was happening in Kocho. At first this worried me. I couldn't imagine what it must be like for them having to escape ISIS or, worse, live under them. As the siege wore on, though, I started to wonder if the teachers were silent not because they were living in fear but because they were happy that ISIS was there. Maybe all along they had considered their students like me to be kuffar. Just the thought made me feel sick to my stomach.

I had all my teachers' phone numbers written down in the back of one of my textbooks, and I used Elias's phone to call Mr. Mohammed. After a few rings, he picked up.

"Merhaba, Ustaz Mohammed," I said, addressing him politely in Arabic. I thought about the days I'd spent in Mr. Mohammed's class, trying to follow his lessons, knowing that if I passed, I would move up to the next grade, closer to graduation and the rest of my life. I trusted him.

"Who is this?" My teacher sounded normal, and his calmness made my heart race.

"Nadia, *ustazi,*" I said. "From Kocho."

"Nadia, what is it?" he asked. His voice quickened slightly. He sounded cold and impatient.

I explained that Baso had been captured by ISIS and taken to Tal Afar. "They said that the school is painted red," I told him. "That's all we know. We can't leave Kocho, Daesh has surrounded the village, and they said they will kill anyone who tries to leave. Can you help us talk to Baso? Do you know where the school is?"

For a moment, my teacher was silent. Maybe he couldn't hear

me. Maybe Daesh had cut service, or maybe Elias was out of credits. When Mr. Mohammed finally spoke, he sounded like a different person from the man who had taught me only months before. His voice was distant and cold. "I can't talk to you, Nadia," he said in a whisper. "Don't worry about your niece. They will ask her to convert, and someone will marry her." He hung up before I could respond. I looked at the phone in my hand, a piece of cheap, useless plastic.

"The son of a bitch," Elias said, grabbing the lamb by the collar and steering it toward the path home. "We've been calling and calling, and none of them are responding."

In that moment something within me changed, maybe forever. I lost hope that anyone would help us. Maybe my teacher was like us: scared for himself and his family and doing whatever he needed to do to stay alive. Or maybe he had welcomed ISIS and the chance to live in the world it envisioned, one guided by their brutal interpretation of Islam—a world without Yazidis, or anyone who didn't believe precisely what they believed. I didn't know. But in that moment I was sure that I hated him.

Chapter 8

THE FIRST TIME I SAW AN ISLAMIC STATE MILITANT UP close was six days into the siege. We had run out of flour and drinkable water, so I went with Adkee and two of our nieces, Rojian and Nisreen, to Jalo's house to get supplies. It was only a few minutes' walk from our house to Jalo's, through a narrow alley, and it was unusual to see Islamic State members on the village roads. They stayed on the outskirts of the village, manning the checkpoints to make sure no one tried to escape.

Still, we were terrified to leave home. Stepping out of the front door was like walking onto another planet. Nothing about Kocho seemed familiar or comforting. Normally the alleyways and streets would be full of people, kids playing and their parents shopping in the small convenience stores or the pharmacy, but now the village was empty and quiet. "Stay close to me," I whispered to Adkee, who walked ahead, braver than the rest of us. We moved quickly, shuffling through the alley in a huddle. I was so scared I felt as if I were hallucinating. We ran from our own shadows.

My mother told us to go. "You don't need the men," she said, and we agreed. We had been sitting around the house doing nothing but watching TV and crying, growing thinner and weaker by the day. My brothers at least went to the jevat, and when they came home, after telling us what the mukhtar or Islamic State commander said, they punched numbers into their cell phones, still trying to find someone who would help us, until they collapsed from hunger and exhaustion. My brothers were fighters, like our father, and I had never seen them so hopeless. It was my turn to do something to help.

There is no grand design to Kocho, no one who mapped out all the homes and streets when the village was settled so it would all make sense in the end. If you own land, you can build whatever you want on it, wherever you want, and so the village is haphazard and can be dizzying to walk through. Houses expand in such unpredictable ways that they can seem alive, and the alleyways zigzag around these houses in a maze that would confuse anyone who hadn't memorized the layout of the village. And memorizing it takes a lifetime of walking from home to home.

Jalo's house was at the very end of the village, and all that separated him from the world outside Kocho was a brick wall. Beyond that the desert-like Sinjar stretched toward Mosul, which was now the capital of the Islamic State in Iraq. We pushed through the metal gate and walked into the kitchen. The house was empty and tidy, with no sign that Jalo and his family had left in a rush, but I was scared being inside. It seemed haunted by their absence. Finding some flour and water and a case of baby formula, we loaded the supplies into bags as quickly as we could, without talking.

On our way out, Rojian pointed to the garden wall, where a brick had fallen out, leaving a hole at about waist height. None of us had been brave enough to look for long at the militants we could see from our roof, where we felt too exposed. The wall, though, provided some cover and through that hole we would be able to see one of the first checkpoints leading out of Kocho. "Do you think there is Daesh out there?" Rojian wondered, and walked into the garden, crouching beside the wall. Looking at one another, the three of us dropped what we carried and joined her, pressing our foreheads against the wall to get a good view of the world outside.

About two hundred yards away, a few militants manned a checkpoint that used to belong to the peshmerga, and the Iraqi Army before them. They were dressed in baggy black pants and black shirts, and their weapons hung by their sides. We watched their movements as though they held a code—their feet tapping on the sandy road, their hands moving while they talked to one another—and each gesture filled us with dread.

A few minutes earlier we had been so scared at the possibility of running into a militant on our walk, but now we couldn't tear ourselves away from the sight of them. I wished we could hear what they were saying. Maybe they were planning something, and we could understand better what was waiting for us, bring some news to help our brothers fight. Maybe they were gloating about taking Sinjar; if we heard that we would get so angry we would fight back.

"What do you think they're talking about?" Rojian whispered.

"Nothing good," Adkee said, snapping us back to reality. "Come on, let's go. We promised Mom we'd deliver these things quickly."

We walked home in a state of disbelief. Nisreen broke the silence. "They're the same as the people holding Baso captive," she said. "She must be so scared."

The alley felt even narrower, and we walked as quickly as we could, trying to stay calm. But when we got home and told my mother what we had seen—how close they were to the home where Jalo's children had slept only days before—Nisreen and I couldn't help it. We began to cry. I wanted to be hopeful and strong, but I needed my mother to understand how scared I was so that she would comfort me.

"They're so close," I said. "We're in their hands. If they want to do anything bad to us, they can."

"We have to wait and pray," my mother replied. "Maybe we'll be rescued. Maybe they won't hurt us. Maybe we'll be saved somehow." Not a day went by that she didn't say something like that.

OUR CLOTHES TURNED gray from dust and sweat, but we didn't think about changing. We stopped eating and drank only small amounts of tepid water out of plastic bottles that had been left in the sun. The power went out and stayed out for the rest of the siege. We ran the generator just enough to charge our cell phones and to watch TV when the news was showing reports on the war with ISIS, which it almost always was. The headlines made us feel hopeless: close to forty children had died on top of Mount Sinjar from starvation and dehydration, and many more had died while fleeing. Bashiqa and Bahzani, two major Yazidi villages close to Mosul, had been taken over by ISIS, but luckily most of the people there had been able to flee to Iraqi Kurdistan. Thousands of Yazidi women and girls from across Sinjar had been abducted; we heard that ISIS was using them as sex slaves.

Qaraqosh, a majority Christian town in Nineveh, had fallen, and almost its entire population had fled to Iraqi Kurdistan, where they were living as refugees in half-built malls and tents set up in church gardens. Shiite Turkmen in Tal Afar were struggling to escape their own siege. ISIS had almost made it all the way to Erbil, but the Americans had stopped them—to protect their consulate, they said, while also giving cover to the Yazidis trapped on Mount Sinjar with air strikes. Baghdad was in chaos. The American president, Obama, was calling what was happening to the Yazidis a "potential genocide." But no one talked about the siege of Kocho.

We were living in a new world. Life in Kocho stopped as people stayed inside for fear of being seen by ISIS. It was strange to be so removed from the other families in the village. We were used to visitors coming over until late at night, spending mealtimes with friends, and talking across rooftops before going to sleep. With ISIS surrounding Kocho, even whispering to the person lying next to you at night seemed dangerous. We tried to go unnoticed, as though ISIS might forget we were there. Even getting skinnier seemed like a way of protecting ourselves, as though if we stopped eating, eventually we would become invisible. People ventured from home only to check on relatives, get more supplies, or help out if someone was sick. Even then they walked quickly and always toward shelter, like insects running away from a broom.

One night, though, in spite of ISIS, we gathered together as a village to celebrate Batzmi, a holiday observed mostly by Yazidi families originally from Turkey. It normally takes place in December, but a villager named Khalaf, whose family celebrates the holiday, thought we needed the ceremony now, when fear kept us from one another and we were close to losing hope. Batzmi is a time to pray to Tawusi Melek, but even more important to us during the siege, it is also a time to remember Yazidis who have been forced to leave their homeland, Yazidis like Khalaf's ancestors, who had once lived in Turkey, before the Ottomans drove them out.

All of Kocho was invited to Khalaf's house, where four men who were thought to have clean souls because they were unmarried were going to bake the holy Batzmi bread. We waited until the sun set, and then people began pouring out of their homes toward Khalaf's. On the way, we cautioned one another not to draw attention to what we were doing. "Don't make noise," we whispered as we walked through the village streets. I was with Adkee, and we were both terrified. If ISIS discovered us, I knew, Khalaf would be punished for conspiring to perform an infidel's ritual, but I didn't know what else the militants might do. I hoped it wasn't too late to bring our case before God.

The lights were on inside Khalaf's house, and people crowded around the baking bread, which is left to puff up on a special dome before being blessed by the head of the household. If the bread stays whole, it brings good luck. If it breaks, something bad might happen to the family. The bread was plain because we were under siege (normally it's studded with nuts and raisins), but it was sturdy and round and showed no sign of breaking.

Except for the sound of soft crying and the occasional pop of the wood in the oven, Khalaf's house was quiet. The familiar smell of the smoke from the oven settled over me like a blanket. I didn't look around to see if Walaa or other school friends, whom I hadn't seen since the siege started, were there. I wanted to focus on the ritual. Khalaf began to pray. "May the God of this holy bread take my soul as a sacrifice for the whole village," he said, and the weeping grew louder. Some of the men tried to calm their wives, but I thought it was brave, not weak, to cry there in Khalaf's house where the sound might carry out to the checkpoints.

Afterward Adkee and I walked home in silence, retracing our steps back through the front door and onto the roof, where those who had stayed behind to guard the house sat upright on their mattresses, relieved that we had returned safely. The women had all taken to sleeping on one side of the roof, the men on the other. My brothers were still constantly on their phones, and we wanted to spare them our crying, which we knew would only make them feel worse. That night I managed to sleep a little, until just before the sun came up and my mother nudged us awake. "It's time to go downstairs," she whispered, and I tiptoed down the ladder into the dark courtyard, praying that no one could see us.

———

IN MY FAMILY it was Hajji, one of my half brothers, who talked the most about villagers rebelling against ISIS. Militants still told the men at the jevat that if we didn't convert to Islam, they would take us to Mount Sinjar, but Hajji was sure they were lying. "They just want to keep us calm," he insisted. "They want to make sure we won't fight back."

Every once in a while, I saw Hajji whispering over our garden wall with our neighbors, and it looked as if they were planning something. They watched closely as Islamic State convoys drove by the village. "They've just come from a massacre," Hajji would say, turning his head as they raced by. Sometimes he would stay up all night watching TV, anger filling him until the sun was high the next morning.

Hajji wasn't the only one in the village thinking about ways to revolt. Many families, like ours, hid weapons from ISIS, and they discussed ways to get them and attack the checkpoints. The men had trained as fighters and wanted to prove themselves, but they also knew that no matter how many Islamic State members they managed to kill with their buried knives or AK-47s, there would still be more along the road, and that eventually, no matter what they did, a lot of people from the village would end up dead if they tried to fight. Even if we all got together and killed the militants who were stationed just around the village, we would have nowhere to go. They controlled every road out of Kocho and had cars and trucks and all the weapons they seized from us and the Iraqi Army. Uprising wasn't a plan; it was a fantasy. But for men like Hajji, the thought of fighting back was all that kept them sane while we waited.

Every day men from the village gathered in the jevat to try to come up with a plan. If we couldn't escape, or fight our way out, or hide, could we trick the militants? Maybe if we told them that we would convert to Islam, they would give us more time. It was decided that if a militant threatened or touched one of Kocho's women or girls, then, and only then, would we stall by pretending to convert. But the plan was never carried out.

When the women plotted, it was to try to come up with ways

we could hide the men if ISIS came to kill them. There were plenty of places in Kocho where the militants wouldn't know where to look—deep, barely wet wells and basements with hidden entrances. Even bales of hay and sacks of animal feed might keep the men safe long enough for them to avoid being killed. But they refused to consider hiding. "We would rather be slaughtered than leave you alone with Daesh," they said. And so, while we waited to find out our fate at the hands of ISIS and lost hope that anyone was coming to save us, I tried to face every possibility of what could happen to me and my family. I started to think about dying.

Before ISIS came, we weren't used to young people dying, and I didn't like talking about death. Just the thought of it frightened me. Then in early 2014 two young people from Kocho had died suddenly. First, a border policeman named Ismail was killed in a terrorist attack while working south of Kocho in Al Qaeda–influenced areas where ISIS was already taking root. Ismail was about Hezni's age, quiet and devout. It was the first time someone from Kocho was killed by ISIS, and everyone started to worry about their family members who had taken jobs with the government.

Hezni was at the police station in Sinjar when they brought Ismail's body in, and so we heard about his death before most people in the village, even before his own wife and family. They were poor, as we were, and Ismail had joined the military, as my brothers had, because they needed the money. That morning I walked the long way to school, avoiding his house. I couldn't bear passing by, knowing that he was dead when his family inside had yet to find out. As word spread through the village, men began firing their rifles into the air in mourning, and all the girls in the classroom screamed when they heard the shots.

Yazidis consider it a blessing to prepare a body for burial, sometimes sitting with it for hours until the sun comes up. My brother Hezni prepared Ismail. He washed the body, braided his hair, dressed him in white, and when his widow brought him the blanket they had slept in on their first night as a married couple, Hezni wrapped her husband in it. A long line of villagers followed his body to the edge of town, before it was loaded onto a truck to be driven to the graveyard.

A few months later, my friend Shireen was accidentally shot by her nephew while he played with a hunting rifle on their farm. I had been with Shireen the night before she was killed. We talked about exams and her two mischievous brothers who had been arrested for fighting. Shireen brought up Ismail. She had a dream the night before he died, she told me. "In the dream something really huge happened in Kocho. Everyone was crying," she said. Then, sounding a little guilty, she confessed, "I think it was about Ismail dying." Now I am sure the dream must have been about her own death, too, or about her nephew, who refused to leave the house after the accident, or even about ISIS coming to Kocho.

My mother prepared Shireen. My friend's hands were stained brownish red with henna and then tied loosely together with a white scarf. Because she was unmarried, her hair was arranged into a single long braid. If she had any gold, it was buried with her. "If man can be buried, then gold can be buried, too," Yazidis say. Like Ismail, Shireen was washed and shrouded in white, and her body was marched in front of a long, mournful crowd to the edge of town, where a truck waited to take her the rest of the way.

These rituals are important because the afterlife, according to Yazidism, is a demanding place, where the dead can suffer like humans. They rely on us to take care of them, showing us what they need through our dreams. Often someone will see a loved one in a dream who tells them that they are hungry or who, they notice, is wearing threadbare clothing. When they wake up, they give food or clothing to the poor, and in return, God gives their dead food and clothing in the afterlife. We consider these good deeds vital to being a pious Yazidi partly because we believe in reincarnation. If you were a good person and a faithful Yazidi during your lifetime, your soul will be born anew, and you will rejoin the community that mourned you. Before that can happen, you have to prove to God and his angels that you deserve to go back to earth, to a life that might even be better than the one you left.

While our souls travel the afterlife, waiting to be reincarnated, what happens to our bodies, our flesh after our souls have no more use for it, is much simpler. We are washed and then buried wrapped in cloth, and the grave is marked with a ring of stones. There should be very little separating us from the dirt, so we can more easily give our bodies back, clean and whole, to the earth that made us. It's important that Yazidis are buried properly and prayed for. Without these rituals, our souls may never be reborn. And our bodies may never go home to where they belong.

Chapter 9

ON AUGUST 12 AN ISLAMIC STATE COMMANDER VISITED THE jevat with an ultimatum: we either convert to Islam and become part of the caliphate, or suffer the consequences. "We have three days to decide," Elias told us all, standing in the courtyard of our house, his eyes darting with a crazy energy. "First they said, if we don't convert, we will have to pay a fine."

I was in the shower when Elias came back with the news, and through a crack in the stall door I could see him speaking to our mother. They both began to cry. Without rinsing the soap out of my hair, I grabbed the first dress I saw, one of my mother's that fell over my small body like a tent, and ran to join my family in the courtyard.

"What happens if we don't pay the fine?" my mother asked.

"Right now they are still saying that they will take us to the mountain and live in Kocho themselves," Elias said. His handmade white undershirt, worn by observant Yazidi men, had turned gray with dirt and grime. His voice was steady, and he was no longer crying, but I could tell he was panicked. No Yazidis in Sinjar had been given the option of paying a fine instead of converting, as Iraqi Christians had. Elias was sure that the militants were lying when they said we would be given that choice, maybe even just taunting us. He breathed slowly; he must have told himself to stay calm for us, practiced what he would say on the way home from the jevat. He was such a good brother. He couldn't help it when he said next, to no one in particular, "Nothing good will come of this," and then repeated, "Nothing good will come of this."

My mother snapped into action. "Everyone, pack a bag," she told us, running into the house herself. We gathered together whatever we thought we might need—a change of clothes, diapers, baby formula, and our Iraqi IDs, the ones that state plainly that we are Yazidi. We swept up any valuables we had, though we didn't have much. My mother packed the state-issued ration card she received when my father died, and my brothers threw extra cell phone batteries and chargers into their bags. Jilan, longing for Hezni, packed one of his shirts—a black one with buttons down the front that she had held close to her throughout the siege.

I opened a drawer in the bedroom I shared with my sisters and Kathrine, pulling out my most prized possession—a long silver necklace inlaid with cubic zirconia and a matching bracelet. My mother had bought them for me in Sinjar City in 2013, after a cable connected to our tractor snapped while I was loading hay into the trailer behind it. The cable hit me across the midsection with the force of a horse kick, nearly killing me, and while I lay unconscious in the hospital, my mother raced to the bazaar to buy the jewelry. "When you get out of here, I will buy you earrings to match," she whispered, squeezing my hand. It was her way of betting on me surviving.

I hid the necklace and bracelet inside sanitary pads, which I ripped open at the seam and stuffed back into their packaging. Then I laid them on top of the extra clothes in a small black bag and zipped it shut. Next, my mother started taking photographs down from the walls. Our house was full of family photos—Hezni and Jilan at their wedding; Jalo, Dimal, and Adkee sitting in a field outside Kocho; Mount Sinjar in the spring, in such bright colors it looked almost artificial. These photos told the history of our family, from when we were desperately poor and crammed into a small house behind my father's, through years of struggle, and into our happier recent lives. Now all that was left were faint rectangles on the walls where the photos once hung. "Find the albums, Nadia," she said, noticing me standing there. "Bring everything out to the courtyard, to the tandoor."

I did what my mother asked, filling my arms with photo albums and heading to the courtyard where she knelt in front of our oven, holding out her hands for the photos my siblings took out of frames, then methodically throwing them into its wide mouth. The squat oven was the center of our home, and all bread, not just the holiday loaf baked for Batzmi, is holy to Yazidis. My mother would make extra bread to hand out to Kocho's poorest, which was a blessing for our family. When we were poor, bread from that oven kept us alive, and every meal I can remember included a tall stack of flat, blistered round loaves.

Now, as the photos turned to ash, the tandoor spat out a black chemical smoke. There was Kathrine as a baby in Lalish, being baptized in the White Spring that starts in the Lalish valley and runs underneath the old stone temple. There was my first day of school, when I cried at the thought of being separated from my mother. There was Khairy's wedding to Mona, the bride's hair crowned with flowers. *Our past is ashes,* I thought. One by one the photographs disappeared into the fire, and when they were gone, my mother picked up a pile of her white clothing, all but what she had on, and added it to the high flames. "I won't have them seeing who we were," she said, watching the pure white cloth curl and turn black. "Now they can't touch them."

I couldn't watch the photos burn. Back inside, in the small room I shared with the other girls, I opened the tall armoire. Checking to make sure I was alone, I pulled out my thick green photo album and opened it slowly, gazing at the brides. Women in Kocho would prepare for days before their weddings, and it showed in the photos. Intricate braids and curls, highlighted blond or dyed red with henna, were hair-sprayed high on a bride's head, her eyes lined thickly with kohl and decorated with bright blue or pink eye shadow. Sometimes she would weave small beads into her hair, and sometimes she would top it all with a sparkly tiara.

When the bride was ready, she was presented to the villagers, who fawned over her, then everyone would dance and drink until the sun came up and they noticed that the bride and groom had, as they were supposed to, left for their wedding night. As early as they could, the bride's girlfriends visited her to get the whole story of that first night. They giggled, examining the bedsheet, stained with a little telltale blood. To me, weddings defined Kocho. Women carefully practiced their makeup while men watered patches of earth so that the next day they wouldn't be too dusty to dance on. We were known throughout Sinjar for throwing elaborate parties, and even, some said, for having particularly beautiful women, and I thought each bride in my album looked like a piece of art. When I opened my salon, the album would be the first thing I put in it.

I understood why my mother asked us to burn the family photos. I also felt sick thinking about the militants looking at them and touching them. I imagined that they would sneer at us, the poor Yazidi family who thought they deserved to be happy in Iraq, who thought they could go to school and get married and live forever in the country where they had been born. The idea made me furious. But instead of taking the green album to the courtyard to be burned, I put it back in the armoire, then closed the doors and, after a moment, locked it as well.

If my mother knew that I was hiding the album, she would have told me that it wasn't good to burn our own photos to stop ISIS from finding them but to keep other people's, and I know that she would have been right. The armoire wasn't even a safe place to hide the album; militants could easily break in to it, and as soon as they opened it, the green album would be the first thing they saw. If my mother had found out and asked me why I saved the photos, I wouldn't have known what to tell her. I still don't know exactly why they meant so much to me. But I couldn't bear to see the photos destroyed, all because we were scared of terrorists.

That night after we climbed onto the roof, Khairy received a phone call. It was a Yazidi friend who had stayed on the mountain even after the PKK established the safe passage to Syria. A lot of Yazidis decided not to leave the mountain, although life up there was very hard. They stayed because they felt safest high up with a steep, rocky slope separating them from ISIS, or because their religious devotion meant they would rather die than leave Sinjar. Eventually they would build a large refugee settlement, stretching from east to west on the plateau, guarded by PKK-affiliated soldiers, many of them the brave Yazidi men who had defended Sinjar as long as they possibly could.

"Look at the moon," Khairy's friend told him. Yazidis believe that the sun and the moon are holy, two of God's seven angels, and the moon that night was bright and big, the kind of moon that would have lit up our farm when we worked at night and kept us from tripping on our walk home. "We are all praying to it right now. Tell the people in Kocho to join us."

One by one Khairy woke up any of us who were sleeping. "Look at the moon," he said. Instead of crouching low so that ISIS couldn't see us on the roof, he told us just this once to pray standing up as we normally would. "Who cares if they see you? God will protect us."

"Just a few at a time," my mother cautioned. In small groups, we stood. The moon lit up our faces and made my mother's white dress glow. I prayed with my sister-in-law, who was lying on a mattress next to me. I kissed the small red and white string brace-let I still wear around my wrist and whispered, simply, "Don't leave us in their hands," before quietly lying back down beneath that enormous moon.

––––––

THE NEXT DAY, Ahmed Jasso, still trying to be the diplomat, invited five leaders from a neighboring Sunni tribe—the same tribe whose members had kidnapped Dishan—to the jevat for lunch. Women in the village prepared an elaborate meal for the tribal leaders, boiling rice, chopping vegetables, and filling clear tulip-shaped glasses with a half-inch of sugar in expectation of the sweet tea they would drink after the meal. The men slaughtered three sheep for the guests to eat, which was a huge honor for visiting tribal leaders.

Over lunch, our mukhtar tried to persuade the Sunni leaders to help us. Out of all our neighbors, this tribe was the most religiously conservative and the most likely to have leverage with ISIS. "Surely there is something you can say to them," Ahmed Jasso said. "Tell them who we are, that we mean no harm."

The leaders shook their heads. "We want to help you," they told Ahmed Jasso. "But there is nothing we can do. Daesh doesn't listen to anyone, not even us."

After the tribal leaders left, a cloud hung over our mukhtar. Naif Jasso, Ahmed's brother, called from Istanbul, where he had taken his sick wife to the hospital. "On Friday they will kill you," he told his brother.

"No, no," our mukhtar insisted. "They said that they will take us to the mountain, and they will take us to the mountain." He was hopeful until the end that there was a solution, even though no one in Baghdad or Erbil was willing to intervene, and the authorities in Washington told Haider, Jalo's friend, that they could not conduct air strikes in Kocho because the risk of civilian death was too great. They thought that if they bombed around Kocho, we all would die along with ISIS.

Two days later Islamic State militants walked through Kocho, delivering ice. It was welcome in the hottest days of August, after nearly two weeks drinking water that had been baking in the sun. Ahmed Jasso called Naif to tell him what was happening. "They swear that nothing bad will happen to us as long as we do what they tell us," he told his brother. "Why would they give us ice if they planned to kill us?"

Naif was not convinced. He paced in the Istanbul hospital room waiting for his phone to ring with updates. Forty-five minutes later, Ahmed called Naif again. "They told all of us to gather in the primary school," he said. "From there, they will take us to the mountain."

"They won't," Naif said to his brother. "They will kill all of you."

"There are too many of us to kill all at once!" Ahmed Jasso insisted. "It's impossible." And then, like the rest of us, he did what ISIS said and started walking toward the school.

We were making food when we heard. Unaware of anything but their own hunger, the children had been crying for a meal, and very early that morning we slaughtered a few of our young chickens to boil for them. Normally we would have let the chickens get older and waited until they had given us eggs before we ate them, but we had nothing else to feed the children.

The chickens were still boiling when my mother told us to get ready to go to the school. "Wear as many layers as you can," she said. "They might take our bags from us." We turned off the gas underneath the pot of greasy water and did what she said. I put on four pairs of stretchy pants, a dress, two shirts, and a pink jacket—as many clothes as I could stand to have on in the heat. Sweat immediately started streaming down my back. "Don't wear anything too tight, and don't show skin," my mother said. "Make sure you look like a decent woman."

Next, I added a white scarf to the bag, along with two dresses— one of Kathrine's cotton dresses and a bright yellow one Dimal had helped design herself with fabric bought in Sinjar City, and which she had barely worn. When I was young, we wore our clothes until they fell apart. Now we had enough money to afford one new dress a year, and I couldn't bear to leave our newest ones behind. Then, without thinking, I put my collection of makeup in the armoire with the album of bride photos and locked it again.

Already a slow stream of people had begun walking in the direction of the school. I could see them through the window, carrying their own bags. Babies hung their heads limply in their mothers' arms, and little kids dragged their feet in exhaustion. Some elderly people had to be pushed in wheelbarrows; they looked dead already. It was dangerously hot. Sweat soaked through the men's shirts and the women's dresses, staining their backs. The villagers were pale, they had lost weight. I heard them groaning but couldn't make out any words.

Hezni called from our aunt's house. As distressed as we were, he sounded like a wild animal, shouting at us that he wanted to come back to Kocho. "If something bad is going to happen to all of you, I need to be there, too!" he screamed.

Jilan shook as she spoke on the phone, trying to comfort him. They had recently decided to have children, and they expected that one day they would have the big family they both wanted. When ISIS came to Sinjar, they had just finished putting a roof on their new concrete house. My mother told us to memorize Hezni and Saoud's cell phone numbers. "You might need to call them," she told us, and I can still recite both by heart.

I walked through my house toward the side door. Even more than usual, each room felt alive with memories. I passed through the living room, where my brothers sat on long summer evenings drinking strong, sugary tea with other men from the village; the kitchen, where my sisters spoiled me by cooking my favorite meal, okra and tomatoes; my bedroom, where Kathrine and I would condition our hair with olive oil, falling asleep with our heads wrapped in plastic and waking up to the peppery smell of the warm oil. I thought of eating meals in the courtyard, the family sitting around a floor mat pinching bits of rice slick with butter between pieces of fresh bread. It was a simple house and could feel overcrowded. Elias was always threatening to move out with his family to give them more room, but he never did.

I could hear our sheep, crowded together in the courtyard. Their coats would grow thick while their bodies shrank with starvation. I couldn't bear the thought of them dying or being slaughtered for the militants to eat. They were all we had. I wish I had known to memorize every one of these details in my house—the bright colors of the cushions in the living room, the spices perfuming the kitchen, even the sound of the water dripping in the shower—but I didn't know I was leaving my home for good. I paused in the kitchen beside a stack of bread. We had taken it out for the children to eat with their chicken, but no one had touched it. I grabbed a few round loaves, which had gone cool and a bit stale, and put them into a plastic bag to take with me. It seemed like the right thing to do. Maybe we would be hungry, waiting for whatever was coming, or maybe the holy food would protect us from ISIS. "May the God who created this bread help us," I whispered, and followed Elias out onto the street.

Chapter 10

FOR THE FIRST TIME SINCE AUGUST 3, KOCHO'S ROADS AND alleyways were full of people, but they were ghosts of themselves. No one greeted anyone or kissed each other on the cheeks or the top of the head as usual. No one smiled. The stench of all our bodies, unwashed and wet with sweat, stung my nostrils. The only sounds were people groaning in the heat and the shouts of the Islamic State militants who had taken positions along the route and on rooftops, watching us and pushing us in the direction of the school. Their faces were covered up to their eyes, which followed us on our slow, labored walk.

I walked with Dimal and Elias. I didn't cling to them, but having them nearby made me feel less alone. As long as I was with my family and we were all going to the same place, I knew that at least we would have the same fate, no matter what happened. Still, leaving my home, for no reason except fear, was the hardest thing I had ever done.

We didn't say a word to one another as we walked. In the alleyway beside our house, one of Elias's friends, a man named Amr, ran up to us. He was a new father, and he was panicked. "I forgot baby formula!" he shouted. "I need to go back home!" He was jumpy, ready to run as fast as he could against the tide of people.

Elias put his hand on Amr's shoulder. "It's impossible," he told him. "Your house is too far away. Just go to the school—people will have formula." Amr nodded, and fell back in line with the others walking in the direction of the school.

We saw more militants where the alleyways emptied into the main road. They watched us, holding their guns ready. Just looking at them terrified us. Women put on headscarves, as though the scarves would protect them from the militants' gazes, and looked down as they walked, watching the small puffs of dry dust collect around their feet with each step. I moved quickly to the other side of Elias, putting my eldest brother between me and ISIS. People walked as if they had no control over their movements or direction. They looked like bodies without souls.

Every house on that walk was familiar. The daughter of the village doctor lived along the way, as did two girls from my class at school. One of them had been taken on August 3, when ISIS first came to Sinjar and her family tried to escape. I wondered what had happened to her.

Some of the homes were long and made of mud bricks, like ours, while others were concrete, like Hezni's. Most were whitewashed or left gray, but some were painted bright colors or decorated with elaborate tiles. Those homes would have taken a lifetime or two to pay for and build, and their owners expected their children and grandchildren to live there long after they died, then give the house to their children and grandchildren. Kocho's houses were always full of people, loud and crowded and happy. Now they sat empty and sad, watching us as we walked. Livestock ate absentmindedly in the courtyards, and sheepdogs barked helplessly from behind the gates.

An elderly couple near us were struggling to walk, and they stopped on the side of the road to rest. Immediately a militant barked at them, "Keep going! No stopping!" but the man seemed too exhausted to hear. He fell onto the road beneath a tree, his skinny body fitting into the small amount of shade. "I won't make it to the mountain," he told his wife, who begged him to stand up. "Just leave me here in this shade. I want to die here."

"No, you have to keep going." His wife propped him up under his shoulder, and he leaned on her as they continued walking, her body like a crutch. "We are almost there."

The sight of that old couple moving slowly toward the school made me so angry that suddenly all my fear went away. Breaking free from the crowd, I ran toward a house where a militant stood guard on the roof and threw my head back, spitting at him with all the force I could muster. In Yazidi culture, spitting is unacceptable, and in my family, it was one of the worst things you could do. Even though I was too far away from the militant for my spit to land on him, I wanted him to know how much I hated him.

"Bitch!" The militant rocked back onto his heels and began shouting down at me. He looked as if he wanted to jump off the roof and grab me. "We are here to help you!"

I felt Elias's hand on my elbow, pulling me back into the crowd.

"Keep walking," Dimal said in a loud, terrified whisper. "Why did you do that? They'll kill us." My brother and sister were furious, and Elias held me tightly to him, trying to hide me from the militant, who was still screaming at us.

"I'm sorry," I whispered, but I was lying. The only thing I regretted was that the militant had been too far away for me to spit directly onto his face.

In the distance, we could see the mountain. Long and narrow and bone-dry in the summer, it was our only source of hope. It seemed to me divine that Mount Sinjar existed at all. All of Sinjar was flat, practically a desert for most of the year, but there in the middle was Mount Sinjar, with its man-made steppes green with tobacco, plateaus good for a picnic, and peaks high enough to be in the clouds and covered in snow in the wintertime. At the very top, perched on the edge of a terrifying cliff, is a small white temple, rising out of the clouds. If we could get there, we could worship at that temple, hide in the mountain villages, maybe even bring our sheep to feed on its grass. In spite of my fear, I still expected that we would end up at Mount Sinjar. It seemed like the mountain existed in Iraq only to help Yazidis. I couldn't think of another purpose.

There was so much I didn't know as I walked with my village to the school. I didn't know that Lalish had been evacuated of everyone but our holiest priests and was being guarded by temple servants, men and boys who went there to scrub the floors and light the olive oil lamps. They were now defending the temple using whatever weapons they could find. I didn't know that in Istanbul, Naif Jasso was frantically calling Arab friends to find out what was going on and that in America, Yazidis were still pleading with leaders in Washington and Baghdad. People all over the world were trying to help us, and they were failing.

I didn't know yet that one hundred and fifty miles away in Zakho, Hezni would hear about what was happening in Kocho and lose his mind, sprinting from our aunt's house toward a well where our family members would have to restrain him to keep him from drowning himself. My brother would call Elias's phone constantly for two days after, letting it ring and ring, until one day it just stopped.

I didn't know how much ISIS hated us and what they were capable of doing. As scared as we all were, I don't think any of us on that walk could have predicted how viciously they would treat us. But while we were walking, they had already started to carry out their genocide. Outside one of our villages in north Sinjar a Yazidi woman lived in a small mud brick shed next to the highway. She wasn't very old, but she looked as if she had lived for hundreds of years because she had spent most of her adult life deep in grief. Her skin was translucent because she rarely went outside, and deep lines surrounded her eyes, which were cloudy from years of weeping.

Decades earlier, all her sons as well as her husband had died fighting in the Iran-Iraq War, and after that she saw no point in trying to live her old life. She moved from her house to the mud brick shed and wouldn't let anyone inside for long. Every day a villager stopped to leave her food or clothing. They couldn't get near her, but she must have eaten the food because she stayed alive, and the clothes disappeared, too. She was alone and she was lonely, and every moment she thought about the family she had lost, but at least she was alive. When ISIS came to Sinjar and found her outside of the village and unwilling to move, they went into her room and set her on fire.

PART II

Chapter 1

I HADN'T REALIZED HOW SMALL MY VILLAGE WAS UNTIL I saw that all of Kocho could fit into its schoolyard. We stood huddled on the dry grass. Some whispered to one another, wondering what was going on. Others were silent, in shock. No one understood yet what was happening. From that moment on, every thought I had and every step I took was an appeal to God. The militants pointed their guns at us. "Women and children, on the second floor," they shouted. "Men, stay down here."

They were still trying to keep us calm. "If you don't want to convert, we will let you go to the mountain," they said, and so we went to the second floor when they told us to, barely saying goodbye to the men we left in the yard. I think if we had known the truth of what was going to happen to the men, no mother would have let her son or husband go.

Upstairs, women huddled together in groups on the floor in the common room. The school where I had spent so many years learning and making friends now looked like a different place. Weeping filled the room, but if anyone screamed or asked what was happening, an Islamic State militant would scream back to shut up, and the room would fall into a terrified quiet again. Everyone, except the very old or the very young, was standing. It was hot and hard to breathe.

A set of barred windows were open to let air in, and from them we could see just beyond the school walls. We rushed toward the windows to try to see what was happening outside; I struggled for a view behind a row of women. No one looked in the direction of the town; everyone tried to pick their sons or brothers or husbands out of the crowd below and see what was happening to them. Some of the men sat forlornly in the garden, and we pitied them. They looked so hopeless. When a line of pickup trucks arrived at the front gate of the school, crowding together haphazardly with their engines still running, we started to panic, but the militants told us to be quiet so we couldn't shout the names of the men or scream as we wanted to.

A few militants began walking around the room holding large bags and demanding that we hand over our cell phones, jewelry, and money. Most women reached into the bags they had packed before leaving the house, dropping their things into the open bags, terrified. We hid what we could. I saw women take IDs out of their bags and remove earrings from their ears, stuffing them under their dresses and into their bras. Others pushed them deeper into their bags when the militants weren't looking. We were scared, but we weren't giving up. Even if they took us to the mountain, we suspected they would want to rob us first, and there were some things we refused to part with.

Still, the militants filled three large bags with our money and cell phones, wedding rings and watches, state-issued IDs and ration cards. Even small children were searched for valuables. One militant pointed his gun at a young girl wearing earrings. "Take them off and put them in the bag," he instructed. When she didn't move, her mother whispered, "Give them to the man so we can get to the mountain," and the girl removed the earrings from her ears and put them in the open bag. My mother gave up her own wedding ring, the most valuable thing she owned.

Through the window, I saw a man in his early thirties sitting in the dry dirt against the garden wall beside a skinny, fragile tree. I recognized him from the village, of course—I recognized everyone—and knew that like all Yazidi men, he prided himself on his bravery and considered himself a fighter. He didn't seem like someone who would give up easily. But when a militant approached and gestured at his wrist, the man said nothing and did nothing to resist. He just held out his hand and looked away as the militant pulled off his watch and threw it into his bag, then let go of the man's hand, letting it fall back to his side. At that moment I understood how dangerous ISIS was. They had brought our men to the point of hopelessness.

"Give them your jewelry, Nadia," my mother ordered quietly. I found her in the corner with some of our relatives, all of whom were clinging to one another, petrified. "If they look and they find it, they will kill you for sure."

"I can't," I whispered. I held tightly to the bag where my valuables were hidden in the sanitary pads. I had even pushed the bread to the bottom, worried that the militants would make me give it up.

"Nadia!" my mother tried to argue, but only for a second. She didn't want to draw any attention to us.

Downstairs Ahmed Jasso was on the phone with his brother Naif, who was still in the Istanbul hospital with his wife. Later he told Hezni all about these terrible calls. "They are taking our valuables," Ahmed told his brother. "Then they said they will take us to the mountain. There are already trucks outside the front gate."

"Maybe, Ahmed, maybe," Naif said. *If this is our last phone call,* he thought to himself, *let it be as happy as possible.* But after he spoke to Ahmed, Naif called an Arab friend in a nearby village. "If you hear gunshots, call me," he told the man, then hung up the phone and waited.

Finally the militants demanded that our mukhtar hand over his cell phone. They asked, "You represent the village. What have you decided? Will you convert?"

Ahmed Jasso had spent his life serving Kocho. When there

was a dispute between villagers, he called the men to the jevat to try to resolve it. When tension rose between us and a neighboring village, Ahmed Jasso was in charge of trying to smooth things over. His family made Kocho proud, and we trusted him. Now he was being asked to decide the fate of the entire village.

"Take us to the mountain," he said.

―――――

THERE WAS A commotion by the open windows, and I forced my way back toward them. Outside, militants had ordered the men onto the trucks parked outside the school, and they were pushing them into lines and onto the trucks, cramming as many men as would fit onto each one. Women whispered together as they watched, scared that if they raised their voices, a militant would close the window, blocking their view. Boys, some of them only thirteen years old, were being put on the trucks along with the men, and they all looked hopeless.

I scanned the trucks and the garden, searching for my brothers. I saw Massoud standing in the second truck, staring straight ahead along with the other men, avoiding looking up at the crowded window or back at the village. With his twin Saoud safe in Kurdistan, Massoud had barely said ten words to us during the siege. He had always been the most stoic of my brothers. He liked quiet and solitude, and his work as a mechanic suited him. One of Massoud's closest friends had been killed when he and his family tried to escape Kocho and go to the mountain, but Massoud never said a word about him or Saoud or any of the others. He had spent the siege watching reports from Mount Sinjar on TV, as we all did, and at night he would come up to the roof to sleep. But he didn't eat, he didn't talk, and unlike Hezni and Khairy, who were always more emotional, he never cried.

Next I saw Elias, walking slowly in line toward the same truck. The man who had been a father to all of us after our own father died looked completely defeated. I glanced at the women around me and was relieved to see that Kathrine wasn't at the window; I didn't want her to see her father like this. I couldn't turn away. Everything around me faded—the noise of the women weeping, the militants' heavy footsteps, the harsh afternoon sun, even the heat seemed to disappear as I watched my brothers being loaded onto the trucks, Massoud in the corner and Elias in the back. Then the doors closed, and the trucks drove away to behind the school. A moment later we heard gunshots.

I fell away from the window as the room erupted in screams. "They killed them!" the women shouted, while the militants swore at us to be quiet. My mother was now sitting on the floor, motionless and silent, and I ran to her. My whole life, whenever I'd been scared, I'd gone to my mother for comfort. "It's okay, Nadia," she would tell me, stroking my hair after I had a nightmare or if I was upset over a fight with one of my siblings. "It will be okay." I always believed her. My mother had lived through so much and never complained.

Now she sat on the floor with her head in her hands. "They've killed my sons," she sobbed.

"No more screaming," a militant ordered, pacing the crowded room. "If we hear another sound, we will kill you." Sobs turned into choking sounds as the women tried their best to stop crying. I prayed that my mother hadn't seen her sons loaded onto the trucks, as I had.

———

NAIF'S ARAB FRIEND called him from his village. "I heard shots," he said. He was crying. A moment later, in the distance, he saw the figure of a man. "Someone is running toward our village," he told our mukhtar's brother. "It's your cousin."

When Naif's cousin got to the village, he fell down, panting. "They killed everyone," he said. "They lined us up and made us climb down into the ditches"—shallow trenches that, in wetter months, hold rainwater for irrigation. "The younger-looking ones they made lift up their arms to check for hair, and if they had none, they were taken back to the trucks. They shot the rest of us." Almost all the men had been killed right there, their bodies falling on one another like trees all hit at once by lightning.

Hundreds of men were taken behind the school that day, and only a small number survived the firing squad. My brother Saeed was shot in the leg and shoulder, and after he fell, he closed his eyes and tried to calm his heart and stop breathing so loudly. A body fell on top of him. It belonged to a big, heavy man who was even denser now that he was dead, and Saeed bit his tongue to keep from groaning under the crushing weight. *At least this body will hide me from the militants,* he thought, and closed his eyes. The ditch smelled of blood. Beside him another man who was not yet dead groaned and cried from the pain, begging someone to help him. Saeed heard the footsteps of the militants as they walked back in his direction. One of the militants said, "That dog is still alive," before letting go another deafening round of automatic fire.

One of the bullets hit Saeed in the neck, and it took all his power not to cry out. Only when the militants sounded far away—moving down the line of hundreds of men—did Saeed dare move a hand to his neck to try to stop the blood. Nearby a teacher named Ali was also wounded but alive. He whispered to Saeed, "There's a farmer's shed nearby. I think they're far enough away that we can make it there without them seeing us." My brother nodded, grimacing in pain.

A few minutes later Saeed and Ali heaved the bodies of their neighbors off them and crawled slowly out of the ditch, looking in both directions to make sure there weren't any militants nearby. Then they walked to the shed as quickly as they could. My brother had been shot six times and most of the bullets were in his legs; he was lucky that none of them had pierced his bones or organs. Ali was wounded in his back, and although he could walk, fear and blood loss had made him delirious. "I left my glasses back there," he kept telling Saeed. "I can't see without them. We have to go get them."

"No, Ali, my friend, we can't," Saeed told him. "They will kill us if we do."

"Okay," Ali said, sighing and leaning against the shed wall. Then a moment later, he'd turn to Saeed again and plead, "My friend, I can't see." And it went on like this while they waited, with Ali begging to return to get his glasses and Saeed telling him gently that they couldn't.

My brother scraped up dirt from the shed floor and pressed it into their wounds, trying to stop the bleeding. He worried that the loss of blood would kill them. Light-headed and still shaking from fear, he listened for sounds from the school and from the field behind him, wondering what was happening to the women and if ISIS had begun to bury the bodies of the men. At one point, a sound like a bulldozer passed by the shed, and he thought they must be using that to fill in the ditch with dirt.

Khaled, my half brother, was taken to the opposite side of the village where men were also being lined up and shot. Like Saeed, he survived by playing dead and then running for safety. His arm hung useless by his side, shattered by a bullet to the elbow, but at least his legs worked, and he ran away as quickly as he could. Watching him leave, a man lying nearby whimpered for help. "My car is parked in the village," the man told Khaled. "I have been shot, and I can't move. Please get my car and come get me. We can go to the mountain. Please."

Khaled stopped and looked at the man. His legs had been crushed by bullets. There was no way to move him without drawing attention to them both, and the man would die unless he got to a hospital. Khaled wanted to tell him he would come back, but he couldn't find the words to lie. So he just stared for a moment at the man. "I'm sorry," he said, and then he ran.

ISIS militants shot at Khaled from the roof of the Kocho school as he ran by, and Khaled saw three men from Kocho take off from the ditch in the direction of the mountain, an Islamic State truck following close behind them. When the militants on top of the truck began firing, Khaled threw himself between two of the round bales of hay that were scattered across the farm and stayed there until the sun went down, shaking and nearly passing out from pain, all the time praying that a strong wind didn't roll away the hay bales, exposing him. Then, when it was dark, he walked by himself through the farmlands to Mount Sinjar.

Saeed and Ali stayed in the shed until the sun went down. While Saeed waited, he watched the school through a small window. "Can you see what is happening to the women and children?" Ali asked from the corner where he sat.

"Not yet," my brother said. "Nothing is happening yet."

"If they are going to kill them, too, wouldn't they have done it by now?" Ali wondered.

Saeed was quiet. He didn't know what was going to happen to us.

When it was almost dark, the trucks returned to the village and parked at the entrance of the school while women and children streamed out of the building, militants ushering us onto the trucks. Saeed craned his neck, trying to find us in the crowd. When he recognized Dimal's headscarf moving in line toward one of the buses, he started to weep.

"What's happening?" Ali asked.

Saeed didn't know. "They are putting the women on the trucks now," he said. "I don't know why." When the trucks were full, they drove away.

To himself, Saeed whispered, "If I survive, I swear to God I will become a fighter and I will rescue my sisters and my mother." And when the sun was down completely, he and Ali started walking as quickly as their wounded bodies would allow in the direction of the mountain.

Chapter 2

I N THE SCHOOL, WE COULD HEAR THE GUNSHOTS THAT
KILLED the men. They came in loud bursts and lasted for an
hour. Some of the women who stayed by the window said they
could see puffs of dirt rising up behind the school. When it was
quiet, the militants turned their attention to us. Women and children were all that was left of Kocho. We were panicked but trying
not to make any noise, not wanting to anger the militants who
watched us. "The home of my father is torn apart," my mother
whispered from where she sat. It's a saying we use only in the
most desperate times; it means that we have lost everything. My
mother sounded like she was completely without hope. Maybe
she *had* seen Elias and Massoud get onto the trucks, I thought.

A militant ordered us downstairs, and we followed him to the
first floor. There the only men were Islamic State militants. A
twelve-year-old boy named Nuri, who was a little tall for his age,
had been taken along with Amin, his older brother, to the ditch.
Amin was shot along with the men, but Nuri had been returned
to the school after the militants, asking him to raise his arms over
his head, discovered that he had no armpit hair. "He's a child—
take him back," the commander said. At the school, the boy was
encircled by worried aunts.

On the stairwell, I saw Kathrine reach down and pick up a roll
of American dollars—hundreds, it looked like—that must have

fallen out of one of the bags. She stared at it in her hand. "Keep it," I told her. "Hide it. We've already given them everything else."

But Kathrine was too scared to keep the money, and she thought that if they saw how cooperative she was, they would take pity on her and her family. "Maybe if I give them the money, they won't do anything to us," she said, and handed the roll to the next militant she saw, who took it without saying anything.

When we saw that the trucks had returned to the school gates, we stopped crying for the men and started screaming for ourselves. Militants began pushing us into groups, but it was chaos. No one wanted to let go of their sister or their mother, and we kept asking, "What have you done to our men? Where are you taking us?" The militants ignored us, pulling us by the arms onto the truck beds.

I tried to hold on to Kathrine, but we were pulled apart. Dimal and I, along with sixteen or seventeen other girls, were loaded onto the first truck, a red pickup with an open flatbed like the ones I used to love riding in. Somehow the other girls got between me and my sister, and while I stayed in the back, Dimal was pushed into a corner in the front where she sat, shoulder to shoulder with other women and children, staring at the floor. We started moving before I saw what happened to everyone else.

The driver sped away from Kocho, driving fast along the narrow, bumpy road. He drove as if he were angry and in a hurry, and every jerky movement threw us against one another and the metal railings so hard, I thought my back might break. Thirty minutes later we all groaned in relief as he slowed down, and we entered the outskirts of Sinjar City.

With only Sunni Muslims left in Sinjar City, I was amazed to see that life was going on as usual. Wives shopped for food at the markets while their husbands smoked cigarettes at tea shops. Taxi drivers scanned the sidewalks for passengers, and farmers drove their sheep out to pasture. Civilian cars filled the road in front of us and behind us, the drivers barely glancing at the trucks full of women and children. We couldn't have looked normal, stuffed into the backs of trucks, crying and holding on to one another. So why wasn't anyone helping us?

I tried to stay hopeful. The city was still familiar, and that comforted me. I recognized some of its streets, lined with cramped groceries and restaurants selling fragrant sandwiches, the oil-slicked driveways of its auto shops, and the produce stands stacked with colorful fruits. Maybe we were going to the mountain after all. Maybe the militants hadn't been lying and they just wanted to get rid of us, to drop us at the foot of Mount Sinjar and let us run away from them toward the grueling conditions on the top. They could think that was equal to a death sentence. I hoped they did. Already our homes were occupied and our men were probably dead, but at least on top of the mountain, we would be around other Yazidis. We could find Hezni and start to mourn the people we had lost. After a little while, we would start to put what was left of our community back together.

I could see the outline of the mountain on the horizon, tall and flat on the top, and I willed our driver to continue straight toward it. But the truck turned east and began driving away from Mount Sinjar. I didn't say anything, although the wind through the truck grates was so loud I could have screamed without anyone noticing.

The moment it became clear that we were not being taken to the mountain, I reached into my bag, looking for the bread I had taken with me from home. I was furious. Why hadn't anyone helped us? What had happened to my brothers? By now, the bread was hard and stale and covered with bits of dust and lint. It was supposed to protect me and my family, and it hadn't. As Sinjar City retreated into the background, I pulled the bread out of the bag and tossed it over the side of the truck, watching as it bounced off the road into a pile of trash.

———

WE ARRIVED IN Solagh a little bit before sunset and pulled up in front of the Solagh Institute, a school just outside the town. The large building was silent and dark. Dimal and I were among the first to be unloaded from the trucks, and we sat, exhausted, in the yard, watching women and children tumble out of the other trucks as they pulled up. As members of our family were pulled off the trucks, they walked through the gates toward us in a daze. Nisreen couldn't stop crying. "Just wait," I told her. "We don't know what will happen."

Solagh was famous in Kocho for its homemade brooms, and once a year my mother or someone from my family would travel there to buy a new one. I went once, shortly before ISIS came. On that trip I had found the town beautiful, lush and green, and I had felt special to be included on that trip. Now it was like another country.

My mother was on one of the last trucks. I'll never forget how she looked. The wind had pushed her white headscarf back on her head, and her dark hair, normally parted neatly down the middle, was wild and messy, her scarf covering only her mouth and her nose. Her white clothes were dusty, and she stumbled when she was pulled down to the ground. "Get going," a militant yelled at her, pushing her toward the garden, laughing at her and other older women who couldn't move quickly. She came through the gates and walked toward us in a trance. Without saying a single word, she sat down and rested her head on my lap. My mother never lay down in front of men.

A militant hammered at the locked door of the institute until it swung open and then he ordered us inside. "First, take off your headscarves," he said. "Leave them here by the door."

We did as he said. With our hair uncovered, the militants

looked at us more closely, then sent us inside. As the women arrived by the truckful at the institute gate—children clinging to their mothers' skirts, young wives with eyes bright red from crying over their lost husbands—the pile of headscarves grew, the gauzy white traditional material mixing with the colorful scarves favored by young Yazidi women. When the sun was nearly down and the trucks stopped pulling up, a militant, whose own long hair was partly covered by a white scarf, poked the barrel of his gun into the pile of headscarves, laughing. "I'll sell you these back for two hundred fifty dinars," he said to us, knowing that it was a pitifully small amount of money—about 20 U.S. cents—and also that we had no money at all.

With all of us stuffed into one room, it was unbearably hot. I wondered if I had a fever. Pregnant women groaned and stretched their legs out in front of them, leaning their backs against the wall and closing their eyes as though trying to block out the room. Other than that, the only sound was the shuffling of clothes and muffled sobs. Suddenly a woman a bit younger than my mother, started screaming at the top of her lungs. "You've killed our men!" she yelled over and over, and her rage spread through the crowd. More women began weeping and screaming, demanding answers or just howling as though her outburst had unlocked their own grief.

The noise made the militants angry. "Stop crying, or I will kill you here," a militant said, pointing his gun at the woman and slapping her across her forehead. But it was as if she were possessed—she couldn't stop. Some women went to comfort her, walking in front of the militant and his gun. "Don't think about what happened to the men," one said to her. "We have to help ourselves now."

They gave us some food—potato chips and rice, along with bottles of water. Although few of us had had anything to eat or drink since leaving our homes that morning, we had no appetite and were too frightened to eat what they gave us. They pushed the packages into our hands when we ignored them. "Eat," they commanded, as though they felt insulted by our refusal. Then they handed some of the older boys plastic bags and told them to walk around the room collecting garbage.

It was late, and we were exhausted. My mother's head still rested on my lap. She hadn't said anything since she arrived, but her eyes were open and she wasn't sleeping. I assumed we would spend the night crammed together in the institute, and I wondered if I would be able to sleep at all. I thought about asking my mother what she was thinking, but it was too hard to talk. I wish I had said something. After we ate, the militants began separating us into smaller groups and ordering most of us back outside to opposite ends of the garden. "Married women, over here with your children, but only the little ones," they shouted, pointing toward one end of the room. "Older women and girls, outside."

We started panicking, not knowing what it meant. Mothers held on to their older children, refusing to let them go. Around the room militants were forcefully pulling apart families, pushing young, unmarried girls toward the door. Back in the garden, Kathrine and I held tightly to my mother, who was again sitting on the ground; Kathrine was even more petrified at the thought of leaving her than I was, and she buried her head into my mother's arm. A militant came up to us. "You!" he barked, pointing my mother toward the south side of the garden. "Go over there."

I shook my head, leaning in closer to my mother. The militant crouched down and pulled on my sweater. "Come on," he said, but I didn't respond. He pulled harder and I looked away. He shoved his hands under my armpits and picked me up off the floor, tearing me away from my mother and pushing me toward the garden wall. I screamed. Then he did the same to Kathrine, who held on to my mother's hand as though glued to her, and begged him not to separate them. "Let me stay with her!" she said. "She's not well." They didn't listen, they carried Kathrine away from my mother while my niece and I both howled.

"I cannot move, I feel I am going to die," I heard my mother say to the militant.

"Come on," he told her, impatiently. "We will take you to a place with air-conditioning." And my mother heaved herself off the ground and followed him slowly, away from us.

To save themselves, some of the older single women began lying, telling the militants that they were married or grabbing children they knew and claiming they were their own. We didn't know what was going to happen to us, but at least the militants seemed less interested in the mothers and married women. Dimal and Adkee pulled two of our nephews close to them. "These are our sons," they told the militants, who stared at them a moment, then passed them by. Dimal hadn't seen her children since her divorce, but she played a convincing mother, and even Adkee, who had never been married and was less maternal, filled the role well. It was a decision made in one split second, a matter of survival. I didn't get to say goodbye to my sisters before they were herded upstairs with the young boys still clutched to their sides.

It took an hour for all the women to be separated. I sat outside with Kathrine, Rojian, and Nisreen; we waited and held one another. Again, the militants offered us chips and water, and although we were too scared to eat, I drank a little water, then a little more. I hadn't realized how thirsty I was. I thought about my mother and my sisters upstairs and wondered whether ISIS would take pity on them, and what that pity might look like. The faces of the girls crowded around me were red from crying. Their hair was falling out of braids and ponytails, their hands clutching at the person nearest them. I was so tired I felt like my head was sinking into my body and any moment the world would go dark. But I didn't lose all hope until I saw the three buses pull up to the school. They were enormous, the kind normally used to transport tourists and religious pilgrims around Iraq and to Mecca, and we instantly knew they were for us.

"Where are they taking us?" Kathrine wailed. She didn't say it, but we were all terrified that they were going to take us to Syria. Anything seemed possible, and I was sure that we would die in Syria.

I held my bag close to me. It was a bit lighter without the bread, and now I regretted throwing it away. Wasting bread was a sin. God doesn't judge Yazidis based on how often we pray or go on pilgrimages. We don't have to build elaborate cathedrals or attend years of religious schooling in order to be a good Yazidi. Rituals, like baptism, are performed only when the family has enough money or time to make the trip.

Our faith is in our actions. We welcome strangers into our homes, give money and food to those who have none, and sit with the body of a loved one before burial. Even being a good student, or kind to your spouse, is an act equal to prayer. Things that keep us alive and allow poor people to help others, like simple bread, are holy.

But making mistakes is part of being human, which is why we have brothers- and sisters-of-the-hereafter—members of the Yazidi sheikh caste whom we choose to teach us about our religion and help us in the afterlife. My sister-of-the-hereafter was a bit older than me, beautiful and very knowledgeable about Yazidism. She had been married once, then divorced, and when she came back to live with her family, she devoted herself to God and her religion. She had managed to escape before ISIS came close to her home, and she was now safe in Germany. The most important job these brothers and sisters have is to sit with God and Tawusi Melek and defend you after you have died. "I knew this person when she was alive," your sister or brother will say. "She deserves to have her soul return to earth. She is a good person."

When I died, I knew my sister-of-the-hereafter would have to defend me for some of the sins I committed while I was alive—stealing candy from the Kocho store, for instance, or the times I was too lazy to go to the farm with my siblings. Now she would have to defend me for a great deal more, and I hoped she could forgive me first—for defying my mother by saving the bridal photos, for losing faith and throwing away the bread, and now for getting on that bus and whatever came after.

Chapter 3

GIRLS LIKE ME WERE LOADED ONTO TWO OF THE BUSES. THE boys, including teenagers like Nuri and my nephew Malik who had been spared in Kocho because they were young, got onto the third. They were as terrified as we were. Armored jeeps full of Islamic State militants waited to escort the buses as if we were going to war, which maybe we were.

While I waited in the crowd, a militant walked over to me. It was the same man who had earlier been poking through the scarves with his gun, and he still held that weapon in his hands. "Will you convert?" he asked me. As he had been when he played with our scarves, he was smirking, mocking us.

I shook my head.

"If you convert, you can stay here," he said, gesturing back at the institute, where my mother and sisters were. "You can be with your mother and sisters and tell them to convert, too."

Again, I shook my head. I was too scared to say anything.

"Fine." He stopped smirking and scowled at me. "Then you will get on the bus with all the others."

The bus was huge, with at least forty rows of six seats cut down the middle by a long lit aisle and surrounded by windows that were covered by drawn curtains. As the seats filled, the air quickly became heavy and hard to breathe, but when we tried to open the windows, or even the curtains so that we could see outside, a militant yelled at us to sit still. I was close to the front and could hear the driver talking on his phone. I wondered if he would reveal where we were going. But he spoke in the Turkmen language, so I couldn't understand him. From my seat on the aisle, I watched the driver and the road through the wide windshield. It was dark when we pulled away from the institute, so all I could see when he turned on the headlights was a small patch of black asphalt and the occasional tree or bush. I couldn't see behind us, and so I didn't get to watch the Solagh Institute retreat into the background with my mother and sisters inside it.

We drove quickly, the two buses full of girls in the front and one with boys in the back, and the white jeeps leading and following our caravan. Our bus was eerily quiet. All I could hear were the footsteps of a militant pacing the aisle and the sound of the engine. I started to feel carsick and tried to close my eyes. The smell of sweat and body odor filled the bus. A girl in the back vomited into her hand, violently at first and then, when a militant yelled at her to stop, as quietly as she could. Her vomiting created a sour odor that spread through the bus and was almost unbearable, and some girls close to her started throwing up as well. No one could comfort them. We weren't allowed to touch or talk to one another.

The militant pacing the aisle was a tall man about thirty-five years old named Abu Batat. He seemed to enjoy his job, stopping at certain rows to peer at the girls, singling out the ones who cowered or pretended to be asleep. Eventually he started pulling certain girls from their seats and sending them to the back of the bus, where he made them stand against the wall. "Smile!" he told them, before taking a photo on his cell phone, laughing while he did it as though amused by the panic that overwhelmed each girl he chose. When they looked down in fear, he would yell, "Raise your head!" and with each girl, he seemed to grow bolder.

I closed my eyes and tried to block out what was happening.

In spite of how terrified I was, my body was so exhausted that I quickly fell asleep. I couldn't rest, though, and every time sleep came, my head snapped back up, and I opened my eyes, startled, and sat there staring through the windshield and remembering, after a moment, where I was.

I couldn't tell for sure, but it seemed like we were on the road to Mosul, which was serving as the capital of the Islamic State in Iraq. Taking over the city was a huge victory for ISIS, and videos online showed celebrations after they occupied the streets and municipal buildings and blocked the roads around Mosul. The Kurdish and central Iraqi forces, meanwhile, swore that they would take the city back from the Islamic State militants, even if it took years. *We don't have years,* I thought, and fell asleep again.

Suddenly I felt a hand on my left shoulder and opened my eyes to see Abu Batat standing over me, his green eyes glowing and his mouth contorted into a smile. My face was almost level with the pistol he had strapped to his side, and I felt like a rock sitting there, unable to move or to talk. I closed my eyes again, praying that he would go away, and then I felt his hand move slowly across my shoulder, brushing my neck, and then down the front of my dress until it stopped over my left breast. It felt like fire; I had never been touched like that before. I opened my eyes but didn't look at him, I just looked straight ahead. Abu Batat reached inside my dress and grabbed my breast, hard as if he wanted to hurt me, and then walked away.

Every second with ISIS was part of a slow, painful death—of the body and the soul—and that moment on the bus with Abu Batat was the moment I started dying. I was from a village and raised in a good family. Whenever I left the house, no matter where I was going, my mother would examine me. "Button up your shirt, Nadia," she would say. "Be a good girl."

Now this stranger was touching me savagely, and there was nothing I could do. Abu Batat continued to walk up and down the bus, groping the girls who sat on the aisle, passing his hand over us as if we were not human, as if he had no fear that we would move or get angry. When he came to me again, I grabbed his hand, trying to stop him from putting it under my dress. I was too scared to talk. I began crying, and my tears fell on his hand, but still he didn't stop. *These are the things that happen between lovers when they get married,* I thought. This had been my view of the world, and of love, my entire life, from the moment I was old enough to know what marriage was, through all the courtships and celebrations in Kocho, until the very moment that Abu Batat touched me and shattered that idea.

"He's been doing that to all the girls sitting on the aisle," the girl sitting in the middle seat next to me whispered. "He's been touching all of them."

"Please switch with me," I begged her. "I don't want him to touch me again."

"I can't," she replied. "I'm too scared."

Abu Batat continued walking up and down the aisle, pausing in front of the girls he liked best. When I closed my eyes, I could hear the swish of his baggy white pants and his sandals slapping against his feet. Every few moments a voice in Arabic would come in on the radio he held in one hand, but it was too staticky to make out exactly what it was saying.

Each time he passed me, he ran his hand along my shoulder and over my left breast, then walked away. I was sweating so much I felt as if I were in the shower. I noticed that he avoided the girls who had been vomiting earlier, and I pushed my hand into my mouth trying to make myself throw up, hoping that I could cover my entire dress in vomit and keep his hand off me, but it was useless. I gagged painfully, and nothing came out.

The bus stopped in Tal Afar, a majority Turkmen city about thirty miles from Sinjar City, and militants started talking on their cell phones and radios, trying to figure out what their superiors wanted them to do. "They said to drop the boys off here," the driver said to Abu Batat, and they both left the bus. Through the windshield, I saw Abu Batat talking to other militants, and I wondered what about. Three-quarters of Tal Afar's residents were Sunni Turkmens, and months before ISIS came to Sinjar, the city's Shiites had fled, leaving it open for the militants.

The left side of my body ached where Abu Batat had groped me. I prayed that he wouldn't get back on the bus, but after a few minutes he did, and we started moving again. As we backed away, I could see through the windshield that we were leaving one of the buses behind. Later I learned that it was the bus full of boys, including my nephew, Malik, whom ISIS would try to brainwash into fighting in their terrorist group. As the years went by and the war continued, they would use the boys as human shields and suicide bombers.

As soon as he was back on the bus, Abu Batat resumed molesting us. He had chosen his favorites, and he visited us most often and kept his hand on us longer, gripping us so hard, it felt like he wanted to tear our bodies apart. About ten minutes after leaving Tal Afar, I couldn't take it anymore. When I felt his hand on my shoulder again, I screamed. It tore open the silence. Soon other girls started screaming as well, until the inside of the bus sounded like the scene of a massacre. Abu Batat froze. "Shut up, all of you!" he shouted, but we didn't. *If he kills me, I don't care,* I thought. *I want to be dead.* The Turkmen driver pulled over, and the bus stopped with a jolt, jerking me in my seat. The driver shouted something into his phone. A moment later one of the white jeeps that had been driving in front of us stopped, too, and a man got out of the passenger seat and started walking toward our bus.

I recognized the militant, a commander named Nafah, from Solagh. At the institute, he had been particularly cruel and harsh, shouting at us without an ounce of humanity. I thought he was like a machine. The driver opened the door for the commander, and Nafah stormed onto the bus. "Who started this?" he asked Abu Batat, and my tormentor pointed at me. "She did," he said, and Nafah walked over to where I sat.

Before he could do anything, I started talking. Nafah was a terrorist, but didn't ISIS have rules about how the women were treated? Surely if they considered themselves to be good Muslims, they would object to the way that Abu Batat was abusing us. "You brought us here, on this bus. You made us come, we had no choice, and this man"—I pointed at Abu Batat, my hand shaking out of fear—"he has been putting his hand on our breasts the entire time. He's been grabbing us, and he won't leave us alone!"

Nafah was quiet after I spoke. For a moment I had hope that he would punish Abu Batat, but that hope disappeared when Abu Batat started to talk. "What do you think you are here for?" he said to me, his voice loud enough for everyone in the bus to hear. "Honestly, don't you know?"

Abu Batat walked over to where Nafah stood and grabbed my neck, pushing my head against the seat and pointing his gun at my forehead. Girls around me shrieked, but I was too scared to make a sound. "If you close your eyes, I will shoot you," he said.

Nafah walked back toward the bus door. Before he left, he turned to us. "I don't know what you thought we had taken you for," he said. "But you have no choice. You are here to be *sabaya*, and you will do exactly what we say. And if any of you scream again, trust me, things will be even worse for you." Then, with Abu Batat still pointing his gun at me, Nafah left the bus.

It was the first time I had heard the Arabic word applied to me. When ISIS took over Sinjar and began kidnapping Yazidis, they called their human spoils sabaya (*sabiyya* is singular), referring to the young women they would buy and sell as sex slaves. This was part of their plan for us, sourced from an interpretation of the Koran that had long been banned by the world's Muslim communities, and written into the fatwas and pamphlets ISIS made official before they attacked Sinjar. Yazidi girls were considered infidels, and according to the militants' interpretation of the Koran, raping a slave is not a sin. We would entice new recruits to join the ranks of the militants and be passed around as a reward for loyalty and good behavior. Everyone on the bus was destined for that fate. We were no longer human beings—we were sabaya.

Abu Batat let go of my neck and put his gun away, but from that moment on until we arrived in Mosul about an hour later, I was his primary target. He still touched other girls, but he focused on me, stopping by my seat more frequently and pushing his hand against my breast with so much force, I was sure I would be bruised. The left side of my body went numb, and although I stayed quiet, fully believing Abu Batat would kill me if I lashed out again, inside my head I never stopped screaming.

It was a clear night, and through the windshield I could see the sky, which was full of stars. The sky reminded me of an ancient Arabian love story my mother used to tell us called "Layla and Majnun." In the story, a man named Qays falls so much in love with a woman named Layla and is so open about how he feels, writing poem after poem about his love for her, that the people around him give him the nickname *Majnun*, which means "possessed" or "crazy" in Arabic. When Majnun asks for Layla's hand in marriage, her father turns him down, telling him that he is too unstable to be a good husband.

It's a tragic story. Layla is forced to marry another man and then dies of a broken heart. Majnun leaves his village and wanders the desert alone, talking to himself and writing poetry in the sand, until one day he finds Layla's gravestone. He stays beside it until he dies, too. I loved hearing my mother tell this story, even though it made me cry for the two lovers. The dark sky that usually frightened me became romantic instead. *Layla* means "night" in Arabic, and my mother used to end the story by pointing at two stars in the sky. "Since they couldn't be together in life, they prayed to be together after death," she would tell me. "And so God turned them into stars."

On the bus, I started praying, too. "Please, God, turn me into a star so that I can be up in the sky above this bus," I whispered. "If you did it once, you can do it again." But we just kept driving toward Mosul.

Chapter 4

ABU BATAT DIDN'T STOP TOUCHING US UNTIL WE ARRIVED in Mosul. The clock above the windshield read two a.m. when we stopped in front of a large building, a home that I thought must have belonged to a very wealthy family. The jeeps drove into a garage, and the buses parked in front of the house, opening their doors for us. "Come on! Get out!" Abu Batat shouted, and we began slowly lifting our bodies out of the seats. Few of us had slept, and we were all sore and aching from sitting. My body hurt where Abu Batat had touched me, but I was wrong to think that now that the bus had stopped, he would leave me alone. We lined up to exit, holding on to whatever we had brought with us, and he waited by the open door, putting out his hands to grope girls as they stepped off the bus. He ran his hands over my body, from my head to my feet.

We entered through the garage. I had never seen such a nice house. It was huge, with large sitting rooms and bedrooms and enough furniture, I thought, for a half-dozen families. No one in Kocho, not even Ahmed Jasso, lived in a house like this. The rooms were still full of the clocks and rugs I assumed had belonged to the family that once lived here, and I noticed that one of the militants was drinking from a mug that had been decorated with a posed family photo. I wondered what had happened to them.

There were Islamic State militants everywhere, dressed in uniforms with their radios squawking constantly. They watched us as we were sent into three rooms, each of which opened onto a small landing. From where I sat with Kathrine and a few others, I could see into the other rooms, where women and girls shuffled around in a daze, looking for people they knew but had been separated from on the buses. The room was crowded, and we sat on the floor, leaning against each other. It was almost impossible not to fall asleep.

The two small windows in the room were closed and the curtains drawn, but luckily someone had set up a swamp cooler—the hulking, cheap relatives of air conditioners that are common throughout Iraq—which thinned the air and made it easier to breathe. There was no furniture in our room except for some mattresses stacked up against the walls. A sickening odor was coming out of the hall bathroom. "A girl had a cell phone, and when they came to search her, she tried to flush it down the toilet," someone whispered. "I heard them talking about it when we got here." At the entrance to the bathroom, I could see a pile of headscarves like what we had left in Solagh, lying on the tile floor like flower petals.

After the rooms were full, a militant pointed at where I was sitting. "Come with me," he said, then turned and walked toward the door.

"Don't go!" Kathrine wrapped her small arms around me, trying to keep me from standing up.

I didn't know what he wanted, but I didn't think I could say no to him. "If I don't, they will just force me," I told her, and I followed the militant.

He led me to the garage on the first floor, where Abu Batat and Nafah were waiting along with another militant. The third militant spoke Kurdish and I was shocked when I recognized him; it was Suhaib, who owned a store in Sinjar City. Yazidis visited his store all the time and I am sure many thought of him as a friend.

All three men looked at me angrily. They still wanted to punish me for my outburst on the bus. "What's your name?" Nafah asked, and when I tried to back away he pulled my hair and pushed me against the wall.

I answered him. "Nadia," I said.

"When were you born?" he asked, and I told him. "Nineteen ninety-three."

Next he asked, "Are you here with any of your family?"

I paused. I didn't know if they wanted to punish Kathrine and the others just for being related to me, so I lied. "I'm here with the other girls," I said. "I don't know what happened to my family."

"Why did you scream?" Nafah tightened his grip on my hair.

I was terrified. I felt my body, which had always been small and thin, practically disappear in his hands. I told myself to say whatever I had to for them to let me go back upstairs to Kathrine. "I was scared," I told him honestly. "This guy in front of you"—I gestured toward Abu Batat—"touched me. The whole trip from Solagh, he was touching us."

"What do you think you're here for?" Nafah repeated what he had said on the bus. "You are an infidel, a sabiyya, and you belong to the Islamic State now, so get used to it." Then he spat in my face.

Abu Batat took out a cigarette, which he lit and gave to Nafah. I was surprised; I thought smoking was illegal under Islamic State law. But they didn't mean to smoke the cigarette. *Please don't put it out on my face,* I thought, still concerned, back then, with being pretty. Nafah pushed the lit cigarette into my shoulder, pressing it down through the fabric of the dresses and shirts I had layered on that morning, until it hit my skin and went out. The smell of burned fabric and skin was horrible, but I tried not to scream in pain. Screaming only got you into more trouble.

When he lit another cigarette and put it out on my stomach, I couldn't help it—I cried out.

"She screams now, will she scream tomorrow?" Abu Batat said

to the others. He wanted them to be even harsher with me. "She needs to understand what she is and what she's here for."

"Leave me alone, and I won't do it again," I said.

Nafah slapped my face hard, twice, and then let go of me. "Go back to the other sabaya," he said. "And never make another sound again."

Back upstairs the room was dark and crowded. I pulled my hair over my shoulder and put my hands on my stomach to hide the burns from my nieces, and then I found Kathrine, sitting next to a woman who looked to be in her late twenties or early thirties. The woman wasn't from Kocho; she must have arrived at the center before us. She had two young children with her, one a baby young enough to be breast-feeding, and she was pregnant. She held the infant to her chest, rocking slightly to keep him quiet, and asked me what had happened downstairs. I just shook my head.

"Are you in pain?" the woman asked me.

Although I didn't know her, I leaned against her. I felt very weak. I nodded.

Then I told her everything, about leaving Kocho and being separated from my mother and my sisters, about seeing my brothers being driven away. I told her about the bus and Abu Batat. "They beat me," I said, and I showed her the cigarette burns on my shoulder and on my stomach, raw and painful.

"Here," she said, reaching into her bag and handing me a tube. "It's diaper cream, but it might help with the burns."

I thanked her and took the lotion to the bathroom, where I rubbed some of it onto my shoulder and stomach. It soothed the burns a little. Then I rubbed a bit more onto the parts of my body where Abu Batat had touched me. I noticed that I had my period, and I asked a militant for some sanitary pads, which he handed to me without looking at me.

When I sat back down in the room, I asked the woman, "What has been happening here? What have they done to you?"

"Do you really want to know?" she asked, and I nodded. "On the first day, on August third, about four hundred Yazidi women and children were taken here," she began. "It's an Islamic State center, where the militants live and work. That's why there are so many of them here." She paused and looked at me. "But it's also where we are sold and given away."

"Why haven't you been sold?" I asked.

"Because I am married, they will wait for forty days before giving me to a militant to be his sabiyya," she said. "That's one of their rules. I don't know when they will come for you. If they don't choose you today, they will choose you tomorrow. Each time they come, they take some of the women. They rape them and then they bring them back, or sometimes I think they keep them. Sometimes they rape them here, in a room in the house, and just bring them back when they are done."

I sat there silently. The pain from my burns built slowly, like a pot of water slowly coming to a boil, and I winced. "Do you want a pill for the pain?" she asked, but I shook my head. "I don't like taking pills," I told her.

"Drink something, then," she said, and I gratefully took the bottle from her, drinking a few sips of the lukewarm water. Her baby had quieted down and was close to sleeping.

"It won't take much time," she continued in a softer voice. "They will come, and they will take you, too, and they will rape you. Some girls rub ashes or dirt on their faces, or mess up their hair, but it doesn't matter because they just make them shower and look nice again. Some of the girls have committed suicide, or tried to, by cutting through the veins in their wrists right over there," she gestured to the bathroom. "You can see the blood high on the walls where the cleaners don't notice it." She didn't tell me not to worry or that everything was going to be fine. When she stopped talking, I leaned my head against her shoulder, close to where her baby had just fallen asleep.

———

THAT NIGHT WHEN I closed my eyes, it was only for a moment. I was exhausted but too terrified to sleep. It was summer, so the sun rose early, and when the light came in—hazy and dim through the heavy curtains—I saw that most of the girls had been awake all night like me. They were groggy, rubbing their eyes and yawning into the sleeves of their dresses. Militants came in with some rice and tomato soup for breakfast, on plastic plates that they threw away afterward, and I was so hungry, I ate some as soon as they put it in front of me.

Many of the girls had spent the night crying, and more started again in the morning. A girl from Kocho who was about Dimal's age but who, unlike Dimal, hadn't managed to fool the militants into thinking she was a married woman, sat close to me. "Where are we?" she asked. She hadn't recognized any of the buildings or roads as we were driving.

"I don't know exactly," I told her. "Somewhere in Mosul."

"Mosul," she whispered. We had all grown up so close to the city, but few of us had ever been.

A sheikh entered the room, and we stopped talking. He was an older man with white hair, dressed in the baggy black pants and sandals popular among ISIS militants, and although his pants were shorter than usual and slightly ill-fitting, he walked around the room and stared at us with an arrogance that made me think he must be someone very important. "How old is she?" he pointed to a young girl from Kocho, cowering in the corner. She was about thirteen. "Very young," a militant told him, proudly.

I could tell from the sheikh's accent that he was from Mosul. He must have helped the terrorists take over the city. Maybe he was a wealthy businessman who could help ISIS grow, or maybe he was a religious figure or had been important when Saddam was in power and had been waiting for the moment when he could get back the authority that the Americans and Shiites had taken from him. It was possible, too, that he wholeheartedly believed all the religious propaganda; that's what they all told us, when we asked why they were part of ISIS, even the ones who spoke no Arabic and didn't know how to pray. They told us that they were right and that God was on their side.

The sheikh pointed at us as if he already owned every girl in the room, and after a few minutes, he settled on three—all from Kocho. After handing the militant a fistful of American dollars, he left the room and the three girls were dragged out behind him downstairs, to where his purchases were logged and processed.

The mood in the room shifted to complete panic. By now we knew what ISIS had planned for us, but we had no idea when more buyers would arrive and how they would treat us. Waiting was torture. Some girls whispered about trying to escape, but that was impossible. Even if we could make it out the window, the house, which was clearly some kind of Islamic State center, swarmed with militants. There was no way any of us could slip away without someone noticing. Plus, Mosul is a sprawling, unfamiliar city. If we did manage to somehow slip past the crowds of militants downstairs, we would have no way of knowing what direction to run in. They had driven us here at night, with the windows covered. They would do anything to make sure we didn't get out alive.

The talk soon shifted to suicide. I admit that, at first, it crossed my mind. Anything would be better than what the woman had described to me the night before. Kathrine and I made a pact with a few others. "We would rather die than be bought and used by Daesh," we said. Killing ourselves seemed more honorable than submitting to the militants, our only way of fighting back. Still, it was impossible that we would watch while one of our neighbors took her own life. One girl wrapped her shawl around her neck, saying she was going to strangle herself, but others forced it out of her hands. Some said, "We can't escape, but if we get to the roof, we can jump off." I kept thinking of my mother. For her, nothing in life was bad enough to justify suicide. "You have to believe that God will take care of you," she would tell me whenever something bad happened to me. After my accident on the farm, she had sat beside me in the hospital praying that I would live, and she spent so much money on the jewelry she gave me when I woke up. She had wanted me to live so badly. I couldn't take my own life now.

Quickly, we reversed our pact. We wouldn't kill ourselves; we would help one another as much as we could and take the first opportunity to escape. While we waited in that house, it became clear how vast the slave trade was in ISIS-held Mosul. Thousands of Yazidi girls had been taken from their homes and were being bought and traded, or given as gifts to high-ranking militants and sheikhs, and transported to cities all over Iraq and Syria. It didn't make a difference if one girl killed herself, or even a hundred. ISIS wouldn't be bothered by our deaths, and they wouldn't change what they were doing. Besides, by now, having lost a few slaves, the militants guarded us to make sure that even if we cut our wrists or strangled ourselves with our scarves, we wouldn't die from the wounds.

A militant came through the room demanding whatever documents we had held on to. "Any papers that say you are a Yazidi, give them to us," he said, shoving them into a bag. Downstairs they piled up all the documents—IDs, ration cards, birth certificates— and burned them, leaving the ashes in a mound. It was as though they thought that by destroying our documents, they could erase the existence of Yazidis from Iraq. I handed over everything I had except for my mother's ration card, which I kept tucked into my bra. It was all I had of her.

Inside the bathroom, I splashed some water on my face and arms. A mirror hung over the sink, but I kept my gaze downward. I couldn't look at myself. I suspected that I already wouldn't recognize the girl who looked back. On the wall above the shower, I saw the blood the woman from the night before had warned me about. The small reddish-brown stains high up on the tiles were all that was left of some Yazidi girls who had come before me.

After that we were separated again, this time into two groups. I managed to stay with Kathrine, and we were lined up and put back on the buses. Some others—all girls I knew from Kocho—stayed behind. We didn't get to say goodbye to them, and later we learned that their group was taken across the border to Raqqa, the capital of ISIS in Syria. I was so relieved to be in Iraq. No matter what happened, I thought I could survive as long as I stayed in my country.

I moved quickly to the back of the bus to make sure I got a seat beside a window, where I thought it would be harder for Abu Batat or another militant to reach me. It was strange to be outside in the heavy summer light after spending the past few days inside with the curtains drawn or being moved from city to city in the dark. I peeked through the curtains as the bus moved, watching the Mosul streets. At first they looked completely normal, just as Sinjar City had, with people buying groceries and walking their kids to school. But unlike Sinjar, Mosul was full of Islamic State militants. The men were stationed at checkpoints, patrolling the streets, clustered in the backs of trucks, or just living their new lives in the changed city, buying vegetables and carrying on conversations with neighbors. All the women were completely covered in black abayas and niqabs; ISIS had made it illegal for a woman to leave home uncovered or alone, so they floated through the streets, almost invisible.

We sat quietly, stunned and terrified. I thanked God that I was with Kathrine, Nisreen, Jilan, and Rojian. Their presence gave me the small bit of strength I needed not to completely lose my mind. Not everyone was so lucky. One girl had been separated from everyone she knew back in Kocho, and she started weeping uncontrollably. "Each of you has someone, but I have no one," she said, wringing her hands in her lap. We wanted to comfort her, but no one was brave enough to try.

At close to ten in the morning, we pulled up to a two-story green house, slightly smaller than the first, and were pushed inside. On the second floor, a room had already been cleared of most of the possessions of the family who once lived there, although a Bible on the shelf and a small cross on the wall made it clear that they had been Christians. A few girls were already there when we arrived. They were from Tel Ezeir, and they sat close together. More thin mattresses were piled up along the walls, and the small windows had either been blacked out or covered with heavy blankets, filtering the midday sun into a dim, depressing light. The whole space reeked of cleaning solution, the same fluorescent blue paste women used in Kocho to sterilize our kitchens and bathrooms.

While we sat there waiting, a militant came into the room to make sure the windows were completely covered and no one could see in or out of them. When he noticed the Bible and the cross, he grumbled to himself, picked up a plastic crate, tossed them inside it, then carried the crate out of the room.

On his way out, he yelled at us to shower. "All you Yazidis, do you always stink?" he said with an exaggerated look of disgust on his face. I thought back to Saoud, coming home from Kurdistan and telling us that people there made fun of Yazidis, saying that we smelled bad and how angry that used to make me. But with ISIS, I hoped I did stink. Filth was armor, protecting us from the hands of men like Abu Batat. I wanted the militants to be so put off by our stench—after sitting in hot buses, many of us vomiting from fear—that they wouldn't touch us. Instead, they pushed us toward the bathroom in groups. "Wipe that filth off of you!" they demanded. "We don't want to smell you anymore." We did as we were told, splashing water on our arms and faces from the sinks but unwilling to take off our clothes and be naked so close to the men.

After the militant left, some of the girls whispered to one another and pointed at a desk. A black laptop computer sat, closed, on top of it. "I wonder if it works," one of the girls said. "Maybe it has the Internet! Then we can connect to Facebook and message some people to tell them we are in Mosul."

I had no idea how to work a laptop or any computer—this was the first one I had ever seen—so I watched while a couple of the others approached the table, slowly. The idea of connecting to Facebook had given us some hope, and it spread through the room. Some of the girls stopped crying. Others stood up on their own for the first time since leaving Solagh. My heart raced a little. I wanted so badly for the machine to work.

A girl opened the laptop, and the screen lit up. We gasped, excited, and watched the door for militants. She started tapping on some keys, then harder, frustrated. Soon she closed the lid and turned back to us, hanging her head. "It doesn't work," she said, sounding like she might cry. "I'm sorry."

Her friends surrounded her, comforting her. We were all so disappointed. "It's okay, you tried," they whispered to her. "Besides, if it worked, Daesh wouldn't have left it here."

I looked over to the wall where the girls from Tel Ezeir sat. They hadn't moved or said anything to us since we arrived. They held one another so close, it was hard to tell where one of them stopped and another started. Their faces, when they looked back at me, were like masks made of pure sorrow, and I thought I must look the same.

Chapter 5

THE SLAVE MARKET OPENED AT NIGHT. WE COULD HEAR the commotion downstairs where militants were registering and organizing, and when the first man entered the room, all the girls started screaming. It was like the scene of an explosion. We moaned as though wounded, doubling over and vomiting on the floor, but none of it stopped the militants. They paced around the room, staring at us, while we screamed and begged. Those of us who knew Arabic begged in Arabic, and the girls who knew only Kurdish screamed as loud as they could, but the men reacted to our panic as if we were whining children—annoying but not worth acknowledging.

They gravitated toward the most beautiful girls first, asking, "How old are you?" and examining their hair and mouths. "They are virgins, right?" they asked a guard, who nodded and said, "Of course!" like a shopkeeper taking pride in his product. Some girls told me they had been checked by a doctor to make sure they weren't lying about their virginity, while others, like me, had only been asked. A few insisted that in fact they were not virgins, that they were spoiled, thinking it would make them less desirable, but the militants could tell they were lying. "They are so young, and they are Yazidi," they said. "No Yazidi girl would have sex unless she was married." Now the militants touched us anywhere they wanted, running their hands over our breasts and our legs, as if we were animals.

It was chaos while the militants paced the room, scanning girls and asking questions in Arabic or the Turkmen language. Nafah, who had arrived when the market opened, chose a very young girl, which made some of the other militants laugh. "We knew you would pick her," they teased him. "Let me know when you are done with her—give her to me."

"Calm down!" militants kept shouting at us. "Be quiet!" But their orders only made us scream louder. An older militant appeared in the doorway, a fat man with a huge belly called Hajji Shakir, who turned out to be one of the leaders in Mosul. (*Hajji* is both a common name and a title for respected men.) He had a girl in tow. She was wearing the niqab and abaya worn by all women in Islamic State towns. "This is my sabiyya," he said, pushing her farther into the room. "She is going to tell you how happy she is now that she is Muslim."

The girl lifted up her niqab. Although she was frail, she was extremely beautiful, with smooth dark skin, and when she opened her mouth, a small gold tooth glinted in the light. I thought she couldn't be older than sixteen. "She has been my sabiyya since August third, when we liberated Hardan from the infidels," Hajji Shakir said. "Tell them how at peace you are, to be with me and to no longer be kafir," he said again to her, who remained quiet. "Tell them!"

She looked down at the carpet but didn't say anything. It looked like she couldn't physically speak. Quickly the chaos of the market took over, and when I glanced back toward the door a moment later, the girl was gone. Hajji Shakir, meanwhile, had approached another sabiyya, a young girl I knew from Kocho.

I lost all control. If it was inevitable that a militant would take me, I wouldn't make it easy for him. I howled and screamed, slapping away hands that reached out to grope me. Other girls were doing the same, curling their bodies into balls on the floor or throwing themselves across their sisters and friends to try to protect them. We were no longer scared that we would be beaten, and many of us, myself included, wondered whether we could provoke them into killing us. When a militant slapped me across the face and said, "This is the one who caused all the trouble yesterday," I was surprised by how little his hand hurt me. It was far more painful a moment later when he touched my breast, and after he left, I collapsed onto the floor, where Nisreen and Kathrine tried to comfort me.

While I lay there, another militant stopped in front of us. I had my knees pulled up to my forehead, and all I could see were his boots and calves, as thick as tree trunks, sticking out of them. He was a high-ranking militant named Salwan who had come with another girl, another young Yazidi from Hardan, who he planned to drop off at the house while he shopped for her replacement. I peered up at him. He was the most enormous man I had ever seen, like a giant in a white dishdasha as big as a tent, scowling behind a reddish beard. Nisreen, Rojian, and Kathrine draped their bodies over me trying to hide me, but he didn't go away.

"Stand up," he said. When I didn't, he kicked me. "You! The girl with the pink jacket! I said, stand up!"

We screamed and huddled together more tightly, but this just provoked Salwan even more. He leaned down and tried to pull us apart, clutching at our shoulders and arms. Still, we held on to one another as though we were one person. Our resistance made him furious, and he yelled at us to stand up, kicking at our shoulders and hands. Eventually, the struggle got the attention of a guard, who came over to help, beating our hands with a stick until the pain was so great we had to let go of one another. After we were separated, Salwan loomed over me smirking, and I saw his face clearly for the first time. His eyes were sunk deep into the flesh of his wide face, which seemed to be nearly entirely covered in hair. He didn't look like a man—he looked like a monster.

We couldn't resist anymore. "I'll go with you," I said. "But you have to take Kathrine, Rojian, and Nisreen as well."

Nafah came over to see what was happening. When he saw me, his face turned red with anger. "It's you again?" he shouted, and he slapped each of us across our faces. "I won't go without them!" I screamed back, and Nafah started hitting us faster and harder, hitting us and hitting us until our faces went numb and Rojian started bleeding from her mouth.

Then he and Salwan grabbed me and Rojian and tore us away from Kathrine and Nisreen, dragging us downstairs. Salwan's footsteps sounded heavy on the staircase. I didn't get to say good-bye to Kathrine or Nisreen, or even look behind me as they took me away.

———

ATTACKING SINJAR AND taking girls to use as sex slaves wasn't a spontaneous decision made on the battlefield by a greedy soldier. ISIS planned it all: how they would come into our homes, what made a girl more or less valuable, which militants deserved a sabiyya as incentive and which should pay. They even discussed sabaya in their glossy propaganda magazine, *Dabiq*, in an attempt to draw new recruits. From their centers in Syria and sleeper cells in Iraq, they mapped out the slave trade for months, determining what they thought was and was not legal under Islamic law, and they wrote it down so that all Islamic State members would follow the same brutal rules. Anyone can read it—the details of the plan for sabaya are collected in a pamphlet issued by ISIS's Research and Fatwa Department. And it is sickening, partly because of what it says and partly because of how ISIS says it, so matter-of-fact, like the law of any state, confident that what they are doing is sanctioned by the Koran.

Sabaya can be given as gifts and sold at the whim of the owner, "for they are merely property," the Islamic State pamphlet reads. Women shouldn't be separated from their young children—which is why Dimal and Adkee were told to stay in Solagh—but grown children, like Malik, can be taken away from their mothers. There are rules for what happens if a sabiyya becomes pregnant (she cannot be sold) or if her owner dies (she is distributed as "part of his estate"). An owner can have sex with a prepubescent slave, it says, if she is "fit for intercourse," and if she is not, "then it is enough to enjoy her without intercourse."

Much of it they support with verses from the Koran and medieval Islamic laws, which ISIS uses selectively and expects its followers to take literally. It is a horrible, stunning document. But ISIS is not as original as its members think it is. Rape has been used throughout history as a weapon of war. I never thought I would have something in common with women in Rwanda—before all this, I didn't know that a country called Rwanda existed—and now I am linked to them in the worst possible way, as a victim of a war crime that is so hard to talk about that no one in the world was prosecuted for committing it until just sixteen years before ISIS came to Sinjar.

On the lower floor, a militant was registering the transactions in a book, writing down our names and the names of the militants who took us. Compared to upstairs, the downstairs was orderly and calm. I sat down on a couch next to a few other girls, but Rojian and I were too scared to talk to them. I thought about being taken by Salwan, how strong he looked and how easily he could crush me with his bare hands. No matter what he did, and no matter how much I resisted, I would never be able to fight him off. He smelled of rotten eggs and cologne.

I was looking at the floor, at the feet and ankles of the militants and girls who walked by me. In the crowd, I saw a pair of men's sandals and ankles that were skinny, almost womanly, and before

I could think about what I was doing, I flung myself toward those feet. I started begging. "Please, take me with you," I said. "Do whatever you want, I just can't go with this giant." It still amazes me the kinds of decisions we all made, thinking it possible that one choice would lead to torture while another would save us, not realizing that we were now in a world where all paths led to the same terrible place.

I don't know why the thin guy agreed, but taking one look at me, he turned to Salwan and said, "She's mine." Salwan didn't argue. The skinny man was a judge in Mosul, and no one disobeyed him. I raised my head and almost felt like smiling at Salwan, thinking I had won, but then I felt him grab my hair and pull my head back violently. "He can have you now," Salwan said. "After a few days you will be with me." And then he let my head fall forward.

I followed the thin man to the desk. "What's your name?" he asked me. He spoke in a soft but unkind voice. "Nadia," I said, and he turned to the registrar. The man seemed to recognize the militant right away and began recording our information. He said our names as he wrote them down—"Nadia, Hajji Salman"—and when he spoke the name of my captor, I thought I heard his voice waver a bit, as if he were scared, and I wondered if I had made a huge mistake.

Chapter 6

SALWAN TOOK ROJIAN, WHO WAS SO YOUNG AND SO INNO-cent, and years later I still think of him with the most anger. I dream about one day bringing all the militants to justice, not just the leaders like Abu Bakr al-Baghdadi but all the guards and slave owners, every man who pulled a trigger and pushed my brothers' bodies into their mass grave, every fighter who tried to brainwash young boys into hating their mothers for being Yazidi, every Iraqi who welcomed the terrorists into their cities and helped them, thinking to themselves, *Finally we can be rid of those nonbelievers.* They should all be put on trial before the entire world, like the Nazi leaders after World War II, and not given the chance to hide.

In my fantasy, Salwan is the first to be tried, and all of the girls from that second house in Mosul are in the courtroom, testifying against him. "This is the one," I say, and point to the monster. "This is the huge one who terrified all of us. He watched me be beaten." Then Rojian, if she wants to, can tell the court what he did to her. If she is too scared or too traumatized, I will speak for her. "Not only did Salwan buy her and abuse her over and over, he beat her whenever he could," I would tell the court. "Even that first night, when Rojian was too scared and exhausted to even think about fighting back, Salwan beat her when he discovered that she was wearing layers of clothing, and he beat her and blamed her for me getting away. When Rojian managed to escape, he bought her mother and enslaved her in retaliation. Her mother had a sixteen-day-old baby, which Salwan took from her, even though your own rules say that you should not separate a mother from her children. He told her that she would never see her baby again." (Many of ISIS's rules, I would learn, were made to be broken.) I would tell the court every detail of what he did to her, and I pray to God that when ISIS is defeated, Salwan is captured alive.

That night, when justice was a far-off dream and there was no chance of us being rescued, Rojian and Salwan followed me and Hajji Salman out of the house and into the garden. The screams from the slave market followed us, loud enough to echo through the entire city. I thought about the families in the houses on those streets. Were they sitting down to dinner? Putting their children to bed? There was no way they couldn't hear what was going on in the house. Music and television, which otherwise might have drowned out our screams, were banned by ISIS. Maybe they wanted to hear our anguish, which was evidence of the power of the new Islamic State leadership. What did they think would happen to them in the end, when Iraqi and Kurdish forces fought to get Mosul back? Did they think ISIS would protect them? I shivered at the thought.

We got into a car, with me and Rojian in the back and the men in the front, and drove away from the house. "We'll go to my place," Hajji Salman said into his cell phone. "There are eight girls there now. Just get rid of them."

We pulled up to a large hall, like something for weddings, with a double-doored entrance surrounded by concrete columns, which looked like it was being used as a mosque. Inside, the room was full of Islamic State militants, close to three hundred of them, all praying. None of them paid attention to us as we walked inside, and I stayed close to the door while Hajji Salman grabbed two pairs of sandals from a large stack and handed them to us. They were men's sandals, made of leather, too big and hard to walk in, but Islamic State militants had taken our shoes from us and now we were barefoot. We tried not to trip as we passed the praying men and went back outside.

Salwan waited by another car, and it was clear then that they meant to separate Rojian and me. We held on to each other's hands and pleaded with them not to break us apart. "Please, don't make us go alone," we said, but neither Salwan nor Hajji Salman listened. Salwan grabbed Rojian by the shoulders and ripped her away from me. She looked so small and so young. We screamed each other's names, but it was useless. Rojian disappeared into a car with Salwan, leaving me alone with Hajji Salman and feeling like I might die, right there, from grief.

Hajji Salman and I got into a small white car, where a driver and a young guard named Morteja waited for us. Morteja stared at me as I took the seat next to him, and I thought that if Hajji Salman hadn't been there, he would have tried to touch me like the men at the slave market. I shrank against the window, sitting as far from him as I could.

By then, the narrow streets were nearly empty and pitch-black, lit by the lights of just a few houses powered by loud generators. We drove for about twenty minutes in silence, the darkness so thick it was almost like we were driving into water, and then we stopped. "Out of the car, Nadia," Hajji Salman ordered. He pulled me roughly by the arm through a gate leading into a garden. It took me a moment to realize that we were back at the first house, the Islamic State center where militants had separated a group of girls destined to go across the border. "Are you taking me to Syria?" I asked softly, and Hajji Salman didn't respond.

From the garden, we could hear girls screaming inside the building, and a few minutes later eight girls wearing abayas and niqabs were pulled by militants through the front door. As they walked by, they turned their heads toward me and stared. Maybe they knew me. Maybe it was Nisreen and Kathrine, and they were too terrified to say anything, just as I was. Whoever they were, their faces were lost behind the niqabs, and a moment later they were shoved into a minibus. Then the doors closed, and it drove away.

A guard took me up to an empty room. I didn't see or hear any other girls, but as in the other houses, ISIS had left piles of Yazidi scarves and clothes as evidence of all the girls who had once been there. A small mound of ashes was all that remained of the documents they had taken from us. Only the ID of one girl from Kocho was partially intact; it stuck out from the ashes like a tiny plant.

Because ISIS hadn't bothered to clear the house of the personal belongings of the family who owned it, remnants of their lives were everywhere. In one room, which had been for exercising, the walls were full of framed photos of a boy, who I assumed was the eldest son, lifting enormous weights. Another room was just for playing games, like pool. But the saddest were the children's rooms, still full of toys and brightly colored blankets, ready for the kids to come back.

"Who did this house belong to?" I asked Hajji Salman when he came to join me.

"A Shiite," he told me. "A judge."

"What happened to them?" I hoped they had managed to escape and were safe in the Kurdish areas by now. Even though they weren't Yazidi, I felt heartbroken for them. Just like in Kocho, ISIS had taken everything from this family.

"He's gone to hell," Hajji Salman said, and I stopped asking questions.

Hajji Salman went to take a shower. When he came back, he was dressed in the same clothes as before, and I could smell faintly the sweat from his clothes and his cologne against the soap. He closed the door behind him and sat down on the mattress next to me. Quickly I stammered, "I have my period," and looked away, but he didn't respond.

"Where are you from?" he asked, sitting close to me.

"Kocho," I answered. In my terror, I had barely thought about my home or my family or anything other than what was going to happen to me from one moment to the next. Saying the name of my village hurt. It brought back memories of home and the people I loved, most vividly of my mother quietly laying her uncovered head in my lap while we waited in Solagh.

"Yazidis are infidels, you know," Hajji Salman said. He spoke softly, almost in a whisper, but there was nothing gentle about him. "God wants us to convert you, and if we can't, then we can do what we like to you."

He paused. "What happened to your family?" he asked.

"Almost all of us managed to escape," I lied. "Only three of us were captured."

"I went to Sinjar on August third, when it all began," he said, relaxing on the bed as if he were telling a happy story. "Along the road I saw three Yazidi men in police uniforms. They were trying to escape, but I managed to catch up to them, and when I did, I killed them."

I stared at the floor, unable to talk.

"We came to Sinjar to kill all the men," my captor went on, "and to take the women and the children, all of them. Unfortunately, some made it to the mountain."

Hajji Salman talked like this for close to an hour, while I sat on the edge of the mattress trying not to hear what he was saying. He cursed my home, my family, and my religion. He told me that he had spent seven years in Mosul's Badush prison and wanted to get his revenge against the infidels in Iraq. What had happened in Sinjar was a good thing, he said, and that I should be happy that

ISIS planned to erase Yazidism from Iraq. He tried to convince me to convert, but I refused. I couldn't look at him. His words became meaningless. He paused his monologue only to pick up a phone call from his wife, whom he called Umm Sara.

Even though what he said was meant to hurt me, I hoped he would never stop talking. As long as he did, he wouldn't touch me, I thought. Yazidi rules for girls and boys being together were not as strict as they were in other communities in Iraq, and in Kocho I had taken rides in cars with male friends and walked to school with male classmates without worrying what people would say. But those boys would never have touched me or hurt me, and before Hajji Salman, I had never been alone with a man like this.

"You're my fourth sabiyya," he said. "The other three are Muslim now. I did that for them. Yazidis are infidels—that's why we are doing this. It's to help you." After he finished talking, he ordered me to undress.

I started to cry. "I have my period," I told him again.

"Prove it," he said, and started to take off his clothes. "That's what my other sabaya said, too."

I undressed. Because I really had my period, he didn't rape me. The Islamic State manual does not outlaw sex with sabaya who are menstruating, but it does say that the captor should wait for his slave to finish her menstrual cycle before having sex with her, to be certain that she is not pregnant. Maybe this was what stopped Hajji Salman that night.

Still, he didn't leave me alone. All night we lay on the mattress naked, and he never stopped touching me. I felt like I had on the bus when Abu Batat was reaching into my dress and forcefully holding my breast—my body hurt and went numb wherever Hajji Salman's fingers went. I was too scared to try to fight him off, and besides, there was little point. I was tiny, thin, and weak. I hadn't eaten a real meal in days, maybe longer when I thought back to the days spent trapped in Kocho, and nothing would stop him from doing whatever he wanted.

———

WHEN I OPENED my eyes in the morning, Hajji Salman was already awake. I started putting my clothes on, but he stopped me. "Take a shower, Nadia," he said. "We have a big day."

After my shower, he handed me a black abaya and niqab, which I put on over my dress. It was the first time I had worn the clothes of a conservative Muslim woman, and although the fabric was light, I found it hard to breathe. Outside, hidden behind my niqab, I saw the neighborhood in the daylight for the first time. The Shiite judge had obviously been wealthy; he lived in an upper-class part of Mosul, where elegant homes were set back from the road by gardens and surrounded by walls. The Islamic State's religious propaganda was a strong lure for potential jihadists, but militants from all over the world were also enticed with the promise of money, and when they came into Mosul, they occupied the nicest homes first and looted the rest of anything they wanted. Residents who hadn't abandoned the city were told they would be given back the authority they had lost after 2003, when the United States dismantled Baathist institutions and redistributed power to the Shia in Iraq, but they were also heavily taxed by ISIS, which seemed to me to be a terrorist group run on greed.

ISIS appeared to revel in the way it took over the city's most important buildings, hoisting their black and white flag wherever they went. The local airport, as well as the entire sprawling campus of Mosul University, once one of the best schools in Iraq, became military bases. Militants stormed the Mosul Museum, the second largest in all of Iraq, destroying artifacts they said were anti-Islamic and selling others in a black market devised to fund their war. Even the city's Nineveh Oberoi Hotel, a lopsided five-star hotel built in the 1980s under Saddam, was filled by key members of the terrorist group. The nicest rooms, people said, were reserved for suicide bombers.

When ISIS came in 2014, hundreds of thousands of people left Mosul, waiting for hours at KRG checkpoints to get into Kurdistan, and debris from their escape was still fresh along the roads where Hajji Salman and I drove. Abandoned cars had been burned down to black skeletons; rebar poked out of the rubble of half-flattened houses; scraps of Iraqi police uniforms littered the roads, left by officers who thought they would have a better chance of making it out alive if they shed their uniforms. Consulates, courthouses, schools, police stations, and military bases were now under the control of ISIS, and they left their mark everywhere, hanging flags, blasting speeches from mosque loudspeakers, even blacking out the faces of children on a mural outside an elementary school since they considered these portraits *haram*, or sinful.

Prisoners from Badush prison had been set free and, in return, were told to pledge their loyalty to ISIS. Joining the militants, they blew up Christian, Sufi, and Shiite shrines and holy sites, some that were as much a part of Iraq as the mountains. At least the Mosul grand mosque was still standing in the old city, although it was made ugly the moment Baghdadi stood behind its pulpit and declared Iraq's second most important city the capital of ISIS in Iraq and, by 2017, it was destroyed like so much of the city.

Finally we stopped in front of the Mosul courthouse, a large sand-colored building on the west bank of the Tigris, with thin spires that reminded me of a mosque. A large Islamic State flag decorated the top of the courthouse. The building was crucial to the Islamic State plan for instituting a new order in Mosul, one led not by the laws of the central Iraqi government but by the Islamic State's fundamentalist beliefs. Islamic State IDs replaced our Iraqi ones, and cars were already being outfitted with new Islamic State license plates. In ISIS-controlled Mosul, women had to be covered all the time—in niqabs and abayas—and escorted by men if they wanted to leave the home. ISIS banned television, radios, and even cigarettes. Civilians who didn't join the terrorist group had to pay a fee if they wanted to leave Mosul, then were allowed to be outside the city for only a certain amount of time. If they were gone too long, a member of their family could be punished and their home and property confiscated for "abandoning the caliphate." Many of the trials were carried out in this courthouse.

Inside, crowds waited to be seen by judges and clerks. A line of militants with black-clad women, who I assumed were sabaya like me, waited in front of a particular room. There we would fill out documents that would officially recognize which Yazidi girls were owned by which militants. We would be forced to convert to Islam, and that conversion was recorded as well. Then a judge would declare us the property of the man who had brought us in. This was a contract for rape that the militants, including Hajji Salman, called "marriage."

When the militants working there saw Hajji Salman, they waved us to the front of the line. Overhearing conversations, I was able to better understand what my captor did for ISIS. Hajji Salman was a judge, and his job was to determine whether a defendant who had been found guilty should be executed.

Inside, the room was empty except for a gray-bearded judge sitting behind a long desk, surrounded by paperwork. Behind him a large Islamic State flag waved in the wind from the air cooler, and two more flags decorated the shoulders of his uniform. As we walked inside, I prayed to God furiously to forgive me for what was about to happen. *I will always believe in you,* I prayed. *I will always be Yazidi.*

The judge, Husayn, was stern and efficient. "Lift up your niqab," he ordered, and I did, showing my face to him. "Do you know the *shahada*?" he asked me. "Yes," I said. Everyone knew the simple Islamic prayer, which demonstrates a convert's commitment to Islam and which Muslims recite when they pray. When I finished, Judge Husayn's face brightened. "God bless you," he said to me. "What you are doing is very good." Then he picked up a camera off his desk and took a picture of my bare face.

Afterward he turned to Hajji Salman and said, "She is your sabiyya now. Do with her what you like," and we made our way out of the courthouse.

With these "marriages" ISIS continued their slow murder of Yazidi girls. First, they took us from our homes and killed our men. Then they separated us from our mothers and sisters. Wherever we were, they reminded us that we were just property, there to be touched and abused, the way Abu Batat squeezed my breast as if he wanted to break it or Nafah put cigarettes out on my body. All of those violations were steps in the execution of our souls.

Taking our religion from us was the cruelest. Leaving the courthouse, I felt empty. Who was I if I wasn't Yazidi? I hoped that God knew that even though I had recited the shahada, I didn't mean it. As long as my soul, murdered by ISIS, could be in the afterlife with God and Tawusi Melek, then ISIS could have my body.

"Was the photo for an ID?" I asked Hajji Salman.

"No," he replied. "They will use the photo to keep track of where you are and who you are with." His grip tightened on my arm. "And if you try to escape, they will print hundreds of copies of those photos with my name and phone number next to it and hang them at every checkpoint to make sure that you are returned to me. You will be returned to me."

Of course, I believed him.

Chapter 7

We left the courthouse and drove to a new home where Morteja, the guard, lived with his family. Compared to Hajji Salman's residence, it was a modest house, only one floor, but still grander than what I had grown up in. Since I had just converted, I thought maybe Hajji Salman would take pity on me and tell me what had happened to my family, so I asked him. "Please, just take me to see Kathrine, Nisreen, and Rojian," I begged. "I just want to make sure they are okay."

To my surprise, he said he would try. "I know where they are," he said. "I'll make a phone call. Maybe you can see them, for a moment, but we will have to wait here for now."

Entering through the kitchen, we were immediately greeted by a large older woman who introduced herself as Morteja's mother. "Nadia was an infidel, but she has just converted," Morteja told his mother, and she raised her thick arms in enthusiastic congratulations to Hajji Salman. "It's not your fault that you were born a Yazidi," she said to me. "It is the fault of your parents, and you will be happy now."

I hadn't been in the same room as a non-Yazidi woman since arriving in Mosul, and I stared at Morteja's mother, looking for a glimmer of sympathy. She was a mother, after all, and I thought that might mean more to her than her being Sunni and me being Yazidi. Did she know what Hajji Salman had done to me the night before, and what he planned on doing as soon as I finished my period? Even if she didn't, she knew I was there by force, that I was separated from my family, and that the men in Kocho had been killed. She showed no affection or sympathy toward me, only glee in finding out that because I had been forced to convert to Islam, there was one fewer Yazidi in Iraq.

I hated her, not just because she had let Mosul be taken over by ISIS, but because she had let it be taken over by *men*. Under ISIS, women were erased from public life. Men joined it for obvious reasons—they wanted money, power, and sex. They were too weak, I thought, to figure out how to get these things without using violence, and in any case, the Islamic State militants I had met so far seemed to enjoy making people feel pain. Those men were served by the laws adopted by ISIS, which gave them total authority over their wives and daughters.

I couldn't understand, though, why a woman would join the jihadists and openly celebrate the enslavement of girls the way Morteja's mother did. Any woman in Iraq, no matter her religion, had to struggle for everything. Seats in parliament, reproductive rights, positions at universities—all these were the results of long battles. Men were content to stay in power, so power had to be taken from them by strong women. Even Adkee's insistence on driving our tractor was a gesture of equality and a challenge to those men.

And yet when ISIS came to Mosul, women like Morteja's mother welcomed them and celebrated the vicious policies that would hide women like her and exploit women like me, just as she had stood by while the terrorists killed or pushed out the city's Christians and Shiites, people the Sunnis had lived with for over a thousand years. She chose to stay and watch and to live under ISIS.

If I had ever seen Yazidis in Sinjar attack Muslims the way that ISIS attacked us, there is no way I would have stood by while it happened. No one in my family would have, men or women. Everyone thinks Yazidi women are weak, because we are poor and live outside the cities, and I have heard people say female fighters with ISIS are, in their own way, proving their strength among men. But none of them—not Morteja's mother, not even a suicide bomber—was a fraction as strong as my mother, who overcame so many struggles and who never would have let another woman be sold into slavery, no matter her religion.

I now know that female terrorists are nothing new. Across the world and throughout history, women have joined terrorist organizations, sometimes taking starring roles, and yet their actions continue to astonish outsiders. People assume that women are too docile, particularly in the Middle East, to be violent. But there are many women in ISIS, and like the men, they reject all faiths except for Islam and think that by joining the terrorists, they are helping the greater cause of building their Sunni caliphate. Like the men, they consider themselves victims of sectarian oppression and the American invasion. The women believed ISIS when they said that if the women supported them, their families would have more money, their husbands would get better jobs, and their children would be given the status they deserved in their country. They were told that it was their religious duty to support the men, and they accepted that.

I have heard stories of Islamic State women helping Yazidis. One girl from Kocho was given a cell phone by the wife of her captor, a foreign fighter who had taken his entire family with him on the long journey from their home in the West to Syria. At first the wife had been enticed by Islamic State propaganda, but quickly she became appalled by the enslavement of Yazidi women. Because of this woman, the Yazidi girls in that house were able to coordinate being smuggled out of Syria to safety.

More often, though, I hear stories of women who are even

crueler than the men. They beat and starve their husbands' sabaya, out of jealousy or anger or because we are easy targets. Maybe they think of themselves as revolutionaries—even feminists—and they have told themselves, as people have throughout history, that violence toward a greater good is acceptable. I've heard of all this, and when I think about bringing ISIS to justice for genocide, I feel some pity for the women. I understand better how people could see them as victims. But I don't understand how anyone could stand by and watch while thousands of Yazidis are sold into sexual slavery and raped until their bodies break. There is no justification for that kind of cruelty, and no greater good that could come out of it.

Morteja's mother kept talking to Hajji Salman, trying to impress him. "Other than Morteja, I have a twelve-year-old daughter," she said. "And a son in Syria, fighting with *Dawla*," using a shortened Arabic term for ISIS. She smiled, thinking of him. "He is so beautiful!" she gushed. "God will bless him."

After the greetings were over, Morteja's mother showed me to a small room. "Wait here for Hajji Salman," she said. "Don't try to go anywhere, and don't touch anything." She closed the door behind her.

I sat on the edge of a couch and hugged my arms to my body. I wondered if Hajji Salman was in fact trying to find my nieces, and if I would be able to see them. It wasn't uncommon for sabaya to interact with one another—men often traveled with them—and it was possible he would give me what I wanted to keep me calm, so that later I would fight less. As long as I got to see that Kathrine and the others were still alive, I didn't care what came after.

Suddenly the door opened, and Morteja walked in. I noticed for the first time how young he was, no more than a year older than me, with a scruffy, short beard. It was clear that he was low-ranking among the militants, and I wasn't even sure he had a sabiyya; if he did, there was no evidence of her living with him. Without Hajji Salman nearby, he approached me with more authority, but it seemed put on, like a boy wearing his father's shoes.

He closed the door behind him and sat down on the bed close to me. Instinctively I pulled my legs up to my chest and rested my forehead on my knees, avoiding looking at him. Nevertheless, he started talking. "Are you happy to be here?" he asked. "Or would you be happier if you could escape and be with your family?" He was making fun of me; he knew how any human being would answer that question.

"I don't know anything about what happened to my family," I said. I pleaded with God for him to go away.

"What would you give me if I helped you escape?" he asked me.

"I have nothing to give you," I said, answering sincerely, even though I knew what he was suggesting. "But if you help me, I will call my brother, and he will give you anything you want."

He laughed and asked, "Are you scared?" all the while inching closer to me.

"Yes, I'm scared," I told him. "Of course I'm scared."

"Let me see," he said, and he reached out for my chest. "Let me see if your heart is beating fast because you are scared."

As soon as I saw his hand coming toward me, I stopped talking to him and screamed as loud as I could. I wished my scream would make the walls collapse around us and the ceiling fall down and kill us all.

The door opened, and Morteja's mother appeared. She gave her son an angry look. "Leave her alone," she said to Morteja, "she doesn't belong to you." And Morteja left the room, hanging his head in shame like a child. "She's a kafir," his mother said to him as he left, then scowled at me. "And she belongs to Hajji Salman."

For a moment, I wondered how she would act if it were just the two of us. In spite of who she was, and what she had allowed to happen, if she had just come and sat down next to me and done nothing beyond acknowledge what was happening to me, I think I would have forgiven her. She was close to my mother's age, and her body was fleshy and soft like my mother's. If she had said, "I know they brought you here by force," and if she had asked, "Where are your mother and your sisters?" and not done anything but say those things, I would have felt so relieved. I fantasized about her waiting until Morteja left and then sitting beside me on the bed and taking my hand, calling me her daughter and whispering, "Don't worry, I will help you escape. I'm a mother, I feel for you." Those words would have been like a piece of bread after I hadn't eaten for weeks. But she said nothing. She left, and I was alone again in that little room.

After a few minutes, Hajji Salman came in. "We can go see Kathrine now," he told me, and my heart felt full and empty at the same time. I worried about my niece more than anyone else.

———

KATHRINE WAS BORN in 1998, Elias's oldest daughter, and from the first moment she was born, she was special in our family. It was Kathrine's teary protests that prevented Elias from moving his family out of our house. She loved my mother almost as much as I did, and she loved me. We shared everything, even clothing, and sometimes we dressed alike. At my cousin's wedding, we both wore red, and at one of my brothers' weddings, we both wore green.

Even though I was older, I was behind a few years in school, and so we were in the same classes. Kathrine was smart, but she was practical beyond her years and hardworking, and she dropped out of school after sixth grade to work on the farm. She liked being outside with our family more than she liked studying, and she liked feeling useful. Even though she was young and slight and quiet, she could do everything in the house and on the farm.

Kathrine milked our sheep and cooked as well as Dimal. When someone got sick, she wept over them and said she could feel their illness inside her until they got better. Falling asleep at night, we would talk about our plans for the future. "I will get married at twenty-five," she used to tell me. "I want lots of children and a big family."

During the siege, Kathrine barely moved from the living room, where she sat in front of the television and wept for the people on the mountain. She refused to eat after she heard that Baso, her sister, had been captured. "We have to be optimistic," I would tell her, stroking her face, which had turned yellow from lack of food and sleep. "Maybe we will survive." My mother would tell her, "Look at your father—you have to be strong for him." But Kathrine lost hope very early and never got it back.

Kathrine and I were put on different trucks leaving Kocho, and I didn't see her again until Solagh, when she held on to my mother as tightly as she possibly could, trying to keep ISIS from taking her away. "I'm going with my mother," she told an Islamic State militant. "She can't walk by herself." But he yelled at her to sit down, and she did.

In Mosul, it was Kathrine who had worried about me the most. "Don't scream again," she said. "I know what Abu Batat was doing. He did the same to me." She knew that I had a hard time controlling my temper—she knew me better than anyone—and she wanted to help me avoid being punished. "Don't speak Arabic, Nadia," she'd said while we waited in the house in Mosul to be divided. "You don't want them to take you to Syria." The last I saw of her, I was being torn from her by Salwan and taken downstairs.

Hajji Salman and I left Morteja's home. As we walked to the door, I saw Morteja's mother in the kitchen, where she was busy applying hot glass cups to a man's back—a type of massage that leaves big red circles on the skin and is supposed to help with circulation. Because it was polite to thank the woman of the house—and because in spite of everything, the habits you grow up with become second nature—I looked at her and said, "Salman is here, I am going, thank you."

"God be with you," she said, and turned back to what she was doing.

Hajji Salman and I drove back to the building where the slave market had taken place the night before. "They're upstairs," he told me, and he left me.

Racing up the stairs, I found Kathrine and Nisreen alone in that large room with the blacked-out windows. I could tell they were exhausted; Kathrine was lying down on one of the thin mattresses, her eyes barely open, and Nisreen was sitting beside her. When I opened the door, they just stared at me blankly. I had forgotten to lift up my niqab. "Are you here to recite Koran for us?" Kathrine asked quietly.

"It's me, Nadia," I said, and when they saw my face, they rushed to me. We cried so hard, we felt like we could die from crying. Our muscles hurt, and we could barely breathe. "They told us to wait for a woman who was coming to check to make sure we were virgins," they said. "We thought you were her!"

Kathrine's eyes were swollen and bruised. "I can't see very well," she told me when I sat down beside her.

"You look so weak," I said, taking her hand.

"I'm fasting so that God might help us," she explained. I worried about her collapsing without food, but I didn't say that. Yazidis observe two official fasts a year and we can choose to fast at other times, to reinforce our commitment to God and open up our communication to Tawusi Melek. Fasting can give us strength rather than take it away.

"What happened to you?" I asked Kathrine.

"A man named Abu Abdullah bought me and took me to another house in Mosul," she said. "I told him that I have cancer and he shouldn't touch me, so he beat me and returned me to the market. That's why my eyes are bruised."

"I tried to escape," Nisreen said. "They caught me and beat me and then brought me back here."

"Why are you wearing that?" Kathrine asked me. She was still wearing two Yazidi dresses layered on top of each other.

"They took away my clothes and made me wear this," I said. "I lost my bag. I don't have anything else."

"I have your bag!" Kathrine said, and handed it to me. Then she peeled off her top layer and gave me that as well. It was a pink and brown dress, one of her new ones, and to this day Dimal and I take turns wearing it, because it is beautiful and because it reminds us of our niece. "Wear this under the abaya," she told me, and I kissed her on the cheek.

One of the guards came to the door. "You have five minutes," he said. "Then Hajji Salman wants you downstairs."

After he left, Kathrine reached into the pocket of her dress and handed me a pair of earrings. "Keep them with you. We might not see each other again."

"If you have the chance to escape, you should escape," she whispered to me, taking my hand and walking with me down the stairs. "I will also try." We held hands until we got to the kitchen and Hajji Salman pulled me outside.

We drove in silence back to Hajji Salman's house. I wept quietly for Kathrine and Nisreen, praying to God that they would survive whatever happened to them. When we got there, Hajji Salman told me to go inside with one of the guards and wait for him. "I won't be long," he said, and I started to pray for myself.

Before I went inside, Hajji Salman looked at me for a long time. "When I come back, I don't care if you have your period," he said after a moment. "I promise you, I will come to you."

That's how he put it: "I will come to you."

Chapter 8

OVER THE PAST THREE YEARS, I HAVE HEARD A LOT OF STO-
ries about other Yazidi women who were captured and enslaved by ISIS. For the most part, we were all victims of the same
violence. We would be bought at the market, or given as a gift to
a new recruit or a high-ranking commander, and then taken back
to his home, where we would be raped and humiliated, most of
us beaten as well. Then we would be sold or given as a gift again,
and again raped and beaten, then sold or given to another militant, and raped and beaten by him, and sold or given, and raped
and beaten, and it went this way for as long as we were desirable
enough and not yet dead. If we tried to escape, we would be punished severely. As Hajji Salman had warned me, ISIS hung our
photos at checkpoints, and residents in Mosul were instructed to
return slaves to the nearest Islamic State center. They were told
there was a five-thousand-dollar reward if they did.

The rape was the worst part. It stripped us of our humanity
and made thinking about the future—returning to Yazidi society,
marrying, having children, being happy—impossible. We wished
they would kill us instead.

ISIS knew how devastating it was for an unmarried Yazidi girl
to convert to Islam and lose her virginity, and they used our worst
fears—that our community and religious leaders wouldn't welcome us back—against us. "Try to escape, it doesn't matter," Hajji

Salman would tell me. "Even if you make it home, your father or your uncle will kill you. You're no longer a virgin, and you are Muslim!"

Women tell stories about how they fought against their attackers, how they tried to beat away the men who were much stronger than them. Although they could never have overtaken the militants who were determined to rape them, their fight allowed them to feel better after the fact. "There's not one time that we let them do it quietly," they say. "I would resist, I would hit, I would spit on his face, I would do anything." I heard of one girl who penetrated herself with a bottle so that she would no longer be a virgin when her militant came for her, and others who tried to light themselves on fire. After they were free, they were able to say proudly that they scratched so hard at their captor's arm that they drew blood, or they bruised his cheek while he was raping them. "At least I didn't let him do whatever he wanted," they would say, and every gesture, no matter how small, was a message to ISIS that they did not truly own them. Of course, it was the voices of the women who were not there, who had killed themselves rather than be raped, that spoke the loudest.

I have never admitted this to anyone, but I did not fight back when Hajji Salman or anyone else came to rape me. I just closed my eyes and wished for it to be over. People tell me all the time, "Oh, you are so brave, you are so strong," and I hold my tongue, but I want to correct them and tell them that, while other girls punched and bit their attackers, I only cried. "I am not brave like them," I want to say, but I worry what people would think of me. Sometimes it can feel like all that anyone is interested in when it comes to the genocide is the sexual abuse of Yazidi girls, and they want a story of a fight. I want to talk about everything—the murder of my brothers, the disappearance of my mother, the brainwashing of the boys—not just the rape. Or maybe I am still scared of what people will think. It took a long time before I accepted that just because I didn't fight back the way some other girls did, it doesn't mean I approved of what the men were doing.

Before ISIS came, I considered myself a brave and honest person. Whatever problems I had, whatever mistakes I made, I would confess them to my family. I told them, "This is who I am," and I was ready to accept their reactions. As long as I was with my family, I could face anything. But without my family, captive in Mosul, I felt so alone that I barely felt human. Something inside me died.

———

HAJJI SALMAN'S HOUSE was full of guards, so I went upstairs immediately. About a half hour later, one of the guards, Hossam, came in with a dress, some makeup, and a hair-removal cream. "Salman said you have to take a shower and prepare yourself before he comes," he said, and then he went back downstairs, leaving the things on the bed.

I took a shower and did what Hossam said, using the cream to remove all the hair from my feet to my underarms. It was a brand my mother had often given us to use, and I always hated it, preferring to use the sugar wax popular in the Middle East. The cream had a strong chemical smell that made me feel dizzy. In the bathroom, I noticed that my period had, in fact, stopped.

Next, I put on the dress Hossam left for me. It was black and blue, with a short skirt falling above the knees and only thin straps over the shoulders. There was a bra inside so I didn't have to wear one. It was a type of party dress I would see on television, not modest enough for Kocho or, in fact, for Mosul. It was the kind of dress a wife wore only for her husband.

Putting it on, I stood in front of the bathroom mirror. I knew that if I didn't wear any makeup, I would be punished, so I looked through the pile that Hossam had left for me. Normally, Kathrine and I would have been thrilled at the new makeup, which was a brand I recognized and could very rarely afford. We would have stood in front of the bedroom mirror, painting our eyelids different colors, surrounding our eyes with thick lines of kohl, and covering our freckles with foundation. At Hajji Salman's, I could barely stand to look at myself in the mirror. I put on some pink lipstick and eye makeup—just enough, I hoped, to avoid being beaten.

I looked in a mirror for the first time since leaving Kocho. Before, when I had put on makeup, I always felt that when I finished, I looked like another person, and I had loved that, the possibility of transforming. But that day at Hajji Salman's, I didn't feel that I looked any different. No matter how much lipstick I wore, the face in the mirror reflected exactly what I had been turned into—a slave who, at any moment, was going to be a prize for a terrorist. I sat down on the bed and waited for the door to open.

Forty minutes later I heard the guards outside greet my captor, and then Hajji Salman came into the room. He wasn't alone, but the men who were with him stayed in the hallway. As soon as I saw him, I collapsed, trying to shrink into a ball so that he couldn't touch me, like a child.

"*Salam alakum,*" Hajji Salman said to me, and looked me up and down. He seemed surprised that I had dressed up as he had asked. "I had other sabaya who I had to sell after a few days," he said. "They didn't do what I asked them. You did a good job," he said approvingly, and then he left and closed the door behind him, leaving me feeling exposed and ashamed.

It was early evening when the door opened again. This time Hossam peered into the room. "Hajji Salman wants you to bring tea to the guests," he said.

"How many are there? Who are they?" I didn't want to leave the room dressed as I was, but Hossam refused to answer. "Just come," he said. "And hurry, the men are waiting."

For a moment, I had hope that the rape wasn't going to hap-

From left to right: my sister Adkee, my brother Jalo, and my sister Dimal.

My father, Basee Murad Taha,
as a young man.

My niece Kathrine at a wedding in 2013.

From left to right: my sister-in-law Sester, my sister Adkee, my brother Khairy, my niece Baso, my sister Dimal, my niece Maisa, and me in 2011.

Clockwise from back row, left: my sister-in-law Jilan; my sister-in-law Mona; my mother; my niece Baso; my sister Adkee; my nieces Nazo, Kathrine, and Maisa; and me at our home in Kocho in 2014.

My brother Hezni driving my family's tractor with me and Kathrine (at left) in the back.

My brothers and half brothers in 2014. Back row, from left to right: Hezni, a neighbor, my half brother Khaled, and my brother Saeed. Front row: my half brother Walid, my brother Saoud, and me.

Jilan and Hezni on their wedding day in 2014.

My mother at her grandson Samih's wedding.

From left to right: my brothers Massoud, Saoud, and Hezni.

My half brother Hajji.

At school with a classmate in 2011.

My mother, Shami.

pen that night. *He's just going to give me to one of these men,* I said to myself, and I walked downstairs to the kitchen.

One of the guards had prepared the tea, pouring the strong reddish-brown liquid into small glass cups and arranging them around a dish of white sugar, and left it on a tray on the stairs. I picked up the tray and brought it into the living room, where a group of militants sat on plush couches. "*Salam alakum,*" I said as I entered, then walked around the room, placing teacups on small tables set up by the men's knees. I could hear them laughing and speaking a distinctly Syrian Arabic, but I couldn't pay attention to what they were saying. My hand shook as I served the tea. I could feel them looking at my bare shoulders and legs. The accent in particular scared me. I was still sure that at some point they would take me out of Iraq.

"Syrian soldiers are so terrible," one of the men said, and the others laughed. "They just give up quickly. They are so scared!"

"I remember," said Hajji Salman. "They gave their country to us so easily. Almost as easily as Sinjar!" That last comment was for me, and I hoped I didn't show how much it hurt to hear it. I held out a cup of tea toward Hajji Salman. "Put it on the table," he said, without looking at me.

I went back to the hallway, where I sat cowering and waiting. After twenty minutes, the men got up, and when they had all left the house, Hajji Salman came to see me, holding an abaya. "It's time to pray," he said. "Cover yourself up so we can pray together."

I couldn't recite the words, but I knew the movements of the Islamic prayer, and I stood next to him, trying to mimic exactly what he was doing so that he would be satisfied and not hurt me. Back in the room, he turned on some religious songs, then went into the bathroom. When he came back, he turned off the music and the room was silent again.

"Take off your dress," he said as he had the night before, and he took off his clothes. Then he came to me, as he'd said he would.

Each moment was terrifying. If I pulled away, he roughly pulled me back. He was loud enough for the guards to hear—he shouted as if he wanted all of Mosul to know that he was finally raping his sabiyya—and no one interfered. His touch was exaggerated, forceful, meant to hurt me. No man ever touched his wife like this. Hajji Salman was as big as a house, as big as the house we were in. And I was like a child, crying out for my mother.

Chapter 9

STAYED WITH HAJJI SALMAN FOUR OR FIVE NIGHTS BEFORE he got rid of me. I was always in pain. Every day, whenever he had time, he raped me, and each morning he left after giving me instructions: "Clean the house. Cook this food. Wear this dress." Other than that, all he said to me was "*salam alakum*." He commanded me to act like a wife, and I was so scared I did everything he asked. If anyone had been watching from a distance, far enough away that they couldn't see how much I cried or how my body shook when he touched me, they might have thought we were truly married. I went through the actions of a wife as he commanded me to. But he never called me his wife, only his sabiyya.

A guard called Yahya brought food and tea to the room I shared with Salman. He was young, maybe twenty-three, and he wouldn't even look at me as he laid the tray inside the door. They wouldn't deprive me of food or water—I was too valuable as a sabiyya to risk killing—but I would eat only a few bites of the rice and soup they served me, just enough to stop feeling dizzy. I cleaned the house as Hajji Salman told me to, from top to bottom, scrubbing the bathrooms, which were filthy with six guards and Salman using them, and sweeping the staircase. I picked up the clothes they left strewn all over the house—black Islamic State pants and white dishdashas—and put them in the washing machine. I scraped leftover rice into the garbage and washed their lip prints off the teacups. His house was full of guards, so they didn't worry about me discovering anything or escaping, and I was allowed to go into any room except for the garage, where I think they kept their weapons.

Through the windows, I watched the city move. Hajji Salman lived in a crowded part of Mosul, near a highway that was usually full of cars. The windows on the staircase overlooked a circular access ramp, and I pictured myself trying to run over it to get to safety. Hajji Salman was constantly trying to warn me about escaping. "If you try, Nadia, you will regret it, I promise you," he would say. "The punishment won't be good." His constant reminders gave me some hope. He wouldn't have been so worried unless some girls had managed to escape their captors.

ISIS was so calculating when it came to enslaving Yazidi girls, but they made mistakes and gave us opportunities. The biggest mistake they made was dressing us like all the women in Mosul, in the anonymous black abaya and niqab. Once we were in that clothing, we blended in, and with ISIS in charge, men were much less likely to engage with a woman they didn't know on the street and therefore were less likely to find us out. Sweeping the staircase, I watched women walking through the city, each one dressed just like the others. It was impossible to tell who might be a Sunni woman going to market and who might be a Yazidi girl escaping her captor.

Many of the Islamic State centers were in crowded neighborhoods like Hajji Salman's, which would be helpful if I were ever outside alone. I imagined myself climbing out the big window in the kitchen, putting on my abaya, and blending into a crowd. Somehow I would make my way to the taxi garage and find a seat in a car to Kirkuk, a frequently used checkpoint into Iraqi Kurdistan. If anyone tried to talk to me, I would just say that I was a Muslim from Kirkuk trying to visit my family. Or maybe

I would say I had fled the war in Syria. I memorized the short opening verse from the Koran in case a militant tried to test me, and my Arabic was perfect, and I already knew the shahada. I had even committed two popular Islamic State songs to memory, one of which celebrated military victories: "We've taken Badush and we've taken Tal Afar, everything is good now." I hated the sound of them, but the songs played in my head as I cleaned. The other one went "Give your lives to God and to the religion." Whatever happened, I would never admit to being Yazidi.

For me, though, I knew it was an impossible plan. Salman's center was full of Islamic State militants, and there was no way I could climb through the window and over the garden fence without one of them noticing. Plus, Hajji Salman let me wear my abaya and niqab only when I went outside with him or a guard who could keep an eye on me. In the house, I wore the dresses I brought from Kocho or whatever Hajji Salman picked out for me. Lying in bed at night, anticipating the creak of the door as Hajji Salman came to join me, I would go over my escape fantasies and have to admit to myself that they could never happen, and then I would fall into such a deep sadness that I would pray for death.

One afternoon after he raped me, Hajji Salman told me to prepare myself for guests who were coming that night. "You might know the sabiyya," he told me. "She asked to see you."

My heart leaped in anticipation. Who would it be? As much as I longed to see a familiar face, I wasn't sure I could bear to meet Kathrine or one of my sisters in the clothes Hajji Salman liked me to wear. Normally when Salman asked me to dress for visitors, he wanted me to wear things like the short blue and black dress, and I was mortified at the thought of another Yazidi girl seeing me like that. Luckily, I was able to find a black dress that, although it had thin straps, at least covered my knees. I pulled my hair back and put on a little lipstick but nothing on my eyes. When Hajji Salman was satisfied, we went downstairs.

The visiting militant turned out to be Nafah, the man from the first center who had punished me for screaming on the bus. He scowled at me but addressed only Hajji Salman. "My sabiyya hasn't stopped asking to see yours," he said. "We will have to sit with them and listen to what they say, though, because I don't trust Nadia."

Nafah's sabiyya was Lamia, my friend Walaa's sister, and we ran to hug and kiss each other on the cheek, so relieved to see a familiar face. Then the four of us sat together, and when Salman and Nafah began to talk together, ignoring us, Lamia and I switched from Arabic to Kurdish.

Lamia was wearing a long dress and a hijab over her hair. We didn't know how long we would have together, so we spoke quickly, trying to get as much information as we could. "Did he touch you?" she asked me.

"Did he touch you?" I asked her back, and she nodded yes.

"He made me convert, and then we were married at the courthouse," she confessed to me, and I told her the same thing had happened to me. "You shouldn't look at it like a marriage, though," I said. "It's not like getting married in Kocho."

"I want to escape," she said. "But people are always visiting Nafah, and it's impossible to leave."

"Same thing with Salman," I told her. "There are guards everywhere, and he told me that if I try to escape, he will punish me."

"What do you think he would do?" she asked quietly, glancing at our captors. They were talking to each other, oblivious to what we were doing.

"I don't know. Something bad," I said.

"We told you girls to speak in Arabic!" Salman yelled. They had overheard us and were angry that they couldn't understand what we were saying.

"What happened to Walaa?" I asked Lamia in Arabic. I hadn't seen my friend after we left Kocho.

"The same night they took me, they distributed all the other girls," Lamia told me. "I don't know what happened to Walaa. I've been asking Nafah to find her, but he won't. What about Dimal and Adkee?"

"They stayed in Solagh," I said, "with my mother." We were quiet for a moment, letting the weight of their absences fall on top of us.

Thirty-five minutes later Nafah got up to leave. Lamia and I kissed each other goodbye. "Take care of yourself and don't be upset," I told her as she pulled her niqab down over her face. "We are all going through the same thing." Then they left, and I was alone with Salman again.

We walked upstairs to my room. "This is the first time I've seen your expression change at all," he said to me when we reached my door.

I turned to him. I didn't pretend not to be angry. "What do you want my face to look like when you lock me up and do things to me that I don't want?" I said back.

"You'll get used to it," he said. "Go inside." He opened the door and stayed in the room with me until morning.

———

HAJJI SALMAN WOULD tell me over and over, "I will punish you if you try to escape," but he never said exactly what he would do. He would almost certainly beat me, but it wouldn't be the first time he did that. Salman hit me all the time. He hit me when he was displeased with the way I cleaned the house, when he was angry about something from work, if I cried or kept my eyes closed while he raped me. Maybe, if I tried to escape, the beating would be severe enough to scar or disfigure me, but I didn't care. If a wound or a scar prevented him or anyone else from raping me, I would wear it like a jewel.

Sometimes after he raped me, he would tell me that there was no point in even trying to escape. "You are no longer a virgin," he would say, "and you are a Muslim. Your family will kill you. You are ruined." Even though I had been forced, I believed him. I felt ruined.

Already I had thought about ways to make myself ugly—in the center, girls had smeared ashes and dirt on their faces, tangled their hair into knots, and avoided showering so that their stench might repel buyers—but I couldn't think of anything other than slashing my face or cutting off all my hair, which I assumed would make Salman beat me. If I tried to disfigure myself, would he kill me? I didn't think so. I was more valuable alive, and he knew that death would be a welcome relief. I could only imagine what Salman would do to me if I tried to escape. Then one day the opportunity came to test him.

In the evening, Salman came home with two men, militants I had never seen before who were traveling without their sabaya. "Did you finish cleaning the house?" he asked, and when I said I had, he told me to spend the rest of the evening in our room, alone. "There is food in the kitchen. If you are hungry, tell Hossam, and he will bring some up for you." I was to stay out of their way and wait for him.

First, though, he told me to bring everyone tea. He wanted to show off his sabiyya. I did as I was told, putting on one of the dresses that he liked and taking the tea from the kitchen into the living room. As usual, the militants there were talking about Islamic State victories in Syria and Iraq. I listened for any mention of Kocho, but I didn't hear them say anything about my home.

The room was crowded with men, only two of whom were visitors. All the center's guards appeared to be joining Salman and his guests for dinner, leaving their stations unmanned for the first time since I arrived. I wondered if that was why he had been so insistent that I stay in my room until the guests left. If all the guards were joining them, it meant there would be no one patrolling the garden or watching to make sure that if I closed the door to the bathroom, I didn't try to crawl out the window. There would be no one outside my door, listening to what was going on inside.

When I finished serving the tea, Hajji Salman dismissed me, and I went back upstairs. A plan was already forming in my head, and I moved quickly, knowing that if I stopped to think about what I was doing, I might talk myself out of it, and that a chance like this might never come again. Instead of going to my room, I went into a living room, where I knew the closets were still full of clothes left by Yazidi girls and the family who owned the house, looking for a spare abaya and niqab. I found the abaya quickly and slipped it on over my dress. To cover my hair and face, I settled on a long black scarf in place of a niqab, hoping that I would find safety before anyone noticed the difference. Then I walked to the window.

We were on the second floor but not very high up, and the wall below the window was built so that some of the sand-colored bricks stuck out a few inches. It was a popular design in Mosul, not meant for anything but decoration, but I thought those bricks could be used as a ladder to climb down to the garden. I poked my head out the window, looking for the guards who usually walked the garden at all hours, but it was empty. An oil drum leaned against the garden fence; it would be a perfect step stool.

Beyond the garden wall the highways rumbled with cars, but the streets were beginning to thin out as people went home for dinner, and in the dusk I thought it was less likely that anyone would notice that the black scarf was not a proper niqab. Hopefully I could find someone who would help me before I was discovered. Other than my jewelry and my mother's ration card, which I tucked into my bra, I left everything behind in the room.

Carefully I put one leg through the open window and then another. With my body halfway through the window and my torso still inside, I moved my feet, trying to feel for one of those bricks. My arms shook, holding on to the windowsill, but I quickly steadied myself. I could tell the climb wouldn't be too difficult. I was just beginning to look for lower bricks when I heard the sound of a gun being cocked just below me. I froze, my body folded over the windowsill. "Go inside!" a male voice yelled up at me, and without looking down, I quickly heaved myself back up and through the window, falling onto the floor below it, my heart racing with fear. I didn't know who had caught me. All of Hajji Salman's guards were in the living room with him. I curled up on the floor beneath the window until I heard footsteps come toward me, and when I looked up and saw Hajji Salman standing over me, I ran as quickly as I could back to my room.

The door opened, and Hajji Salman came in, carrying a whip in his hands. Screaming, I threw myself onto the bed and pulled a thick comforter over my entire body and my head, hiding the way a child hides. Salman stood beside the bed and without a word started beating me. The whip came down hard, over and over, so fast and with so much anger that the thick blanket did little to protect me. "Get out of there!" Hajji Salman shouted, louder than I had ever heard him. "Get out from under that blanket and get undressed!"

I had no choice. I lifted the blanket off and, with Salman still hovering over me holding the whip, slowly took off my clothes. When I was completely naked, I stood still, waiting for what he would do to me and crying silently. I assumed he would rape me, but instead, he started walking toward the door. "Nadia, I told you that if you tried to escape something really bad would happen to you," he said. His soft voice had returned. Then he opened the door and walked through it.

A moment later Morteja, Yahya, Hossam, and the three other guards walked in, staring at me. They stood where Salman had been a moment before. As soon as I saw them, I understood what my punishment would be. Morteja was the first to come to the bed. I tried to stop him, but he was too strong. He pushed me down, and there was nothing I could do.

After Morteja, another guard raped me. I screamed for my mother and for Khairy, my brother. In Kocho, they came whenever I needed them. Even if I just burned my finger a little bit, if I asked for them, they would come to help me. In Mosul, I was alone, and their names were all I had left of them. Nothing I did or said stopped the men from attacking me. The last thing I remember from that night is the face of one of the guards as he came toward me. I remember that before it was his turn to rape me, he took off his glasses and carefully put them down on a table. I guess he worried they would break.

———

WHEN I WOKE up in the morning, I was alone and naked. I couldn't move. Someone, one of the men I supposed, had put a blanket over me. My head spun when I tried to get up, and my body ached when I reached out for clothes. Every movement felt like it would push me back into unconsciousness, as if a black curtain had been halfway drawn in front of my eyes or everything in the world had become a shadow of itself.

I went to the bathroom to take a shower. My body was covered in filth left by the men, and I turned on the water and stood under it for a long time, crying. Then I cleaned myself very well, scrubbing my body, my teeth, my face, my hair, and the entire time praying and asking God to help me, and to forgive me.

Afterward I went back to my room and lay down on the sofa. The bed still smelled like the men who had raped me. No one came to see me, although I could hear them talking outside my room, and after a moment I managed to sleep. I didn't dream about anything. When I next opened my eyes, Salman's driver was standing over me, poking me on the shoulder. "Wake up, Nadia. Get up, get dressed," he said. "It's time to go."

"Where am I going?" I asked, stuffing my things into my black bag.

"I don't know—away from here," he said. "Hajji Salman has sold you."

Chapter 10

WHEN I WAS FIRST CAPTURED AND LEARNED WHAT WAS happening to Yazidi girls, I prayed that I would be held by only one man. Being bought once as a slave, having your humanity and dignity taken from you, was bad enough, and I couldn't stand the thought of being passed from militant to militant, moved from house to house, and maybe even transported across the border into ISIS-held Syria, like an object at the market, like a sack of flour in the back of a truck.

Back then I didn't understand how cruel one man could be. Hajji Salman was the worst man I had ever met, and after he allowed his guards to rape me, I prayed to be sold. I didn't care to whom and I didn't care where they took me. Even the possibility of going to Syria, where it was much harder to escape and which I had once thought of as a death sentence, seemed better to me than staying with Salman. When I fantasize about putting ISIS on trial for genocide, I want to see Hajji Salman, like Salwan, captured alive. I want to visit him in jail, where he will be surrounded by Iraqi military officers and guards with guns. I want to see how he looks and hear how he talks without the power of ISIS behind him. And I want him to look at me and remember what he did to me and understand that this is why he will never be free again.

I packed my bag and followed the driver outside. Hajji Salman was somewhere in the house, but I didn't see him when I left.

I willed myself not to look at Morteja and the other guards as I passed by them. It was getting dark by the time we left Hajji Salman's, but the air was still hot, with only a little breeze blowing sand onto my face, which no one had asked me to cover. Although I was outside, I didn't feel any sense of freedom. Knowing that there was no person in the whole of Mosul who would help me made me feel hopeless.

A new guard, a man I didn't recognize, sat in the front of a small white car with the driver. "Are you hungry?" he asked me as we left. I shook my head no, but we pulled over to a restaurant anyway. The driver went inside and brought back some sandwiches wrapped in foil, one of which he tossed onto the backseat beside me along with a bottle of water. Outside the car, people walked around, bought food and sat and ate, talked on their phones. I wished I could just open the door and show myself to them. I wished that as soon as they knew what was happening, they would help me. But I didn't think they would. A strong smell of meat and onions rose through the foil, and I closed my eyes as we started driving, trying not to throw up.

Soon we arrived at the first checkpoint out of Mosul. It was manned by Islamic State militants carrying automatic weapons and pistols. I looked out the window, wondering if they were in fact posting photos of escaped sabaya as Hajji Salman had said they were, but it was too dark to see anything. "Why isn't your wife wearing the niqab?" a militant asked the driver.

"She's not my wife, hajji," he said. "She's a sabiyya."

"Congratulations to you," the militant said, and waved us through.

By now it was completely dark. We drove along the highway east out of Mosul, passing a few cars and trucks along the way. In the darkness, the flat Iraqi landscape seemed to have no end. When they ran, where did the escapees go? How did they get through the checkpoints in Mosul? If they managed to, how did they know where to run through the fields, who might help them and who would turn them in, how long could they go without dying of thirst? They were so brave to try.

"Look!" the driver said, pointing a bit ahead of us on the side of the road at a box, glowing white in our headlights. "I wonder what it is?"

"Don't stop," the guard warned. "It could be an IED. You know this road is full of them."

"I don't think so," the driver said, pulling over and stopping about ten feet from the box. There were pictures and lettering on the side, but from the car it was impossible to tell what it was. "I bet it's something that was looted and fell off a truck." He was excited: as a lowly driver, he wouldn't have been able to get as much new stuff as higher-ranking men in ISIS.

While the guard kept protesting—"No one would have left anything good on the road!" he said. "If it explodes, it will kill all of us!"—the driver got out of the car and walked toward the box. He crouched and examined it without touching it. "Whatever it is, it's not worth it," the guard muttered to himself. I pictured the driver greedily opening the lid and a huge bomb going off, blowing him apart and launching our car into the middle of the desert. If I died, it didn't matter, as long as the two men died, too. *Let it be a bomb*, I prayed.

A minute later the driver picked up the box and triumphantly carried it back to the car. "Fans!" he said, putting it in the trunk. "Two of them, and they run on batteries."

The guard sighed and helped him shove the box into the trunk. I sank back into the seat, disappointed. After the second checkpoint, I asked the driver, "Hajji, where are we going?"

"Hamdaniya," he told me. Apparently Hamdaniya, a district in the north of Nineveh, had been taken over by ISIS. My half brother Khaled had been stationed there with the military, and he hadn't told me that much about it, but I knew that there was a large

Christian population there, who would all by now be gone or dead. Along the way we passed the charred, upturned remains of an Islamic State vehicle, evidence of the battle to take over the area.

In Kocho, during the siege, we followed the Islamic State attacks on the Christian villages closely. Like us, the villagers there had lost all their belongings and the houses they had spent their life's earnings to build. Iraqi Christians were also being forced from their homes just because of their religion. Christians in Iraq were often under attack, and, like Yazidis, they struggled to stay in their homeland. Over the years, the population has gotten smaller and smaller as they have left for countries where they feel more welcome. After ISIS arrived, many Christians said that soon there would not be a single one of them left in all Iraq. When ISIS came to Kocho, though, I felt envy for the Christians. In their villages, they had been warned that ISIS was coming. Because, according to ISIS, they were "people of the book" and not kuffar like us, they had been able to take their children, their daughters, to safety in Kurdistan, and, in Syria, some had been able to pay a fine rather than convert. Even those who had been expelled from Mosul without anything at least had been spared enslavement. Yazidis had not been given the same chance.

Soon we arrived at a city in Hamdaniya district. The entire city was dark without electricity, and it smelled terrible, like rotting animal flesh. Streets were quiet, and homes had been emptied of regular people. Only terrorists remained, and only the Islamic State headquarters was lit up, powered by a huge generator that made a loud noise in the still night.

When ISIS first came to Iraq, they promised that they would restore services to cities and towns that lacked them. Their propaganda, when it wasn't celebrating their violence, flaunted these promises—for electricity, better garbage collection, and nicer roads—as though they were a normal political party. We were told that people believed them and thought they would serve them better than the Iraqi government, but I didn't see anything in Mosul that made me think that life was better for the average person there. This city was like a shell of itself, empty and dark, smelling of death and populated only by the terrorists who made the empty promises in the first place.

We stopped at the Islamic State headquarters and went inside. As in Mosul, it was full of militants. I sat quietly and waited to be told what to do; I was exhausted and desperate to sleep. A militant walked in. He was short and so old that his back was hunched, and the teeth he had left were rotting in his mouth. "Go upstairs," he told me. I was terrified, sure that Hajji Salman was continuing his punishment of me by selling me to the old man and that he was sending me to the room where he planned to rape me. When I opened the door to the room, though, I saw that there were other girls there. It took me a moment before I recognized them.

"Jilan! Nisreen!" It was my sister-in-law and my niece. I had never been so happy to see anyone in my life, and we rushed toward one another, kissing and weeping. They were dressed like me and looked as if they hadn't slept in weeks. Nisreen was really small—I didn't know how she coped with being a sabiyya—and for Jilan, separated from the husband she loved so much, I thought that rape must be even worse than it was for me. Quickly, knowing we could be taken from one another at any moment, we sat on the floor and started telling one another our stories.

"How did you get here?" I asked them.

"We were both sold," Nisreen said. "I was sold twice in Mosul and then brought here."

"Do you know what happened to Kathrine?" Nisreen asked me.

"She's in a center, too, in Mosul," I said.

I told them what Lamia had told me about Walaa, and some of what had happened to me. "I was held by a terrible person," I said. "I tried to escape, but he caught me." I didn't tell them everything. Some of it I wasn't ready to say out loud. We held one another as close as we could. "The nasty-faced old man downstairs—I think he's the one who bought me," I said.

"No." Nisreen looked down. "He owns me."

"How can you stand it, when this disgusting old man comes to you at night?" I said to Nisreen.

Nisreen shook her head. "I don't think about me," she said. "What about Rojian, taken by that enormous guy? After she left, we all went crazy. We cried as much as we could. For once, we weren't even thinking about what had happened in Kocho—all we thought about was Rojian with that monster."

"What happened in Kocho?" I was scared to ask. "Do you know for sure?"

"I saw on TV that all the men were killed," Nisreen said. "Everyone was killed, every man. It was on the news."

Even though I had heard the bullets being fired behind the school, until that moment I had held out hope that the men had survived. Hearing my niece confirm it was like hearing the bullets again, round after round of them until it was the only thing in my head. We tried to comfort one another. "Don't cry because they are dead," I told them. "I wish we had been killed with them." Being dead was better than being sold like merchandise and raped until our bodies were in shreds. Among our men there had been students, doctors, the young, and the elderly. In Kocho, my brothers and half brothers had stood side by side as ISIS killed almost all of them. But their deaths took just a moment. When you are a sabiyya, you die every second of every day, and just like the men, we would never see our families or our homes again. Nisreen and Jilan agreed. "We wish we had been with the men when they killed them," they said.

The militant with the rotting teeth—Nisreen's captor—came to the door and pointed at me. "Time to go," he said, and we all started begging. "You can do whatever you want to us, just please keep us together!" we screamed, holding on to one another just as we had that night in Mosul. And just like that night, they tore us apart and dragged me downstairs before I could say goodbye.

In Hamdaniya I lost all hope. It was ISIS controlled, so there was no way of escaping, and no way to dream that someone walking in the streets would be moved to help if they saw a Yazidi girl in distress. There was nothing but empty houses and the smell of war.

Fifteen minutes later we arrived at the second center in Hamdaniya. I had the sinking feeling that here I would meet my new owner, and I walked slowly from the car, feeling like my body was made of cement. This center was made up of two houses, and when the car pulled up, a middle-aged man walked out of the smaller one. He wore a long black beard and the Islamic State black pants. The driver indicated that I was to follow him inside. "That's Abu Muawaya," he told me. "Do what he says."

The house was only one story, but it was very tidy and beautiful, having once belonged to a wealthy Christian family. There were no girls there to greet me, but Yazidi clothes were piled everywhere, brighter and bolder than the typical dress of a conservative Muslim Iraqi woman, as well as remnants of the family that had fled the house. It was like entering a tomb. Abu Muawaya joined another, younger man in the kitchen where they ate bread and yogurt and drank black tea.

"How many days will I be here?" I asked the men. "I have family members in the other center. Can I be with them?"

They barely looked at me, and Abu Muawaya answered. "You are a sabiyya," he said calmly. "You don't give orders—you take them."

"Nadia, did you convert?" the other man asked.

"Yes," I said, wondering how they knew my name and what else they knew about me. They didn't ask me any questions about where I was from or what happened to my family, but those details may not have mattered to them. All that mattered was that I was there, and I belonged to them.

"Go and shower," Abu Muawaya said. I wondered how much Hajji Salman had sold me for. Sabaya who were no longer virgins sold for less money, I knew that, and I might have had a reputation as a troublemaker because of the incident on the bus and because I tried to escape. Was this further punishment for that attempt? Maybe Salman had been so eager to get rid of me he had given me as a present, or maybe he had found the most brutal man he could and simply given me to him. That happened, I knew. Yazidi girls were passed from terrorist to terrorist for no money at all.

"I showered this morning," I told him.

"Then go wait for me in that room," Abu Muawaya pointed to a bedroom, and I obediently walked through the doorway. It was a small room with a narrow brown bed, covered by a blue-and-white-striped blanket. Shoes filled two shelves against the wall, and a large bookshelf was full of books. On top of a desk a computer sat dead, its screen dark. The room must have belonged to a student, I thought, a boy about my age; the shoes were the kind of loafers worn by college students, and they weren't that big. I sat on the bed and waited. I avoided looking into the large mirror hanging on the wall, and I didn't think about whether I was small enough to fit through the air vent that was there in place of a window. I didn't want to open the closet or look through his things to learn more about him. I didn't even check to see what the books were on the shelf. Probably the boy was still alive somewhere, and it didn't seem right for a dead person to go through the things of the living.

Chapter 11

EVERY ISLAMIC STATE MEMBER TREATED ME CRUELLY, AND
the rape was always the same, but I remember a few small dif-
ferences between the men who abused me. Hajji Salman was the
worst, in part because he was the first to rape me and in part because he acted the most like he hated me. He hit me if I tried to
close my eyes. For him, it was not enough just to rape me—he humiliated me as often as he could, spreading honey on his toes and
making me lick it off or forcing me to dress up for him. Morteja
acted like a child who had been allowed a treat he had been whining for when he came to rape me, and I will never forget the other
guard's glasses, the way he was so gentle with them and so vicious
with me, a person.

Abu Muawaya, when he came into the room around eight
p.m., took me by the jaw and pushed me against the wall. "Why
aren't you resisting?" he asked. It seemed to make him angry. I
assumed from the amount of Yazidi clothing in his house that he
had been with many sabaya, and perhaps they all resisted except
for me. Maybe he liked proving that he could have them even if
they fought back. He was small, but he was very strong. "What's
the point?" I said to him. "It's not just one man or two or three—
you all do this. How long do you expect me to resist?" I remember
that he laughed when I said that.

After Abu Muawaya left, I fell asleep alone and was woken

up later that night by a body behind me in bed. It was the man who had been eating bread and yogurt with Abu Muawaya in the kitchen; I don't remember his name. I remember that my throat hurt from thirst, and when I got up to get some water, he grabbed my arm. "I just need to drink something," I said. I was shocked by my own hopelessness. After what happened with the guards at Hajji Salman's, I lost all fear of ISIS and of rape. I was just numb. I didn't ask this new man what he was doing, I didn't try to convince him not to touch me, I didn't talk to him at all.

At some point, there was rape and nothing else. This becomes your normal day. You don't know who is going to open the door next to attack you, just that it will happen and that tomorrow might be worse. You stop thinking about escaping or seeing your family again. Your past life becomes a distant memory, like a dream. Your body doesn't belong to you, and there's no energy to talk or to fight or to think about the world outside. There is only rape and the numbness that comes with accepting that this is now your life.

Fear was better. With fear, there is the assumption that what is happening isn't normal. Sure, you feel like your heart will explode and you will throw up, you cling desperately to your family and friends and you grovel in front of the terrorists, you cry until you go blind, but at least you do something. Hopelessness is close to death.

I remember that Abu Muawaya's friend acted offended when I pulled away from him in the morning after I opened my eyes and saw, to my horror, that my leg was resting over his. Since I was a child, whenever I sleep next to someone I love, like my sister, mother, or brother, I put my leg over them, to be close to them. When I saw I had done that with a terrorist, I immediately jerked away. He laughed and asked, "Why did you move?" I hated myself. I worried that he would think I cared for him. "I'm not used to sleeping next to anybody," I said. "I want to rest a little." He checked the time on his phone and then left to go to the bathroom.

Abu Muawaya laid out breakfast on a floor mat and told me to come eat. Even though it meant sitting in the kitchen and sharing a meal with two men who had raped me, I rushed to the food. I hadn't eaten since leaving Salman's, and my hunger was powerful. The food was familiar and good—dark honey, bread, eggs, and yogurt. I ate in silence while the men talked about the mundane chores that would fill their days—where to get more gasoline for the generators, who would be arriving at what center. I didn't look at them. When we finished, Abu Muawaya told me to take a shower and put on an abaya. "We will leave here soon," he said.

Back in the room, out of the shower, I looked in the mirror for the first time. My face was pale and yellow, and my hair, which was almost to my waist, was matted and tangled. My hair used to bring me so much happiness, but now I wanted to have nothing to remind me of how I used to want to be pretty. I looked through the drawers for a pair of scissors to cut it off, but I couldn't find any. It was so hot in the room, I felt that my head was on fire. Suddenly the door opened, and the second man walked in. He had a blue dress with him and told me to put it on. "Can't I wear this instead?" I asked, showing him one of my Yazidi dresses. It would have felt comforting to have that on, but he said no.

He watched me as I dressed and came close to me, touching me everywhere. "You stink," he said, covering his nose. "Didn't you shower? Do all Yazidi girls stink like you?"

"This is how I smell," I told him. "I don't care if you like it or not."

On the way out of the house, I noticed a small plastic disc—a memory card for a cell phone—on the table, near Abu Muawaya's phone. I wondered what could be on it. Pictures of sabaya? Pictures of me? Plans for Iraq? In Kocho I used to love to take people's memory cards and put them into Khairy's phone, just to see what was on them. Each one was a small mystery to be solved, and they usually said a lot about their owners. For a moment I fantasized about stealing the terrorist's memory card. Maybe there were secrets on it that could help Hezni find me or the Iraqi Army retake Mosul. Maybe there was evidence of the crimes ISIS was committing. But I left the card; I was so hopeless that I couldn't imagine anything changing no matter what I did. Instead I just followed the men outside.

A van, about the size of an ambulance, was parked on the street outside, and a driver stood by the gate, waiting. He had come from nearby—Mosul or Tal Afar—and while we stood there, he updated Abu Muawaya on how the militants were faring in those cities. "We have great support in both places," he said. Abu Muawaya nodded his approval. They stopped talking when the door to the van opened and three women stepped out.

Like me, the women were covered fully in abayas and niqabs. They huddled together outside the van. One of the figures was much taller than the other two, and the smaller figures clutched at the larger figure's abaya and her gloved hands, as though waiting for the folds of her abaya to swallow them. They paused at the foot of the van, turning their heads from left to right, looking around them, taking in the Hamdaniya compound. Their eyes, peering through the gap in the niqab, were full of fear when they landed on Abu Muawaya, who watched them closely.

The tall one had her hand on the smallest one's shoulder and was pulling her very close to her plump body. The smallest girl might have been as young as ten. I thought it must be a mother and her two young daughters, and that they had all been sold together. "It is not permissible to separate a mother from her prepubescent children through buying, selling, or giving away [a slave]," the Islamic State pamphlet on sabaya reads. Mothers stay with their children until those children are "grown and mature." After that, ISIS can do whatever it wants with them.

Staying close together, the threesome walked slowly away from the van toward the small house where I had spent the night, the two girls moving around their mother like chicks around a hen, clinging to the slippery fabric of her gloves. Had I been exchanged for them? As they passed us, I willed them to make eye contact with me, but by then they were looking straight ahead. One by one they disappeared into the darkness of the small house, and the door shut behind them. It must be terrible to watch your children or your mother or sisters go through what we were going through. Still, I envied them. They were lucky; ISIS often violated their own rules and separated mothers from their children. And it was so much worse to be alone.

Abu Muawaya gave the driver some Iraqi dinars and we began driving out of Hamdaniya. I didn't ask where we were going. My hopelessness was like a cloak—heavier, darker, and more obscuring than any abaya. In the car, the driver played the kind of religious music so popular in ISIS-held Mosul, and the noise and the motion of the car made me dizzy. "Please pull over," I told Abu Muawaya. "I need to throw up."

The car stopped on the side of the highway, and I pushed open the door, running a few feet into the sand where I lifted up my niqab and threw up breakfast. Cars whizzed by, and the smell of gasoline and dust made me throw up again. Abu Muawaya got out and stood a small distance away, watching me to make sure I didn't try to run, either into the field or into traffic.

On the road connecting Hamdaniya and Mosul, there is a large checkpoint. Before ISIS came to Iraq, it was manned by the Iraqi Army, which wanted to monitor the movements of Al Qaeda–linked insurgents. Now that checkpoint was part of ISIS's scheme to control the roads, thereby controlling the country. You could say that Iraq is a country of checkpoints, and the one connecting Hamdaniya and Mosul is just one of many that flew the terrorists' black and white flag.

In Kurdistan, the checkpoints are decorated with the bright yellow, red, and green Kurdish flag and staffed by peshmerga. Elsewhere in Iraq the checkpoints that are covered in the black, red, white, and green Iraqi flag tell you that you are in territory controlled by the central government. In the northern Iraqi mountains connecting us to Iran, and now in parts of Sinjar, the YPG fly their flags over their own checkpoints. How can Baghdad or the United States say that Iraq is a unified country? You would have to have never traveled along our roads, waited in line at our checkpoints, or been questioned solely based on the city written on your license plate to think that Iraq isn't broken into a hundred pieces.

At around eleven-thirty in the morning we stopped at the checkpoint. "Get out, Nadia," Abu Muawaya told me. "Go inside." I walked slowly into the small concrete building that served as the guards' office and lounge, feeling light-headed and fragile from nausea. I assumed they needed to do some additional checking while I waited, so I was surprised when I saw the van drive through the checkpoint and continue along the road to Mosul, leaving me alone.

The building was made up of three small rooms: the main room, where a militant sat behind a desk covered in paperwork, as well as two smaller rooms that seemed to be lounges. One of the doors was ajar, and I could see the iron frame of a twin bed. A girl was sitting on top of the mattress talking to another girl in Arabic. "*Salam alakum*," the militant said to me, looking up from his work. I started walking toward the room with the girls, but he stopped me. "No, you will go into the other room." My heart sank; I would be alone in there.

The small room looked as if it had been recently cleaned and painted. A television sat dark in the corner, and a prayer rug was rolled up beside it. Some fruit had been left on a plate next to the TV, and the faint, sweet odor from the warm apples made me remember my nausea. I drank from a watercooler that was gurgling against the wall, then sat on a mattress that was on the floor. I was dizzy—I felt like the room was going in circles.

Another militant appeared in the doorway. He was young and very skinny. "Sabiyya, what's your name?" He stood still, looking at me.

"Nadia," I said, wincing from a headache.

"Do you like it here?" he asked me.

"Why," I said, "am I going to stay here?" Was I going to be kept at this checkpoint, a place that wasn't even a place?

"You're not going to stay long," he said, then left.

The room started spinning faster, and I gagged and coughed, trying to keep the water in my stomach. I was scared that if I threw up, I would get into trouble.

Someone knocked on the door. "Are you okay?" the skinny man's voice came from outside the room.

"I want to throw up," I said. "Is it okay if I throw up?"

"No, no, not here," he said. "This is my room, I pray here."

"Let me go to the bathroom, then," I said. "I want to wash my face."

"No, no." He wouldn't open the door. "You're fine. You're fine, just wait."

A moment later he came back with a mug of something hot. "Drink this," he said, holding it out to me. "You'll feel better." The liquid was tinted green and smelled of herbs.

"I don't like tea," I told him.

"It's not tea," he said. "It will make your headache go away." He sat on the mattress facing me, pursing his lips together and putting his hand on his chest. "Drink it like this," he demonstrated, breathing in the steam and then sipping the liquid.

I was terrified. I thought for sure this was the man who had bought me, and any moment he would take his hand off his own chest and put it on mine. Even if he wanted to cure my headache, it was just so that I would be well enough for him to molest.

My hands shook while I drank the liquid. Once I had taken a few sips, he took the mug out of my hands and put it on the floor next to the mattress.

I started to cry. "Please," I said. "I just came from other men this morning. My head hurts. I'm really sick."

"You will be okay," he said. "You will be okay," and he started pulling at my dress. It was so hot in the room that I had taken off my abaya, and all I was wearing was the blue dress Abu Muawaya's friend had brought me that morning. I tried to resist him, yanking my skirt down as soon as he pulled it up, and he quickly lost his temper, hitting me hard on my thighs and saying again, "You're going to be okay." This time it sounded like a threat. He started raping me with my dress half on and was very fast, and when he finished, he sat up, straightened his shirt, and said, "I'll be right back. I am going to see if you can stay here or not."

When he left, I pulled my dress back down and wept a little, then picked up the mug and started drinking the herbal water again. What was the point of crying? The liquid was lukewarm, but it helped with my headache. Soon the militant came back, as though nothing had happened between us and asked me if I wanted more to drink. I shook my head.

It was clear by now that I didn't belong to the skinny militant or to any particular man. I was a sabiyya at the checkpoint, and any Islamic State member could come into the room and do whatever he wanted with me. They would keep me in a locked room with nothing but a mattress and a bowl of rotting fruit, just waiting for the door to open and another militant to enter. This was my life now.

I was still very dizzy when the skinny man left, and I thought maybe it would help to stand up and walk around. There was nothing for me to do but pace around that room in circles like a prisoner, past the watercooler, past the fruit bowl, past the mattress and the TV that I never tried to turn on. I ran my hand along the white wall, feeling the small clots of paint as if they contained messages. I took off my underwear to see if maybe I had my period, but I didn't. I sat back down on the mattress.

Soon after another militant came inside. He was huge and spoke in a loud, arrogant voice. "Are you the sick one?" he asked.

"Who else is here?" I said back to him, but he refused to answer. "None of your business," he said, then repeated, "Are you the sick one?" This time I nodded, yes.

He came in and locked the door. He had a gun attached to his belt, and I imagined grabbing it and putting it to my head. *Just kill me,* I wanted to say to him, but then I thought that if he saw me reaching for the gun, he would think of a punishment worse than death, and so I didn't try to do anything.

Unlike the skinny guy before him, the new militant locked the door. This sent me into a panic. I stepped away from him, and then dizziness took over, and I fell onto the floor, not completely unconscious but sick and foggy. He came and sat next to me and said, "I think you're scared." His tone wasn't kind—it was mocking and cruel.

"Please, I'm really sick," I said to him. "Please, hajji, I'm really sick." I repeated it over and over, but he still came over to where I was lying and dragged me by the shoulders onto the mattress. The floor scraped against my bare feet and my calves.

Again, he mocked me. "Do you like it here?" He laughed. "Do you like how they treat you here?"

"You all treat me the same," I said. My head was floating, and I could barely see. I lay where he had dragged me, closing my eyes and trying to block him out and forget about the room. I tried to forget who I was. I tried to lose all ability to move my limbs, to talk, to breathe.

He continued to taunt me. "You are sick—don't talk," he said, putting his hand on my stomach. "Why are you so thin? Don't you eat?"

"Hajji, I am really sick." My voice faded into the air while he lifted up my dress.

"Don't you know how much I like you when you're like this?" he said. "Don't you understand that I like it when you are weak?"

Chapter 12

EVERY SABIYYA HAS A STORY LIKE MINE. YOU CAN'T IMAGINE the atrocities ISIS is capable of until you hear about them from your sisters and cousins, your neighbors and schoolmates, and you realize that it wasn't that you were particularly unlucky, or that you were being punished for crying out or trying to escape. The men were all the same: they were all terrorists who thought it was their right to hurt us.

Other women saw their husbands killed in front of them before they were abducted, or listened to their captors gloat about the slaughter in Sinjar. They are held in homes or hotels, even in prisons, and systematically raped. Some of them are children and are attacked no matter whether they have started their period or not. One girl had her hands and legs tied when her captor raped her, and another was raped for the first time while she slept. Some girls were starved and tortured if they disobeyed their captors, and others even if they did everything the militant asked them to do.

One woman from our village was being transported from Hamdaniya to Mosul when her captor decided he couldn't wait to rape her, and so he pulled over to the side of the road and raped her in the car. "It was right there on the road, with the door open and my legs stuck outside the car," she told me. When they got to his home, he made her dye her hair blond and pluck her eyebrows and behave like a wife.

Kathrine was taken by Dr. Islam, a specialist who used to travel to treat Yazidis before he joined ISIS. Every week he bought a new girl and got rid of an old one, but he held on to Kathrine, his favorite. He forced her to groom herself and wear makeup, as Hajji Salman had done to me, and then he would make her pose for photos of the two of them together. In one set they are wading in a river, Dr. Islam holding Kathrine in his arms like newlyweds. She has her niqab flipped up over her head and is smiling so wide it looks like her face might split. Dr. Islam forced her to look happy and to pretend she loved him, but I know her and I can tell that behind that forced smile is pure terror. She tried to escape six times and was turned in by the people she went to for help. Each time when she was delivered back to Dr. Islam, he punished her viciously. The stories are endless.

I was at the checkpoint for one night. Early the next morning the militant's two-way radio went on, waking him up. "Are you feeling better?" he asked me. I hadn't slept at all. "I don't feel better," I answered. "I don't want to be here."

"Then you need something. I'll show you later how you can feel better," he said, then started answering the calls on his radio and, soon after, left the room.

They locked me inside. I could hear cars passing through the checkpoint and militants talking into their radios, and I thought they might keep me there until I died. Banging on the door to be let out, I began throwing up again, this time just allowing the vomit to go onto the floor and the mattress. The skinny militant came back and told me to take off my hijab, then poured water over my head while I threw up. For fifteen minutes I heaved out little more than a thin dribble of sour-smelling liquid, as if my body were being drained. "Go to the bathroom," he told me. "Wash yourself." Abu Muawaya's van had returned to take me the rest of the way back to Mosul.

In the bathroom, I splashed water over my face and arms. My

body shook as if I had a fever, and I could barely see or stand. I had never felt so weak. That feeling changed something inside of me.

Since leaving Kocho, I had begged for death. I had willed Salman to kill me or asked God to let me die or refused to eat or drink in the hopes I would fade away. I had thought many times that the men who raped and beat me would kill me. But death had never come. In the checkpoint bathroom, I began to cry. For the first time since I left Kocho, I thought I actually might die. And I also knew for sure that I didn't want to.

———

ANOTHER MILITANT HAD arrived to take me the rest of the way to Mosul. His name was Hajji Amer, and I assumed that he was my new owner, although I was too sick to ask. It was a short distance between the checkpoint and the city, but because I had to stop every few minutes to throw up, the drive took us nearly an hour. "Why are you so sick?" Hajji Amer asked, and I didn't want to tell him that I thought it was because of the rape. "I haven't eaten or had much water," I said. "And it's so hot here."

When we got to Mosul, he went into a pharmacy and bought me some pills, which he gave me after we arrived at his house. I was crying quietly the whole time, and he chuckled the way my brothers would when they thought I was being overly dramatic. "You are bigger than this," he told me. "You shouldn't cry."

His small house was painted dark green with a white stripe, and it looked as if it hadn't been occupied by ISIS for long. It was clean, and there were no Islamic State clothes or dresses left by Yazidi girls. I went to the sofa and fell asleep the moment I lay down, and it was evening before I woke up and my headache and nausea were gone. The driver was lying on another couch with his phone next to him. "Are you feeling better?" he asked when he saw that I was awake.

"A little," I said, though I still wanted him to think I was too sick to touch. "I'm dizzy. I think I need to eat something." I hadn't eaten since breakfast with Abu Muawaya, the morning before, and I had vomited up all that food.

"Read a little Koran and pray," he told me. "Then the pain will disappear."

I went to the bathroom, taking my bag with me. I worried that if I left it in the living room, he would take it from me, even if he thought it held only clothes and sanitary pads. Locking the door behind me, I checked to make sure that my jewelry was safely tucked inside the pads, hidden enough that no one could tell it was there unless they chose to lift up each pad individually, which I couldn't imagine any man doing. I picked up my mother's ration card and held it in my hand for a moment, remembering her. Then I left the bathroom, determined to get the militant to give me some information.

It was strange to be with a man who didn't rape me the moment we were alone. At first I wondered if it was possible that Hajji Amer, in spite of being with ISIS, had some pity in him when he saw that I was so sick. Perhaps he was low-ranking enough that his only job was to watch me. Back in the living room, though, he was waiting for me the way Hajji Salman had every evening, with a cruel, entitled look on his face, and although he didn't rape me, he assaulted me. After he had finished, he relaxed back on the couch and began talking in a normal tone as though we knew each other.

"You're going to stay in this house for a week," he told me. "After that you might go to Syria."

"I don't want to go to Syria!" I begged. "Take me to another house in Mosul, but don't send me to Syria."

"Don't be afraid," he told me. "There are many sabaya like you in Syria."

"I know there are," I said. "I still don't want to go."

Hajji Amer paused and looked at me. "We'll see," he said.

"If I'm going to be here a week, can I see my nieces Rojian and Kathrine?" I asked him.

"Maybe they are in Syria," he said. "Maybe if you go to Syria, you can see them."

"I saw them not that long ago in Mosul," I replied. "I think they must still be somewhere in this city."

"Well, I can't help you," he said. "All I know is that you are supposed to wait here. You could be in Syria as early as tomorrow."

"I am telling you, there is no way I am going to Syria!" I was angry now.

Hajji Amer smiled. "Who do you think controls where you go?" he told me, his voice never rising. "Think about it. Where were you yesterday? And where are you today?"

He went to the kitchen, and a moment later I heard the loud pop of eggs frying in hot oil. I followed him. A plate of eggs and tomatoes was waiting for me on the table, but in spite of my hunger I no longer wanted to eat. The thought of going to Syria terrified me. I could barely sit. He didn't seem to mind that I wasn't eating.

After he finished his eggs, he asked me if I had any abayas other than the one I was wearing.

"This is my only one," I said.

"You may need more if you are going to Syria," he replied. "I'll go out and buy you some."

He took the keys to the car and walked to the front door. "Stay here," he told me. "I'll be back soon." Then he left, the door slamming behind him.

I was alone. There were no other people in the house, and no noise. We were a little bit outside the city, and the streets were mostly peaceful, with only a few cars driving by, and although the houses were spaced close together, they were small. From the kitchen window, I could see some people walking from house to house, and beyond that the road stretching out of Mosul. The neighborhood seemed peaceful, not frantic like the part of the city around Hajji Salman's house and not destitute like Hamdaniya. I stood looking out that window for almost a half hour before it even occurred to me that the roads were empty not just of people but of ISIS.

For the first time since being punished by Hajji Salman, I thought about escaping. The torture at the checkpoint and the promise that I was going to go to Syria had reignited the urgency to flee. I contemplated climbing out of the kitchen window, but before I did, I walked to the front door to see if the militant had, by some miracle, left it unlocked. The door was heavy and wooden. I turned the yellow handle, and my heart sank. It wouldn't budge. *He wouldn't be so stupid as to leave it unlocked,* I thought. But for good measure, I gave it one last pull and nearly fell over when it swung open.

Dazed, I stepped out onto the stoop and stood perfectly still, expecting at any moment to have a gun pointed at me and to hear the loud voice of a guard. But there was nothing. I walked down the stairs and into the garden. I wasn't wearing my niqab, so I walked with my head slightly turned down, looking out of the corners of my eyes for guards or militants. There were none. No one shouted at me—no one even seemed to notice me. There was a low wall around the garden, but I could easily jump over it if I used a trash can as a step stool. My stomach turned in anxiety.

Quickly, as though something had taken over my body, I ran back inside the house and grabbed my bag and niqab. I moved as fast as I could; who knew when Hajji Amer would come back, and what if he was right and tomorrow they planned on taking me to Syria? I pulled my niqab down over my face, lifted the straps of my bag over my shoulder, and yanked on the door handle again.

This time I used all my strength the first time, and it opened easily. I quickly crossed the threshold onto the stoop, but as soon as the air hit me, I felt a tug on the skirt of my abaya, and I turned around. "I feel sick!" I said, expecting to see a militant standing in the doorway. "I need air!" Even the night with Salman's guards was less terrifying than that moment. There was no way they would believe I was doing anything but trying to escape. But when I looked behind me, I saw that no one was there. The tug I felt was only the corner of my abaya, caught in the door as it closed. I almost laughed, pulling it unstuck, and then I ran into the garden.

Standing on top of a trash can, I peered over the garden wall. The street was empty. To my left was a large mosque that must have been full of Islamic State militants observing the dusk prayer, but to my right and in front of me were normal neighborhood streets whose residents were inside, perhaps praying, perhaps cooking dinner. I could hear cars and the sound of a running hose; next door a woman was watering her yard. Fear stopped me from climbing over the wall. *What if Hajji Amer drives back right this moment?* I thought. *Can I handle the punishment again?*

I considered jumping over the wall into a neighbor's garden rather than onto the street, where I worried Hajji Amer might be driving. None of the houses appeared to have electricity, and it was getting dark out. In my abaya, I might go unnoticed in the shadowy yards. Already I had ruled out going through the garden gate, which I was sure someone would be watching. A woman alone, covered or not, coming out of an ISIS-held house, would raise alarms, and the reward for turning in a sabiyya was too tempting.

I knew that if I thought about it any longer, I would run out of time. I had to decide. But I couldn't move. No matter what choice I played in my head, it always ended with me being captured and punished as Hajji Salman had punished me. I assumed that Hajji Amer had left me alone in the house with the door unlocked and no guards not because he had forgotten. He wasn't stupid. He did that because he thought at this point, having been abused for so long and being so weak from sickness and hunger, I wouldn't think of trying to escape. They thought they had me forever. *They are wrong,* I thought. And in the blink of an eye, I tossed my bag over the wall and then jumped over it myself, landing with a thud on the other side.

PART III

Chapter 1

ON THE OTHER SIDE OF THE GARDEN WALL, I COULD SEE that the road leading straight from the house was in fact a dead end, and since it was time for evening prayer, it would be very risky to pass the large mosque to the left. The only option was to turn right, with no idea where that might lead me. I started walking.

I was still wearing the men's sandals Hajji Salman had given me that first night, taken from the hall that had been turned into a mosque, and it was the first time wearing them that I'd walked a distance greater than from the door of a house to a car. They flopped against the soles of my feet—I worried it was too loud—and sand caught between the straps and my toes. *They're too big!* I thought. I had forgotten, and for a moment I delighted in that observation because it meant that I was moving.

I didn't walk a straight line. Instead I wove between parked cars, turned corners at random, and crossed and recrossed the same streets over and over, hoping that a casual observer would think I knew where I was going. My heart beat so hard in my chest that I worried the people I passed would hear it and know what I was.

Some of the houses I passed were lit by generators and ringed by wide gardens full of purple-flowered bushes and tall trees. It was a nice neighborhood, built for large, well-off families. Since it was dusk, most people were in their homes, eating dinner and putting their kids to bed, but as it grew darker, they came outside to sit in the breeze and chat with their neighbors. I tried not to look at any of them, hoping that no one would notice me.

My entire life, I've been scared of the night. I was lucky to be poor: it meant that I slept in the same room as my sisters and nieces or on the rooftop surrounded by family, and I never had to worry about what hid in the darkness. As I walked that evening in Mosul, the sky was quickly darkening, and my fear of the night became even worse than my fear of ISIS catching me. Without streetlights and with only some of the houses lit, the Mosul neighborhood would soon be pitch-black. Families would begin going to sleep, and the streets would be empty of everyone, I thought, except for me and the men who were looking for me. By now, I assumed, Hajji Amer had returned to the house with my new abayas and discovered that I was missing. He had probably radioed other Islamic State members, maybe a commander or even Hajji Salman specifically, to say that I had escaped. He would then run back to his van to look for the figure of a fleeing girl in the strong headlights. He was probably scared for himself. After all, it was because he had left me alone with the door unlocked that I had escaped so easily. I imagined this made him drive faster and look harder, knocking on doors and questioning people on the street, stopping any woman walking alone. I imagined he'd look well into the night.

My abaya helped me blend in, but I didn't feel invisible, as I'd hoped I would. All I could think about as I walked was the moment they would catch me, what their weapons and their voices would sound like, and then what their hands would feel like dragging me back to the house I had fled from. I had to find somewhere to hide before it got completely dark.

As I passed each house, I imagined walking up to the door and knocking. Would the family that answered turn me in right

away? Would they send me back to Hajji Salman? Islamic State
flags hung from the lampposts and over gates, reminding me that
I was in a dangerous place. Even the sound of children laughing
in their yards frightened me.

For a moment, I wondered if it would be better to go back.
I could climb back over the garden wall and push back through
the heavy front door and be sitting in the kitchen right where
Hajji Amer left me when he returned. Maybe it would be better
to go to Syria than to be caught trying to escape again. But then
I thought, *No, God has given me this chance and has made it easy for
me to leave that house.* The unlocked door, the quiet neighborhood,
the lack of guards, and the trash can by the garden wall—all these
had to be signs that it was time to risk another escape. A chance
like this wouldn't come twice, especially if I was caught.

At first, I jumped at every noise and every movement. A car
drove down the street, its only working headlight shining at me
like a policeman's flashlight, and I pressed myself against a garden wall until it passed. When I saw two young men in track-
suits walking toward me, I crossed the street to avoid them. They
went by, chatting, as if they hadn't seen me. Hearing the creak
of a rusty gate opening in front of a house, I quickly turned a
corner, walking as fast as I could without running, and when a
dog barked, I turned another corner. These fearful moments were
all that was guiding me, but I still couldn't imagine where I was
going. I thought I might walk forever.

As I walked, the houses shrank from the multistory concrete
homes of the wealthier families that ISIS had taken over—with
the fancy cars parked out front and loud generators powering televisions and radios—into more modest dwellings, most of them
one or two stories of gray cement. Fewer lights were on, and the
neighborhoods grew quieter. I could hear babies crying inside the
houses, and I imagined their mothers rocking them, trying to get
them to be quiet. Grassy yards became small plots for vegetables,

and family sedans became farmers' pickup trucks. Streams of sewage and dishwater ran into gutters alongside the road: I was in a poor neighborhood.

Suddenly I felt that this was what I had been looking for. If any Sunni in Mosul was going to help me, it was most likely to be a poor Sunni, maybe a family who'd stayed only because they didn't have the money to leave and maybe was less interested in the politics of Iraq than in their own livelihood. Plenty of poor families joined ISIS. But that night, with nothing to guide me and no reason to trust one stranger over another, I just wanted to find a family like mine.

I didn't know which door to knock on. I had spent so many hours inside Islamic State centers, screaming as loud as I could with the other girls, knowing that the noise reached the people outside and yet none of them had helped. I'd been transported between cities in buses and cars, passing cars packed with families who didn't even glance at us. Every day the militants executed people who disagreed with them, raped Yazidi women they had deemed worth less than objects, and carried out their plan to erase Yazidis from the face of the earth—and still no one in Mosul did anything to help. ISIS had been largely homegrown, and even though a great many Sunni Muslims fled Mosul when the organization took over—and more would be terrorized under Islamic State rule—there was no reason for me to think that behind any of these doors lived a single sympathetic person. I remembered how I'd longed for Morteja's mother to look at me the way she might look at her own daughter, and how instead she'd looked at me with hatred. Were these houses full of people like her?

Still, I had no choice. It was impossible for me to leave Mosul alone. Even if I made it past the checkpoint, which I almost certainly wouldn't, I would be caught walking along the road or would die of dehydration long before I made it to Kurdistan. My only hope of getting out of Mosul alive was in one of these houses. But which one?

Soon it was dark enough that it became hard to see in front of me. I'd been walking for a little under two hours, and my feet ached in my sandals. Each step seemed like a measure of safety, a distance, no matter how small, between me and ISIS. Still, I couldn't walk forever. At one corner I paused beside a large metal door, as wide as it was tall, and raised my hand, about to knock. But then at the last moment, I lowered my hand back down to my side and started walking again. I don't know why.

Around the corner from that house, I stopped by a green metal door, smaller than the first. There were no lights on in the house, which was two stories and concrete, similar to some of the new houses built in Kocho. There was nothing special about the house, nothing to tell me what the family inside was like. But I had walked enough. This time when I raised my hand, I banged my palm twice against the door. It made a loud, hollow thumping sound, and while it vibrated through the metal, I stood on the street waiting to see whether I would be saved.

———

A SECOND LATER the door swung open, and a man who looked to be in his fifties stood on the other side. "Who are you?" he asked, but I pushed past him without saying anything. In the small garden I saw a family sitting in a circle very close to the door, lit only by the moon. They stood up, startled, but didn't say anything. When I heard the garden gate close, I lifted my niqab over my face.

"I beg you," I said. "Help me." They were silent, and so I kept talking. "My name is Nadia," I said. "I am a Yazidi from Sinjar. Daesh came to my village, and I was taken to Mosul to be a sabiyya. I lost my family."

Two young men in their twenties sat in the garden, along with an older couple who I thought must be the parents and a boy who looked to be around eleven years old. A young woman, also in her twenties, sat rocking a baby to sleep. She was pregnant and I thought I saw fear register on her face before anyone else's. The power was out in their small house and they had brought mattresses to the garden where the air was cooler.

For a moment my heart stopped. They could be Islamic State members—the men had beards and were wearing baggy black pants, and the women were dressed conservatively, though their faces were uncovered because they were at home. There was nothing to distinguish them from the people who had held me, and I thought for sure they would turn me in. I froze and stopped talking.

One of the men grabbed my arm and pulled me from the garden into their house. It was hot and dark in the entranceway. "It's safer in here," the older man explained. "You shouldn't talk about those kinds of things outside."

"Where are you from?" the older woman, who I assumed was his wife, asked me once we were inside. "What happened to you?" Her voice was anxious but not angry, and I felt my heart slow down a little bit.

"I'm from Kocho," I told them. "I was taken here as a sabiyya, and I just ran from the last house where Daesh had me. They were going to try to take me to Syria." I told them what happened to me, even the rape and abuse. I thought that the more they knew, the more likely they were to help me. They were a family, so they were capable of pity and love. But I didn't say the names of the militants who had bought or sold me. Hajji Salman was an important figure in ISIS, and who could imagine a more fearful person to defy than the judge who sends people to their deaths? I thought, *If they knew that I belonged to Salman, they would return me right away, no matter how sorry they felt for me.*

"What do you want from us?" the woman asked.

"Imagine that you have a young daughter who was taken away from her family and subjected to all this rape and suffering," I said. "Just, please, think of that when you consider what to do with me now."

As soon as I finished, the father spoke up. "Have peace in your heart," he said. "We will try to help you."

"How can they do that to little girls?" the woman whispered to herself.

The family introduced themselves. They were indeed Sunnis who had stayed in Mosul when ISIS came, because they had no-where else to go, they said. "We don't know anyone in Kurdi-stan to help us get through the checkpoints," they told me. "And besides, we are poor. All we have is in this house." I didn't know whether to believe them—plenty of poor Sunnis had left Mosul, while others stayed and became disillusioned by ISIS only when their own lives got worse, not because of the suffering of others—but I decided that if they helped me, that must mean they were telling the truth.

"We are Azawi," they said, referring to a tribe that has long, close relationships with Yazidis in the area. It meant they would probably know about Yazidism and may even have kiriv in villages near mine. It was a good sign.

Hisham, the older man, was heavyset and wore a long black and white beard. His wife, Maha, had a plump, beautiful face. When I came in, she was only wearing a housedress, but after a moment, because I was a stranger, she went inside to put on her abaya. Their sons Nasser and Hussein were skinny, still growing into men, and they both, especially Nasser, peppered me with curious questions: How did I get here? Where was my family?

At twenty-five, Nasser was the eldest, and he was very tall, with a deep, receding hairline and a large, wide mouth. I worried about the sons the most: if any of the family members would be loyal to ISIS, it would be these young Sunni men. But they swore they hated the militants. "Life has been terrible since they got here," Nasser told me. "We feel we are living in a war."

Nasser's wife, Safaa, was also in the garden. Like Nasser, she was tall, and she had striking eyes set very deep in her head. She didn't say anything, just looked at me while bouncing her baby in her lap and glancing at Nasser's youngest brother, Khaled, who was also very young and was oblivious to what was going on. Out of everyone, Safaa seemed the most worried about me being there. "Do you want a different abaya?" she asked me after I had taken off my dirty one. It was a kind gesture, but something in the way she said it made me think she was judging me for wearing a Yazidi dress in a Muslim house. "No, thank you," I said. I didn't want to wear the unfamiliar clothing any more than I had to.

"Who were you with from Daesh?" Nasser finally asked.

"Salman," I said quietly, and he grunted knowingly but didn't say anything more about my former captor. Instead, he asked me about my family and where I would go if I left Mosul. I felt that he wasn't afraid and that he wanted to help me.

"Have you met other Yazidi girls?" I asked.

"I have seen some before in the court," Hisham said. Hussein, his son, confessed that he had watched buses drive by that he thought were full of slaves like me. "There are signs in Mosul saying that if you turn in a sabiyya, Daesh will give you five thousand dollars," he said. "But we've heard it's a lie."

"We don't like what is happening," Hisham said. "We would have left Mosul long ago, when Daesh first came, but we don't have any money, and we have nowhere to go."

"Four of our daughters are married here," Maha said. "Even if we left, they would have stayed. Their husbands' families might be with Daesh. We don't know—so many people support them. But we can't leave our daughters here alone."

I don't want to sound ungrateful to the family who let me

inside their home. They heard my story without judgment and they offered to help. Still, I couldn't help but wonder where they had been the whole time I was captive. Listening to their excuses made me angry, although I tried not to show it. How could Hussein watch those buses drive by, thinking that on board were young girls and women about to be raped night after night by Islamic State militants? How could Hisham have watched in the court as militants dragged their sabaya into illegal marriages? They were helping me, but only after I showed up at their door. And I was one of thousands. They said they hated ISIS, but none of them had done anything to stop them.

Maybe, I thought, it was asking too much of a normal family to fight back against terrorists like the men in ISIS, men who threw people they accused of being homosexual off rooftops; men who raped young girls because they belonged to the wrong religion; men who stoned people to death. My willingness to help others had never been tested like that. But that was because Yazidis had never been shielded by their religion, only attacked. Hisham and his family had remained safe in ISIS-occupied Mosul because they were born Sunni and therefore were accepted by the militants. Until I showed up, they'd been content to wear their religion as armor. I tried not to hate them for it, because they were showing me such kindness, but I didn't love them.

"Do you have anyone in Kurdistan that we can call to tell them you are with us?" Hisham asked.

"I have brothers there," I told him, and recited Hezni's number, which was etched in my brain.

I watched as Hisham dialed the number and began to speak. Then he took the phone off his ear in confusion and dialed again. The second time the same thing happened, and I worried that I had the wrong number. "Is he picking up?" I asked Hisham.

He shook his head. "A man keeps answering, but as soon as I tell him who I am and where I am calling from, he starts cursing at me," he told me. "It might not be your brother. If it is, I don't think he believes me that you are with me."

Hisham tried again. This time whoever picked up let him talk. "Nadia is here with us, she ran away from her captor," he explained. "If you don't believe me, I know Yazidis who will tell you who I am." Hisham had served in Saddam's military with a connected Yazidi politician from Sinjar. "He will tell you that I am a good person and that I won't hurt your sister."

It was a brief conversation, and afterward Hisham told me that it had been Hezni he was talking to. "At first, when he saw that it was a phone call from Mosul, he thought I was calling to be cruel," he said. "Apparently the men who are holding his wife call him sometimes just to remind him of what they are doing to her. All he can do is curse at them and hang up." My heart hurt for Hezni and Jilan, who had struggled so hard to be together in the first place.

It was getting late, and the women laid out a mattress for me in one of the rooms and asked me if I was hungry. "No," I said. I couldn't imagine eating anything. "But I'm very thirsty." Nasser brought me some water, and as I drank it, he warned me not to go outside, ever. "This neighborhood is full of Daesh members and sympathizers," he told me. "It's not safe for you."

"What has been happening here?" I wanted to know. Were there sabaya nearby? Did militants search homes when one went missing?

"We are living in a dangerous time," Nasser said to me. "Daesh is everywhere. They rule the entire city, and we all have to be careful. We have a generator, but we can't run it at night because we worry that if the American planes see the lights, they will drop a bomb on our home."

In spite of the heat, I shivered, thinking back to the door I had first stopped at and decided not to knock on. Who was behind it?

"Sleep now," Hisham said. "In the morning we will think of a way to get you out of here."

The room was stifling and I slept very little. All night I thought about the houses around me, full of families supporting ISIS. I thought of Hajji Salman scouring the roads in his car, searching for me, his rage keeping him up all night. I wondered what had happened to the militant who had let me escape. Would the promise of a five-thousand-dollar reward persuade Nasser and his family to hand me over? Had they been lying to me, pretending that they were compassionate and willing to help, all the while hating me for being Yazidi? It would be foolish for me to trust them just yet, I thought, even if they were from the Azawi tribe and even if Hisham did have Yazidi friends from his time in the army. There were Sunnis with closer ties to Yazidis who had betrayed their friends to ISIS.

My sisters and nieces who had been separated from me—they could be anywhere. Would they be punished because I escaped? What had happened to the women we left in Solagh, and the girls taken to Syria? I thought about my beautiful mother, her white scarf falling from her hair as she tripped off the truck in Solagh, and how she had laid her head on my lap and closed her eyes to block out the terror that surrounded us. I saw Kathrine being ripped from my mother's arms before we were all loaded onto the buses. Very soon I would find out what had happened to all of them. When I did sleep, it was without dreaming, in total blackness.

Chapter 2

I WOKE UP AT FIVE A.M., BEFORE ANYONE ELSE, AND MY FIRST thought was that I had to get out of there. *It's not safe here,* I told myself. *What are they going to do with me? What are the chances that they are good enough people to take the risk to help me?* But it was morning, and the hot sun was already lighting up the streets, where there wasn't even shade to hide me if I tried to leave. I had nowhere else to go. Lying in bed, I realized that my fate was in the hands of Hisham and his family, and all I could do was pray that they really meant to help me.

Nasser arrived two hours later, with instructions from Hisham. While we talked and waited for his father to join us, Maha served us breakfast. I couldn't eat, but I drank a little coffee. "We will take you to stay with my sister Mina and her husband, Basheer," he told me. "They live a little bit outside the city, and there is less of a chance of Daesh being there and seeing you."

"We know that Basheer doesn't like Daesh," Nasser said. "But we are not sure about his brothers. He says they haven't joined, but you never know, so you will have to be careful. Basheer is a good guy, though."

With my niqab covering my face, I felt safe in the car with Hisham and Nasser. The neighborhood began to thin out as we drove to Mina and Basheer's house, on the outskirts of Mosul. No one looked at us as we walked from the car to the front door, and I didn't see any neighboring houses flying Islamic State flags or that had been spray-painted with Islamic State graffiti.

The couple met us in the entranceway to the house, which was larger and nicer than Hisham's and reminded me of the houses my married brothers had been building slowly in Kocho, with their life savings. It was concrete and built to last, with tile floors covered with green and beige carpets, and couches with thick cushions in the living room.

Mina was the most beautiful woman I had ever seen. She had a pale round face and bright green eyes like jewels, and she was shaped like Dimal—not too thin. Her long hair was dyed a rich brown. She and Basheer had five children, three boys and two daughters, and when I arrived, the whole family greeted me calmly, as though Hisham and Nasser had already answered all the questions they had about me. No one tried to comfort me. Other than Nasser, who seemed curious to know all the details of what had happened to me, the family treated me like I was a duty to fulfill, and I was grateful for that. I wasn't sure yet that I could return their affection if they offered it. "*Salam alakum*," I said to them. "*Alakum asalaam*," Basheer replied. "Don't worry, we will help you."

The plan was to get a fake ID made for me either in Safaa's name or in Mina's—whichever turned out to be easier—and then for one of the men, either Basheer or Nasser, to accompany me from Mosul to Kirkuk, pretending that we were husband and wife. Nasser had friends in Mosul who made IDs—once the standard Iraqi state ID and now the black and white Islamic State one—who would help us. "We will get you an Iraqi ID, not a Daesh one," he told me. "It will seem more authentic and it will make it easier for you to get into Kurdistan, if we get through the Daesh checkpoints."

"If we use Safaa's information, then you will go with Nasser," Basheer said. "If we use Mina's, you will go with me." Mina sat with us, listening but not saying anything. Her green eyes flashed in my direction when her husband said this. It was clear that she wasn't happy, but she didn't object.

"Will Kirkuk be a good place to leave you?" Basheer asked. He thought it might be the easiest entrance into Kurdistan beyond Mosul. If so, they would tell the ID maker to list my birthplace as Kirkuk and to give me a name common in that city.

"Is Kirkuk with ISIS?" I didn't know. Growing up, I had always assumed that Kirkuk was a part of Kurdistan because that's what the Kurdish parties said, but I'd gathered from conversations I'd overheard between Islamic State militants that the region was disputed, like Sinjar, and that it was now coveted not only by the Kurds and the Baghdad government but also by ISIS. The militants had taken over so much of Iraq, I would have believed that they controlled Kirkuk and all its oil fields by now. "I can ask my family. If it's controlled by the peshmerga, then I can go there."

"Fine." Basheer was satisfied. "I will call Hisham's friend in Sinjar to see if he can help you, and Nasser will get you your ID."

That day I spoke to Hezni for the first time since escaping. For most of the conversation, we both managed to stay calm—there was a lot of work to be done if I was going to make it home alive—but when I first heard his voice, I was so happy I could barely speak.

"Nadia," he said. "Don't worry. I think this family is good—they will help you."

Hezni sounded like he always had, confident and emotional at the same time. In spite of what I was going through, I felt sad for him. I supposed I might soon find out what it was like to be one of the saved Yazidis, and all the grief and longing that went along with it, if I was lucky.

I wanted to tell him how I'd escaped. I felt proud of how brave I had been. "It was so strange, Hezni," I said. "After all that, ev-

eryone keeping such a close eye on me, this man left the door unlocked. I just opened the door and climbed over the wall and left."

"It's what God wanted, Nadia," he said. "He wants you to live
and to come home."

"I'm worried that one of the sons here is with Daesh," I told
Hezni. "They are very religious."

But Hezni told me I had no choice. "You have to trust this
family," he said. I told him that if he thought they were good,
then I would stay with them.

Later I would learn about the smuggling networks that had
been established to help Yazidi girls escape from ISIS, in part
because from his container home in the refugee camp, Hezni
would help to arrange the escapes of dozens of girls. Each operation began in panic and chaos, but after the family of the victim
managed to get enough money together, it would begin to unfold
like a business deal, employing a system of smugglers. There are
middlemen—mostly Arab, Turkmen, and Syrian or Iraqi Kurdish
locals—who are paid a few thousand dollars for their part in the
scheme. Some are taxi drivers, who smuggle the girls in their cars;
others serve as spies in Mosul or Tal Afar, letting families know
where the girls are hiding; others help at checkpoints or bribe and
bargain with the Islamic State authorities. A few of the key players inside the Islamic State territories are women; they can more
easily approach a sabiyya without causing alarm. At the head of
the networks are a few Yazidi men, who, using their connections
in the Sunni villages, set up the networks and make sure it all
goes according to plan. Each team works in its own zone—some
in Syria and some in Iraq. As in any business, competition has
developed among them, since it has become clear that smuggling
sabaya is a good way to make money during wartime.

When the plan for my own escape was being made, the smuggling network was just starting to develop, and Hezni was figur-

ing out how he could participate. My brother is brave and good, and he wouldn't let anyone suffer if he could help it, but so many girls had his phone number—all his female relatives had memorized it and passed it to sabaya they met along the way—that he was quickly overwhelmed by phone calls. By the time Hisham called him on my behalf, he'd already reached out to others for help and had been connected to KRG officials working on freeing Yazidis, as well as to local point people in Mosul and elsewhere in ISIS-held Iraq. Quickly, smuggling became his full-time—and unpaid—job.

Not knowing exactly what to expect when I was getting ready for my trip to Kirkuk, Hezni was worried. He wasn't sure that having one of the brothers, Nasser or Basheer, come with me all the way into Kurdistan would work. It wasn't easy for a Sunni man of fighting age to cross a Kurdish checkpoint, and Hezni knew that if ISIS found out that a family in Mosul had helped a sabiyya escape, the punishment would be severe. "We don't want him to be captured because he tried to help you," Hezni told me. "It's our responsibility to make sure nothing happens to Nasser or Basheer when they come with you to Kurdistan. Okay, Nadia?"

"I understand, Hezni," I told him. "I'll be careful." I knew that if we were caught at an Islamic State checkpoint, whoever was with me would be killed, and I would be returned to slavery. At a Kurdish checkpoint, the danger was that Nasser or Basheer would be placed into detention.

"Take care of yourself, Nadia," Hezni told me. "Try not to worry about anything. Tomorrow they will get you an ID. When you get to Kirkuk, call me."

Before we hung up, I asked him, "What happened to Kathrine?"

"I don't know, Nadia," he said.

"What about in Solagh?" I asked.

"ISIS is still in Kocho and Solagh," he said. "We know that

the men have been killed. Saeed survived, and he told me what it was like. Saoud made it here, and he is doing all right. We don't know yet what happened to the women in Solagh. But Saeed is determined to go fight Daesh to liberate it, and I'm worried about him." Saeed was in terrible pain because of his bullet wounds, and he had nightmares about the firing squad every night, which prevented him from sleeping. "I'm worried that he can't cope with what happened," Hezni said.

We said goodbye, and Hezni passed the phone to Khaled, my half brother. He had more information for me. "Yazidis aren't on the run anymore," he told me. "They live in extremely difficult conditions in Kurdistan, waiting for the camps to open."

"What happened to the men in Kocho?" I asked, even though I had already been told. I didn't want it to be true.

"All the men were killed," he said. "All the women were taken. Have you seen any of the women?"

"I saw Nisreen, Rojian, and Kathrine," I told him. "I don't know where they are now."

The news was worse than I expected. Even what I already knew was difficult to hear. We hung up, and I handed the phone back to Nasser. I no longer worried that the family was going to betray me, and so I let myself relax a little bit. I felt more tired than I ever had in my whole life.

———

I STAYED AT Mina and Basheer's house for several days while the escape plan was worked out, and most of the time I kept to myself, thinking about my family and what was going to happen to me. If no one asked me any questions, I was happy to stay quiet. They were a very religious family, praying five times a day, but they said they hated ISIS, and they never asked me about my forced conversion or tried to get me to pray with them.

I was still very sick and my stomach felt like it was on fire, so one day they took me to the local women's hospital. They had to convince me that it was safe to go. "Just put a hot water bottle on my stomach," I told Nasser's mother. "That's enough." But she insisted that I see a doctor. "As long as you wear your niqab and stay with us, you will be fine," she assured me and I was in so much pain that I couldn't argue for long. My head was spinning and I barely noticed when they took me to their car and drove me into town. I was so sick that now, looking back, the hospital visit seems like a dream that I struggle to remember. But after that I got better and stronger, and I waited quietly indoors for the day I would be told it was time to leave.

Sometimes I ate with them, and sometimes I ate alone; they urged me to be careful, to stay away from the windows and ignore the telephone. "If anyone comes to the door, stay in your room and don't make a noise," they told me. Mosul was not like Sinjar. In Kocho, when a visitor comes, they don't bother knocking. Everyone knows everyone else, and we were all welcome in one another's homes. In Mosul a visitor waits to be invited inside, and even a friend is treated like a stranger.

Under no circumstance was I to go outside. Their main bathroom was in an outhouse, but I was instructed to use the smaller one inside instead. "We don't know if any of our neighbors are with Daesh," they said. I did what they told me to do. The last thing I wanted was to be discovered and returned to ISIS and for Hisham and his family to be punished for trying to help me. I had no doubt that they would execute every one of the adults, and just the thought of Mina's two young daughters, both close to eight years old and beautiful like their mother, being taken into Islamic State custody made me sick to my stomach.

I slept in the daughters' room. We barely spoke. They weren't scared of me—they just weren't interested in knowing who I was, and I had no intention of telling them. They were so innocent. On the second day, I woke up to see them sitting in front of their bedroom mirror, trying to wrestle tangles out of their hair. "Can I help?" I asked. "I am very good at doing hair." They nodded, and I sat behind them, running a comb through their long hair until it was soft and straight. It was something I used to do for Adkee and Kathrine every day, and doing it, I felt almost normal.

The television was kept on all day so that the kids could play with their PlayStation. And because the boys were so distracted by their video games, they noticed me even less than the girls. They were around the same age as Malik and Hani, my two nephews who were kidnapped and forced to become ISIS fighters. Before August 2014, Malik had been a shy boy, but smart and interested in the world around him. He loved us, and his mother, Hamdia. Now I had no idea where he was. ISIS had instituted an intense system of reeducation and brainwashing for the teenagers they kidnapped. While the boys were taught Arabic and English, they learned words of war like *gun*, and they were told that Yazidism was a religion of the devil and that their family members who wouldn't convert would be better off dead.

They were taken at an impressionable age, and as I'd eventually learn, the lessons worked on some of them. Later Malik would send photos to Hezni in the refugee camp. They showed him in Islamic State fatigues, smiling and carrying a rifle, his cheeks red with excitement. He would call Hezni's phone just to tell Hamdia that she should come join him.

"Your father is dead," Hamdia would tell her son. "There is no one left to take care of the family. You have to come home."

"You should come to the Islamic State," Malik would reply. "You will be taken care of here."

Hani managed to escape after nearly three years in captivity, but when Hezni tried to arrange Malik's rescue, my nephew refused to go with the smuggler who approached him in a marketplace in Syria. "I want to fight," he told him. He was a shadow of the boy he had been in Kocho and after that, Hezni stopped trying. But Hamdia would always pick up the phone if she saw it was Malik calling. "He's still my son," she would say.

Mina was a good housewife and mother. She spent her days cleaning and cooking for her family, playing with the kids, and nursing the baby. The days were tense, for her as well as for me, and we didn't talk very much. Soon enough either her brother or her husband was going to make the dangerous trip with me to Kurdistan. It was a lot for one family to go through.

Once, passing each other in the hall, she commented on my hair. "Why is it red only at the ends?" she asked.

"I dyed it with henna a long time ago," I said, examining the strands.

"It's pretty," she said, and moved past me, saying nothing else.

One afternoon after lunch Mina struggled to quiet the baby, who needed to eat and wouldn't stop crying. Normally she wouldn't let me help with the housework, but that afternoon when I offered to do the dishes, she nodded, grateful. The sink was in front of a window that overlooked the street, where someone might see me, but she was too distracted by her baby to think about whether we would be caught, and I was happy to have a chance to help her. To my surprise, she started to ask me questions.

"Do you know other people with Daesh?" she asked, cradling the baby against her chest.

"Yes," I said. "They took all my friends and my family, and they separated us." I wanted to ask her the same question, but I didn't want to offend her.

She paused, thinking. "After you leave Mosul, where will you go?"

"To my brother," I said. "He's waiting to go to a refugee camp with other Yazidis."

"What is the camp like?" she asked.

"I don't know," I said. "Almost everyone who survived will go there. My brother, Hezni, says it will be hard. There will be nothing to do, no work, and it's far from cities. But they will be safe."

"I wonder what will happen here," she said. It wasn't really a question, so I didn't say anything. I continued washing the dishes, and she was quiet until I was finished.

By then the baby had stopped crying and was falling asleep in Mina's arms. I went back upstairs to the daughters' room and lay down on a mattress, but I didn't close my eyes.

Chapter 3

IT WAS DECIDED THAT NASSER WOULD BE THE ONE TO GO with me. That made me happy; Nasser liked to talk to me, and in the days leading up to our journey, he was the one I felt more comfortable with. By the time we left, he was almost like a brother.

Like my brothers, Nasser teased me when I got lost in my own head, which was often. We had a running joke together that no one else understood. During the first days at the house, when Nasser would ask me how everything was, I would just answer absentmindedly, "It's very hot, very hot." I was too distracted by fear to say anything else. And so he would ask me when I saw him again, an hour later, "Nadia, how is everything now?" and I would say again, without realizing that I was repeating myself, "Nasser, it is very hot, very hot," just like that. Eventually, he began to answer for me, asking in a joking tone, "Hey, Nadia, how is it? Is it very hot? Or is it very hot, very hot?" and I laughed when I realized what he was doing.

Nasser came back the third day with an ID card. It listed my name as Sousan and my hometown as Kirkuk, but otherwise it contained all of Safaa's information. "Make sure you memorize everything on this ID card," he told me. "If they ask you when or where you were born at the checkpoint, and you don't know . . . that will be the end of it."

I studied the ID day and night, memorizing Safaa's date of

birth—she was a little older than me—and her mother's and father's names, as well as Nasser's date of birth and his mother's
and father's names. On Iraqi IDs, both before and during ISIS,
a woman's father's or husband's information is as important as
her own.

Safaa's picture was pasted into one corner. We didn't look very
much alike, but I didn't worry about the guards at the checkpoints
asking me to lift up my niqab to show my face. I couldn't imagine
an Islamic State member telling a Sunni woman to show her face
in front of her husband, who was presumably also with ISIS. "If
they ask you why you haven't gotten a Daesh ID yet, just tell them
you haven't had time," Hisham said. I was so scared, I memorized
the information quickly, and after that I felt like it was imprinted
on my brain.

Our plan was simple. Nasser and I would pretend to be husband and wife, traveling to Kirkuk to visit my family. *Sousan* was
a popular name in the city. "You tell them you are staying a week
or so," they told me. "Nasser will say that he is accompanying you
and will come back that day or the next, depending on what time
you arrive." That way Nasser wouldn't have to worry about bringing a bag or paying the fine ISIS required of Sunnis who wanted
to stay outside the caliphate for an extended time.

"Do you know anything about Kirkuk?" they asked me.
"Names of neighborhoods, or anything about what it looks like,
in case they ask?"

"I've never been," I said. "But I can ask my brother some things."

"What about her bag?" Nasser asked. I still had the black cotton sack with me. Inside were dresses that had belonged to Kathrine, Dimal, and me, as well as the sanitary pads that hid my
jewelry and my mother's ration card. "It doesn't look like the kind
of bag a Muslim woman packs for a week visiting family."

Hisham went out and returned with a bottle of shampoo and
a bottle of conditioner, as well as a couple of simple dresses in the

style popular among Muslim women, and I added these things to my bag. I started to feel guilty about the money they were spending on me. They were a poor family, like mine, and I didn't want to be a burden. "When I am back in Kurdistan, I will send you something," I told them. They insisted it was fine, but I couldn't get it out of my mind. I still worried that if the money became too much of a strain, they would decide to turn me in.

Hezni told me not to think about it. "The five-thousand-dollar reward is a lie," he said. "Daesh just says that so that girls will be less willing to try to escape. They want you to think that you are like cattle and that every family wants to catch one of you to sell. But they don't pay.

"Anyway, it's good for Nasser to leave Mosul," Hezni told me.

"What do you mean?" I asked, confused.

"You don't know?" Hezni said. "Ask Hisham."

That evening I told Hisham what my brother had said. "What did he mean? Does Nasser want to leave?" I asked.

After a moment, he told me. "We are worried about Nasser," he said. "He's a young man and it's only a matter of time before Daesh forces him to fight."

Nasser grew up poor under a Shiite government during the American occupation, and when he was younger, he had been angry at what he saw as the persecution of Sunnis. Young men like him were prime recruits for ISIS, and his family thought the terrorists wanted Nasser to join their police force. He was already fixing the sanitation systems in buildings around Mosul and everyone worried that even that job, although it was not violent, could brand him a terrorist later on.

By the time I arrived out of nowhere on their doorstep, they had been desperately trying to think of a way to get him out of Mosul. They thought it was possible that if the family helped a Yazidi escape slavery, the Kurdish authorities would eventually let them into Kurdistan.

Hisham urged me not to tell Nasser that I knew and, no matter what, not to tell anyone that he had worked for ISIS, even just repairing toilets. "It doesn't matter what the job was," he said. "The Kurds or the Iraqi Army will put him in prison."

I promised him that I wouldn't tell anyone. I couldn't imagine Nasser becoming an Islamic State policeman, arresting people on the basis of religion or because they had violated some vicious rule or dissented in some way and probably sending them to their death. Would he have to work with Hajji Salman? Nasser was my friend now, and he seemed too gentle and too understanding to take such a job. On the other hand, I had only just met him, and so many Sunnis had turned against Yazidis. I wondered if there had been a part of his life when he thought that all religions in Iraq other than Sunni Islam should be forced out of the country, and whether he had felt that by thinking that, he was taking part in a revolution to take back Iraq. I had heard my brothers talk about the Sunnis who, because of years of oppression under the Americans, Kurds, and Shia, and the Islamic radicalization that came at the same time, had turned so violently against their neighbors. Now one of them was helping me. But was he doing it only to save himself? Did that matter?

———

OVER THE PAST few years, I have thought a lot about Nasser and his family. They took a huge risk in helping me. ISIS would have killed them, and maybe captured the daughters and enlisted the sons, if they had found out that the family had taken in a sabiyya—and they could have easily found out. They were everywhere. I wish that every human being acted with the same courage as Nasser's family did.

Still, for every family like Nasser's, there were thousands more in Iraq and Syria who did nothing or who took an active role in the genocide. Some of them betrayed girls like me who tried to escape. Kathrine and Lamia were turned in six times by people they approached for help, first in Mosul and then in Hamdaniya, and every time they were punished. A group of sabaya who were taken to Syria were hunted in the reeds of the Tigris like escaped criminals after a local farmer called the Islamic State commander to tell him about some slaves who had rushed to him out of the darkness to ask for his help.

Families in Iraq and Syria led normal lives while we were tortured and raped. They watched us walk through the streets with our captors and gathered on the streets to witness executions. I don't know how each individual was feeling. After the liberation of Mosul began in late 2016, families talked about the hardship of living under ISIS, how brutal the terrorists were, and how frightening it was to hear the war planes overhead, knowing they could bomb their homes. They couldn't find enough food to eat, and their electricity was cut off. Their kids had to go to Islamic State schools, their boys had to fight, and everything they did involved a fine and a tax. People were killed in the streets, they said. It was no way to live.

But when I was in Mosul, life seemed normal, even good, for the people there. Why did they stay in the first place? Did they agree with ISIS and consider the idea of their caliphate a good thing? Did it seem like a natural continuation of the sectarian wars they had been fighting since the Americans came in 2003? If life had continued to get better, as ISIS had promised them it would, would they have let the terrorists kill whomever they wanted?

I try to have compassion for these families. I'm sure many of them were terrified, and eventually even those who welcomed ISIS at the beginning would come to hate them and say, after Mosul was liberated, that they had no choice but to let the terrorists do what they wanted. But I think they did have a choice. Had they gathered together, pooled their weapons, and stormed the

Islamic State center where militants were selling girls or giving them as gifts, it's possible we all would have died. But it would at least have sent the message to ISIS, Yazidis, and the rest of the world that not all Sunnis who stayed in their homes supported terrorism. Maybe if some people in Mosul had gone into the streets and shouted, "I am a Muslim, and what you are demanding of us is not true Islam!" the Iraqi forces and the Americans would have gone in earlier, with help from the people living there, or smugglers working to free Yazidi girls could have expanded their networks and gotten us out by the handfuls instead of one at a time like a dripping faucet. But instead they let us scream in the slave market and did nothing.

After I arrived at Nasser's family's house, they told me that they had started thinking about their own role in ISIS. They said they felt guilty that it had taken me showing up on their doorstep, desperate and begging, for them to help a sabiyya; they knew that their survival, and the fact that they had not been displaced, was in some way a collusion with the terrorists. I didn't know how they would have felt about ISIS if life had gotten better, not worse, when the militants took over Mosul. They told me they were changed forever. "We swear that after you leave, we will help more girls like you," they said.

"There are so many others who need you," I told them.

Chapter 4

W E WAITED A FEW DAYS BEFORE NASSER AND I MADE THE trip. I was comfortable being in the house, but I desperately wanted out of Mosul. ISIS was everywhere, and I was sure that they were looking for me. I could imagine Hajji Salman, his skinny frame shaking in anger and his soft, menacing voice threatening me with torture. I couldn't be in the same city as that kind of man. One morning in Mina's house, I woke up covered in tiny red stinging ants and took it as a sign. I wouldn't feel an ounce of real safety until we passed through the first checkpoint, and I knew there was a chance we wouldn't make it at all.

A few days after I arrived at Mina's, Nasser's mother and father came to the house early in the morning. "It's time to go," Hisham said. I put on Kathrine's pink and brown dress and, just before I was to leave, covered it with a black abaya.

"I will read a prayer," Maha said to me. She said it kindly, and so I agreed, listening as she spoke the words. Then she gave me a ring. "You said that Daesh took your mother's ring," she said. "Please take this one instead."

My bag was packed with all the extra things the family had bought for me, as well as the things I still had from Kocho. At the last minute, I took out Dimal's beautiful long yellow dress and gave it to Mina. Kissing her on both cheeks, I thanked her for taking me in. "You will look beautiful in this dress," I said, handing it to her. "It belonged to my sister Dimal."

"Thank you, Nadia," she said. "*Insha'allah* you will make it to Kurdistan." I couldn't watch while the family, and his wife, said goodbye to Nasser.

Before we left the house, Nasser gave me one of the two cell phones he had brought with him. "If you need anything or if you have a question while we are in the taxi, text me," he said. "Don't talk."

"I throw up when I ride in cars for too long," I warned him, and he picked up a few plastic grocery bags from the kitchen and handed them to me. "Use these. I don't want to have to stop.

"At the checkpoints, don't act afraid," he continued. "Try to be calm. I will answer most of the questions. If they turn to you, answer them briefly and keep your voice low. If they believe that you are my wife, they won't ask you to talk very much."

I nodded. "I'll do my best," I said. Already I felt like I might faint from fear. Nasser seemed calm; he never acted afraid of anything.

At around eight-thirty in the morning, we started walking together to the main road. There we would hail a taxi to take us to the Mosul garage, where another taxi that Nasser had hired in advance was waiting to take us all the way to Kirkuk. Nasser stayed a bit ahead of me on the sidewalk, and we didn't talk. I kept my head down, trying not to look at the people we passed, sure that the fear in my eyes would tell them immediately that I was Yazidi.

It was a hot day. Mina's neighbors watered their lawns, trying to revive the dead plants, while their kids raced up and down the streets on brightly colored plastic bicycles. The noise startled me. After being inside so long, the bright streets felt threatening, wide open and full of danger. All the hope I had tried to gather while waiting at Mina's disappeared. I was sure that ISIS would catch up to us, and that I would go back to being a sabiyya. "It's okay," Nasser whispered to me as we stood on the sidewalk of the main road, waiting for a taxi to appear. He could tell I was frightened. Cars sped by, covering the front of my black abaya with a fine yellow dust. I was shaking so much that by the time we got a taxi, it was hard for me to maneuver my body inside it.

Every scenario that ran through my head led to our capture. I saw our taxi breaking down on the side of the highway and us being picked up by a truck full of militants. Or I saw us driving unknowingly over an IED and dying there on the road. I thought about all the girls I knew from home, family and friends, who were now scattered across Iraq and Syria, and my brothers who had been taken behind the school in Kocho. Who was I even going home to?

The Mosul garage was crowded with people looking for taxis to take them to other cities in Iraq. Men bartered with drivers over prices, their wives standing silently beside them. Boys hawked icy bottles of water, and vendors along the edges sold silver bags of chips and candy bars or stood proudly next to elaborate towers of cigarettes. I wondered if any of the women at the garage were Yazidi like me. I hoped they all were, and that the men were like Nasser, helping them. Yellow taxis, marked by small signs on their roofs, parked and idled under signs advertising destinations: Tal Afar, Tikrit, Ramadi. All of them were at least partly under Islamic State control or threatened by the terrorists. So much of my country now belonged to the men who had enslaved and raped me.

While the taxi driver prepared for our trip, he and Nasser chatted. I sat on a bench slightly away from them, trying to act the part of Nasser's wife, and I couldn't hear much of what they were saying. Sweat ran into my eyes, making it hard to see, and I clutched my bag tightly to my lap. The driver was in his late forties. He looked strong even though he wasn't very big, and he wore a small beard. I had no idea how he felt about ISIS, but

I was scared of everyone. While they negotiated, I tried to feel brave, but it was hard to think of any outcome in which I was not recaptured.

Finally Nasser nodded at me to get into the car. He sat beside the driver, and I climbed into the seat behind him, putting my bag down gently beside me. The driver fiddled with the radio as we pulled out of the garage, looking for a station, but everything was static. He sighed and turned it off.

"It's a hot day," he said to Nasser. "Let's buy some water before we start driving." Nasser nodded, and a moment later we pulled up beside a kiosk where the driver bought a few bottles of cold water and some crackers. Nasser handed a bottle to me. Water dripped down the sides of it, pooling on the seat beside me. The crackers were too dry to eat; I tried one, just to appear relaxed, and it stuck in my throat like cement.

"Why are you going to Kirkuk?" the driver asked.

"My wife's family is there," Nasser replied.

The driver looked at me in his rearview mirror. When I saw his eyes, I turned away, pretending to be mesmerized by the city outside my window. I was sure the fear in my eyes would give me away.

The street around the garage was full of militants. Islamic State police cars were parked along the sides, and officers strolled along the sidewalks, guns in their belts. There seemed to be more police than people.

"Will you stay in Kirkuk or come back to Mosul?" the driver asked Nasser.

"We're not sure yet," Nasser said, just as his father had told him. "We'll see how long it takes to get there, and what it's like in Kirkuk."

Why is he asking so many questions? I thought. I was glad that I wasn't expected to talk.

"If you like, I can wait and take you back to Mosul," the driver told us, and Nasser smiled at him. "Maybe," he said. "We'll see."

The first checkpoint was inside Mosul, a large, spider-like structure made of high columns holding up a metal roof. Once an Iraqi Army checkpoint, it was now proudly displaying the Islamic State flag, and Islamic State vehicles, also once belonging to the Iraqi Army, were parked in front of a small office. They, too, were covered in black and white flags.

Four militants were on duty when we pulled up, working out of small white booths where they could take breaks from the heat and fill out paperwork. ISIS was intent on controlling all the traffic in and out of Mosul. Not only did they make sure that no anti-ISIS fighters or smugglers came into the city, they also wanted to know who left, why, and for how long. If they defected, ISIS could punish their families. At the very least, the militants could try to extort money out of them.

Only a few cars were in line ahead of us, and we quickly approached one of the guards. I started shaking uncontrollably and felt tears come out of my eyes. The more I willed myself to be calm, the more I shook and I thought for sure it would give me away. *Maybe I should run*, I thought, and as we slowed down, I put one of my hands on the door handle, preparing to jump out of the car if I needed to. Of course, it wasn't really an option. There was nowhere for me to go. On one side of the car, the hot plain stretched into nowhere, and on the other side and behind us was the city I was so desperate to flee. Militants watched every inch of Mosul, and they would have no trouble catching up with a sabiyya escaping on foot. I prayed to God not to be captured.

Sensing I was scared and without being able to talk to me, Nasser glanced at me in the side mirror. He smiled just for an instant, to calm me down, the way Khairy or my mother would have back in Kocho. Nothing could have stopped my heart from racing, but at least I was no longer imagining myself jumping from the car.

We stopped beside one of the guard booths, and I watched

as the door opened and a militant in full Islamic State uniform stepped out. He looked like the guys who had come to the Islamic State center to buy us, and I started shaking again in fear. The driver rolled down his window, and the militant leaned down. He looked at the driver, then over at Nasser, and then he glanced at me and the bag next to me. "*Salam alakum*," he said. "Where are you going?"

"Kirkuk, hajji," Nasser said, and passed our IDs through the window. "My wife is from Kirkuk." His voice didn't waver.

The militant took the IDs. Through the open door to the guard booth, I saw a chair and a small desk with a few papers and the militant's radio sitting on top of it. A small fan whirred softly on the corner of the desk, and a nearly empty bottle of water teetered close to the edge. Then I saw it. Hanging on the wall, with three others, was the photo that had been taken of me in the Mosul courthouse, the day Hajji Salman forced me to convert. Below it, there was some writing. I was too far away to read what it said, but I guessed it listed my information and what to do if I was caught. I gasped softly and quickly scanned the other three photos. Two of them I couldn't see because of the sun's glare, and the other was of a girl I didn't recognize. She looked very young, and like me, her fear registered on her face. I looked away, not wanting the militant to notice that I was staring at the photos, which would certainly have made him suspicious.

"Who are you going to see in Kirkuk?" the guard was still questioning Nasser and had barely paid attention to me.

"My wife's family," Nasser said.

"For how long?"

"My wife will stay for a week, but I will return today," he said, just as we had rehearsed it. He didn't sound scared at all.

I wondered if Nasser could see my photo hanging in the guard post from where he was sitting. I thought for sure if he could, he would make us turn back. Seeing my photo confirmed that they were actively looking for me, but Nasser just continued answering questions.

The guard circled the car to my side, then motioned for me to roll down my window. I did so, all the while feeling like I might faint from fear. I remembered Nasser's advice to stay calm and answer his questions as quietly and as briefly as possible. My Arabic was perfect, and I had been speaking it from a young age, but I didn't know if there was something in my accent or choice of words that would give me away as being from Sinjar, not Kirkuk. Iraq is a big country, and you can usually tell where someone grew up based on the way they talk. I had no idea how someone from Kirkuk was supposed to sound.

He leaned down and looked through the window at me. I was grateful that my niqab covered my face, and I tried to control my eyes, not to blink too much or too little, and certainly, under no circumstances, to cry. Underneath my abaya, I was soaked in sweat and still shaking from fear, but the image of me in the guard's glasses was of a normal Muslim woman. I sat up and prepared to answer his questions.

They were brief. "Who are you?" His voice was level—he sounded bored.

"I am Nasser's wife," I said.

"Where are you going?"

"Kirkuk."

"Why?"

"My family is in Kirkuk." I spoke softly and looked down, hoping my fear would come across as modesty and my answers didn't seem rehearsed.

The guard straightened up and walked away.

Finally he asked the driver, "Where are you from?"

"Mosul," the driver said, sounding as though he had answered this question a million times.

"Where do you work?"

"Wherever there's a fare!" the driver answered, chuckling. Then without another word, the guard handed our IDs back through the window and waved us through.

We drove over a long bridge, none of us speaking. Beneath us, the Tigris River shimmered in the sun. Reeds and plants hugged the water; the closer they could get, the more likely they were to live. Away from the bank, the plants were less lucky. They were singed by the Iraqi summer sun, and only a few, carefully watered by the people living there or catching some moisture from a rainfall, would sprout again in the spring.

Once we were on the other side, the driver spoke up. "You know, that bridge we just crossed is covered with IEDs," he said, "bombs planted by Daesh in case the Iraqis or the Americans try to retake Mosul. I hate driving over it. I feel like it could explode at any moment."

I turned around to look. Both the bridge and the checkpoint were retreating in the distance. We had made it past both of them alive, but it could have gone very differently. The Islamic State militant at the checkpoint could have asked me more questions—he could have heard something in my accent or noticed something in my demeanor that made him suspicious. "*Get out of the car,*" I imagined him saying, and I would have had no choice but to do what he asked, following him into the guard booth, where he would have commanded me to lift up my niqab, showing him that I was the woman in the photo. I thought of the bridge exploding while we were on it, the IEDs shattering our car and killing all three of us in an instant. I prayed that when the bridge did explode, it would be full of Islamic State militants.

Chapter 5

A S WE DROVE AWAY FROM MOSUL, WE WENT BY SCENES OF past battles. Smaller checkpoints that had been abandoned by the Iraqi Army were piles of burned rubble. The wreckage of a huge truck was left like trash on the side of the road. I had seen on TV that militants burned the checkpoints after the army abandoned them, and I couldn't understand why they would do that. They just wanted to destroy things for no reason. Not even the flocks of sheep walking alongside the road, led by a young shepherd sitting on top of a slow-moving donkey, could make the landscape appear anything close to normal.

Soon we arrived at another checkpoint. This one was manned by only two Islamic State militants, who seemed far less concerned about who we were and where we were going. They ran through the same questions more quickly. Again I could see through the door into the guard booth, but I didn't see any photos hanging inside. They waved us through after only a few minutes.

The road from Mosul to Kirkuk is long and winds through the countryside. Some of it is wide while parts are narrow and two lanes of traffic pass each other head-on. These roads are notorious for accidents. Cars try to speed past huge slow trucks, flashing their lights at oncoming traffic, forcing them to drive onto the shoulder to let them pass. Trucks full of building material spill gravel along the way, chipping cars and windshields, and in places the roads are so uneven, you feel like you are driving off a cliff.

Iraqi cities are connected by a series of these kinds of roads, some more dangerous than others, and they are always crowded. When ISIS came, they were strategic about controlling the roads even before they took the cities, cutting off traffic and isolating people who would otherwise flee. Then they set up checkpoints, making it easy to catch anyone trying to leave. In much of Iraq, the paved highways are the only option for a citizen on the run. In the open plains and deserts, there are few places for people to hide. If the cities and towns are the vital organs of Iraq, the roads are the veins and arteries, and as soon as ISIS controlled them, they controlled who lived or died.

For a while I watched the landscape, which was a dry and desert-like flat plain of sand and rock, so unlike the parts of Sinjar I loved the most, where in springtime everything was covered with grass and flowers. I felt like I was in a foreign country, and in some ways, I guess I was—we weren't out of Islamic State territory yet. As I watched more closely, though, I noticed that the landscape wasn't monotonous at all. Rocks grew bigger until they became small cliffs and then shrank back into sand. Spiky plants appeared in the sand and sometimes grew into skinny trees. Occasionally I would see the teetering head of an oil pump or a small group of mud brick houses making up a village. I watched until carsickness took over and I could no longer look out the window.

I felt dizzy and reached for one of the plastic bags Nasser had given me before we left Mina's house. A moment later I threw up. My stomach had been mostly empty—I had been too nervous to eat breakfast—but the watery vomit filled the taxi with a sour odor that I could tell bothered the driver, who kept his window open until he could no longer tolerate the grit that blew in with the hot air. "Please tell your wife that next time she has to be sick, I can pull over," the driver told Nasser, not unkindly. "It smells terrible in here." Nasser nodded.

A few minutes later I asked him to pull over, and I got out. Cars sped by, creating a strong wind that inflated my abaya around my body like a balloon. I walked as far as I could away from the car—I didn't want the driver to be able to see my face—and lifted up my niqab. The vomit stung my throat and lips, and the smell of the petrol made me retch even more.

Nasser came to check on me. "Are you okay?" he asked. "Can we go, or do you need to stay here longer?" I could tell he was worried, both about me and about being stopped on the side of the road. Every once in a while an Islamic State military vehicle passed by, and I was sure that the sight of a vomiting girl, even one dressed in an abaya and niqab, would turn some heads.

"I'm okay," I told him, walking slowly back to the taxi. I felt weak and dehydrated. I had sweat through my layers of clothing, and I couldn't remember the last thing I had eaten. Back in the car, I sat in the middle seat and closed my eyes, hoping I could fall asleep.

We approached a small town, one built up just on the sides of the road. Stores selling snacks and busy mechanic's shops opened up directly onto the highway, waiting for customers to pull in. A cafeteria-style restaurant advertised typical Iraqi food like grilled meat and rice with tomato sauce. "Are you hungry?" the driver asked us, and Nasser nodded. He hadn't eaten breakfast. I didn't want to stop, but it wasn't up to me.

The restaurant was large and clean, with tiled floors and plastic-covered chairs. Families sat beside one another, but collapsible plastic partitions separated the men from the women, which was normal for more conservative parts of Iraq. I sat on one side of the partition while Nasser and the driver went to get food. "If I eat, I'll just throw up," I whispered to Nasser, but he insisted. "You'll get sicker if you don't eat," he said, and a minute later he came back with some lentil soup and bread, which he put down on the table in front of me before disappearing behind the partition.

I lifted my niqab just far enough from my face so that I could eat without getting the fabric dirty. The soup was delicious, made of lentils and onions like I would have in Kocho and spicier than I was used to, but I could only eat a few spoonfuls. I worried about having to stop along the road again if I got sick.

Because of the partition, I felt like I was alone. A group of women sat at the opposite end of the restaurant, far enough away that I couldn't hear what they were saying. They were dressed like me and ate slowly, methodically lifting their niqabs to take bites of kebab and bread. Men in long white dishdashas, who I assumed were with them, had taken seats on the other side of the partition from them; I saw them when we came in. They ate without talking, and so did we, and it was so quiet in the restaurant that I thought if I could hear the lift and fall of the women's veils, it would sound like someone breathing.

Two Islamic State militants walked toward us in the parking lot when we left. Their truck, one of the beige-painted military vehicles flying an Islamic State flag, was parked near our taxi. One of them had an injured leg, and he walked with a cane, and the other walked slowly beside him so that he could keep up. My heart stopped. Quickly, I dashed over to the other side of Nasser, putting him between me and the militants, but when we passed them, they didn't give us a second glance.

Across the street, an Islamic State police car sat with two police officers inside. Were they here for us? Had they dropped off a colleague who was patrolling the street for me and Nasser? At any moment I expected them to notice us coming out of the restaurant and to run toward us, pointing their guns at our heads. Maybe they wouldn't even bother to ask us questions. Maybe they would kill us right there in the parking lot.

I was scared of everyone. The men in the restaurant in the white dishdashas—were they ISIS? Were the women who were with them their wives or their sabaya? Did they love ISIS the way Morteja's mother had? Every person on the street, from the cigarette seller to the mechanic rolling out from underneath a car, was my enemy. The sounds of cars or kids buying candy were as terrifying as if a bomb had gone off. I rushed to get back in the car. I wanted to get to Kirkuk quickly, and I could tell by the way Nasser followed me that he, too, was anxious to go.

By now it was past noon, and the sun was even hotter. If I looked out the window, I instantly felt nauseous, but if I tried to close my eyes, the darkness behind them swirled and was dizzying. So I stared straight ahead at the back of Nasser's seat, thinking of nothing but myself and what might happen along the road. My fear was unrelenting. I knew we had more Islamic State checkpoints to go through, and after that the peshmerga. The phone Nasser gave me buzzed, and I saw that I had a text message from him.

"Your family has been messaging me," it said. "Sabah will wait for us in Erbil."

Sabah, my nephew, had been working in a hotel in the Kurdish capital when ISIS massacred Kocho's men. We planned on staying with him for a night or two before I made my way to Zakho, where Hezni was waiting. Assuming we made it that far.

At the third Islamic State checkpoint, they didn't ask us any questions, not even our names. They just glanced at our IDs and waved us through. Either the system for catching escaped sabaya wasn't in place yet or the militants were sloppier and less organized than they wanted people to believe.

From there we drove a little bit in silence. I think we were all tired. Nasser didn't send me any more text messages, and the driver stopped searching for radio stations and asking Nasser questions. He just looked straight ahead at the road, driving at a steady pace past the fields and pastures of northern Iraq, mopping sweat off his forehead with a handful of paper napkins until they were worn into small wet pieces.

I felt drained from fear and sickness, and I wondered if Nasser was getting nervous about crossing the Kurdish checkpoints, where the peshmerga were trained to be suspicious of Sunni men trying to enter Kurdistan. I had decided, after my conversation with Hezni, that I wouldn't leave Nasser in Islamic State territory, even if it meant going back to Mosul. I wanted to tell him not to worry, but I remembered my promise to stay quiet, and I wanted to save text messaging for emergencies, so I said nothing. I hoped at that point Nasser knew that I wasn't the kind of person who would leave friends in danger.

————

WE ARRIVED AT a crossroads with one sign pointing toward Kirkuk, and the driver stopped. "I can't take you any further," he said. "You have to walk to the checkpoint from here." Because he had Mosul license plates, he might be questioned and detained by the peshmerga.

"I'll wait here," he said to Nasser. "If they don't let you in, come back, and we will go back to Mosul together."

Nasser thanked him and paid him, and we collected our things from the car. We started walking in the direction of the checkpoint, the only people on the shoulder of the road. "Are you tired?" Nasser asked me, and I nodded. "I'm very tired," I said. I felt drained of everything, and I still wasn't hopeful that we were going to make it all the way. I couldn't help imagining the worst with every step I took—ISIS picking us up now, as we walked, or the peshmerga detaining Nasser. Kirkuk was a dangerous city, often the site of sectarian fighting even before the war with ISIS, and I imagined us getting through only to be caught in a car bomb or IED. We still had a long journey ahead of us.

"Let's just get to the checkpoint and see what happens," he told me. "Where is your family?" he asked.

"Zakho," I told him. "Near Duhok."

"How far is that from Kirkuk?" he asked, and I shook my head. "I don't know," I said. "Far." We walked in silence the rest of the way, side by side.

At the checkpoint, people lined up in cars and on foot to be interviewed by the peshmerga. Since the war with ISIS started, the Kurdistan Regional Government has taken in hundreds of thousands of displaced Iraqis, including a lot of Sunnis from Anbar Province and other Sunni-dominated areas that had become unlivable for anyone not aligned with ISIS. They didn't make it easy for them to get into Kurdistan, though. Most Sunni Arabs needed to have a Kurd sponsor them if they wanted to pass through the checkpoints, and the process could take a long time.

Because Kirkuk is not officially part of the autonomous Kurdish region and has a large Arab population, it is normally somewhat easier for non-Kurds to pass through its checkpoints than, say, the checkpoint into Erbil. Sunni Arab students go through once a week or every day to go to school in the city, and families go to shop or visit relatives. Kirkuk is very diverse—Turkmen and Christians live alongside Arabs and Kurds—and that has long been its charm and its curse.

After ISIS came to Iraq, the peshmerga raced to Kirkuk to secure the city, and its valuable oil fields, from the terrorists. They were the only military force in Iraq that was capable of protecting Kirkuk from the terrorists, but some people living there complained that they were like occupiers in their insistence that the city was Kurdish, not Arab or Turkmen. We didn't know whether it also meant that it would be harder for Nasser to pass through the checkpoint. Since we were coming from the Islamic State's capital in Iraq, they would be suspicious of our explanation that we were going to visit my family, and they might not let us in unless I admitted to being an escaped Yazidi sabiyya. I wasn't willing to do that, though, at least not yet.

Since the massacres in Sinjar, Yazidis had been welcomed into Kurdistan, where the government helped establish camps for the displaced. Some Yazidis were suspicious about the KRG's motives. "The Kurds want us to forgive them for abandoning us," those Yazidis said. "It's just about the bad press. The world watched Yazidis stranded on the mountain, and the KRG wants them to forget what they saw." Others thought that the KRG wanted to resettle Yazidis inside of Kurdistan rather than help them retake Sinjar, so that our numbers might strengthen their bid for independence from Iraq.

Whatever their motives, Yazidis needed the Kurdish government now. KRG camps were being built specifically for Yazidis near Duhok, and the KDP had established an office devoted to helping free Yazidi sabaya like me. Slowly the KRG was trying to repair its relationship with Yazidis and reestablish our trust in them, hoping that we would once again call ourselves Kurds and want to be a part of Kurdistan. But on that day I was not ready to forgive them. I didn't want them to think that, by letting me in, they were saving me when they could have kept my family from being torn apart before ISIS came to Sinjar.

Nasser turned to me. "Nadia," he said, "you can go and tell them you are Yazidi. Tell them who you are, and who I am. Speak to them in Kurdish." He knew that I would be let in instantly if I told them who I really was.

I shook my head. "No," I said. I felt angry seeing the peshmerga in their uniforms, carrying out their work at the Kirkuk checkpoint. They hadn't left Kirkuk, so why had they left us?

"Do you know how many of those men abandoned us in Sinjar?" I asked Nasser. I thought about all those Yazidis who had felt scared with ISIS nearby and had tried to cross into Kurdistan but were turned away. "Don't worry!" they were told at the KRG checkpoints. "The peshmerga will protect you, it's better for you to stay home." If they weren't going to fight to defend us, they should have let us into Kurdistan. Because of them, thousands of people were killed, kidnapped, and displaced.

"I won't tell them I'm Yazidi, and I won't speak Kurdish," I told him. "It won't change anything."

"You have to relax," Nasser said. "You need them now. Be practical."

"There's no way!" I said, almost shouting. "I'm not going to do anything that lets them know I need them." After that, Nasser didn't say anything more about it.

At the checkpoint, the soldier examined our IDs and looked us over. I didn't say a word to them and still spoke to Nasser in Arabic. "Open your bag," the soldier said, and Nasser took it from me and opened it for the peshmerga. They spent a lot of time rummaging through my things, lifting up the dresses and examining the bottles of shampoo and conditioner. I was relieved that they didn't look inside the box of maxi pads, where I still had the jewelry carefully hidden away.

"Where are you going?" they asked us.

"We are staying in Kirkuk," Nasser said. "With my wife's family."

"Who is taking you there?" they asked.

"A taxi," Nasser said. "We'll find one on the other side of the checkpoint."

"Okay," he said, pointing to a large crowd of people standing in a loose crowd by the small checkpoint offices. "Go stand over there and wait."

We stood with the others in the hot sun, waiting for the peshmerga to let us into Kirkuk. Whole families huddled together, carrying huge suitcases and clear plastic bags full of blankets. Old people sat on their things, the women fanning their faces and groaning quietly about the heat. Cars were piled so high with furniture and mattresses that they looked like they might collapse from the weight. I saw a young boy carrying a soccer ball and an old man with a yellow bird in a cage as though those things were the most important things in the world. We were all from different places, of different ages and different religions, but waiting together, unsure and scared, at the Kirkuk checkpoint, we were all the same. We wanted the same things—safety, security, to find our families—and we were running from the same terrorists. *This is what it means to be Iraqi under ISIS*, I thought. *We are homeless. Living at checkpoints until we live at refugee camps.*

Finally a soldier called us over. I spoke to him in Arabic. "I'm from Kirkuk, but I live in Mosul now, with my husband," I said, gesturing to Nasser. "We are going to see my family."

"What are you taking with you?" they asked.

"Just some clothes for the week," I said. "Some shampoo, some personal things . . ." My voice trailed off, and my heart was beating fast. If they turned us away, I didn't know what we would do. Nasser might have to go back to Mosul. We looked at each other nervously.

"Are you carrying any weapons?" they asked Nasser. He said no, but they searched him anyway. Next they scrolled through his phone, looking for photos or videos that might suggest he was with ISIS. They left me alone and didn't ask to look at the phone Nasser had given me.

After a while, the soldier handed us our things back and shook his head. "Sorry, we can't let you in," he said. He wasn't cruel, but he was very efficient. "Every visitor to Kurdistan needs to have someone sponsor them. Otherwise we don't know who you are, really."

"We have to call my father's friend in Sinjar," Nasser said to me when the soldier had left. "He has connections and he can tell them that we should be let in. They will listen to him."

"Fine," I said. "Just as long as he doesn't tell them that I am Yazidi and that you are helping me escape."

Nasser made the call and handed the phone to the soldier, who spoke into it briefly. He looked surprised and a little annoyed. "You should have just called him from the beginning," he told us, giving Nasser back the phone. "You can go."

On the other side, I immediately took off my niqab. The evening breeze felt good on my face, and I smiled. "What, you didn't like wearing it?" Nasser teased, smiling back at me.

Chapter 6

WHEN THE TAXI DRIVER, A BUBBLY KURDISH MAN IN HIS midforties, asked us where we wanted to go, Nasser and I looked at each other blankly. "Take us to Kurdistan," Nasser said, and the driver laughed. "You are in Kurdistan!" he replied, then tried again. "What city do you want to go to? Erbil? Sulaymaniyah?"

Nasser and I laughed. Neither of us knew the geography of Kurdistan. "Which is closest?" Nasser asked him.

"Sulaymaniyah," the driver answered.

"Sulaymaniyah, then," we said. We were exhausted and relieved, and as we settled in for the drive, we forgot to call Sabah, my nephew, as Hezni had told us to.

It was getting dark. From the ring road, all I could see of Kirkuk was the glow of the houses and streetlights from afar. When I was younger, we watched Kurds celebrate Newroz, their New Year, on TV, dancing in huge groups around bonfires and grilling piles of meat on the sides of green mountains. I would say somewhat bitterly, "Look at how great life is in Kurdistan, while we are living in these poor villages," and my mother would scold me. "They deserve good lives, Nadia," she would say. "They went through a genocide under Saddam, you know."

I was a stranger in Kurdistan. I didn't know what the towns

were called or what the people who lived there were like. I had no friends in Kirkuk or Sulaymaniyah, and even though Sabah worked in a hotel in Erbil and Saoud had worked on construction sites near Duhok, they were more like the Bangladeshi or Indian laborers who came to Kurdistan for a paycheck, and they hadn't made Erbil or Duhok their home. Maybe I was a stranger in all of Iraq. I could never go back to Mosul, where I had been tortured. I had never been to Baghdad or Tikrit or Najaf. I had never seen the great museums or ancient ruins. In all of Iraq, all I really knew was Kocho, and now that belonged to ISIS.

Our driver was a proud Kurd, pointing out sites along the way in a happy mixture of Kurdish and Arabic and trying to strike up a conversation with Nasser about life in Mosul. "The whole city is taken over by Daesh?" he asked, shaking his head.

"Yes," Nasser replied. "A lot of people want to get out, but it's hard."

"The peshmerga will run them out of Iraq!" our driver declared. Nasser said nothing.

I was more relaxed in the taxi. There was a chance that Nasser would get interrogated at the next checkpoint, which separated the disputed territory from true Kurdistan, but we had Hisham's friend from Sinjar on our side. Clearly, he had some authority. At least I was no longer looking over my shoulder for Islamic State cars and worrying that the people around me were secretly terrorists.

"See those buildings, close to the mountains?" the driver asked us, pointing his thin fingers at Nasser's window. To our right, massive housing developments were being built in the shadows of Iraq's eastern mountains. Huge billboards proudly advertised the project, with mock-ups of the finished neighborhood. "When they're finished, they will look like American apartment buildings," our driver said. "Very new, very beautiful. Wonderful things are happening in Kurdistan."

"What is your wife's name?" the driver asked, looking at me in his rearview mirror.

"Sousan," Nasser replied, still using the name on my ID.

"Sousan!" the driver said. "What a pretty name. I'll call you Su Su," he said, smiling at me. After that, whenever he pointed something out, he made sure he had my attention. "Su Su! Do you see that lake out there? It's so beautiful in the springtime," or "Su Su, that town we just passed? That place has the best ice cream you have ever tasted."

I remember that drive and wonder if Sinjar could ever do what Kurdistan had, recover from genocide to become even better than it was before. I longed to believe it could, but I had to admit it seemed unlikely. Sinjar is not like Kurdistan, where the population is almost all Kurdish and where the enemy, Saddam's army, came from the outside. In Sinjar, Yazidis and Arabs all live together. We rely on one another for trade, and we pass through one another's towns. We tried to be friends, but our enemy built itself up inside Sinjar, like a disease aimed at killing anything it came into contact with. Even if the Americans and others helped us the way they did after Saddam attacked the Kurds—Yazidis couldn't offer them much in return, so they probably wouldn't—how could we go back to our old lives and live among Arabs again?

"Su Su!" The driver was trying to get my attention again. "Do you like to picnic?" I nodded my head. "Of course you do! Well, you should come here, to the mountains outside Sulaymaniyah for a picnic. You won't believe how beautiful it is in the springtime." I nodded again.

Later Nasser and I would laugh at the driver and the nickname he'd given me. "We didn't let Daesh take you," Nasser said. "But if we'd stayed longer with him, he wouldn't have let you go."

———

WE ARRIVED IN Sulaymaniyah at close to four in the morning, when everything, including the garage where we would need to get a taxi to Erbil, was closed. As we neared the checkpoint, the driver told us not to worry. "I know these guys," he said, and sure enough, after a few words in Kurdish, they waved us through.

"Where should I take you?" the driver asked, but we shook our heads.

"Just take us close to the garage," Nasser said.

"It's closed now," the driver replied. He was kind, and he worried for us.

"That's fine," Nasser said. "We will wait."

The driver pulled over, and Nasser paid him. "Su Su, good luck!" he said, and drove away.

We sat down outside a supermarket near the garage and leaned against the wall. The street was empty, and the whole city was quiet. Tall buildings, their windows dark, loomed over us. One of them was shaped like a sail and lit up bright blue; I later learned it was modeled after a building in Dubai. A soothing breeze blew over us, and the sight of the mountains, which encircle Sulaymaniyah like a necklace, was familiar and comforting. I needed to find a restroom, but I was too shy to tell Nasser, and so we just sat there, exhausted, waiting for the shops to open so we could eat something.

"You've never been here before?" Nasser asked.

"No," I said. "But I knew that it was a beautiful place." I told him about the Newroz celebrations I had watched on TV, but I didn't bring up Saddam or Anfal. "There is a lot of water here, and things stay green much longer," I told him. "There are parks with games and rides for kids. Iranians cross the border just to walk around in the park. And the mountains remind me of home."

"Where will we go tomorrow?" I asked Nasser.

"We'll get a taxi to Erbil," he said. "And meet your nephew at his hotel. Then you will go to Zakho to be with Hezni."

"Without you?" I asked, and he nodded. I felt sorry for him. "I wish your family could come to Kurdistan. I wish you didn't have to live under Daesh."

"I don't know how that could happen," Nasser said. "Maybe one day." He seemed very sad.

My body ached from sitting in cars for so long, and so did my feet from the walk to the first Kurdish checkpoint. Eventually we both fell asleep, but not for long. An hour or two later the sound of morning traffic and the soft light of the dawn sun woke us up. Nasser turned to me. He was happy that I had slept. "The sun rose on you without fear this morning," he said.

"It's a morning without fear," I replied. "It's beautiful here."

Our stomachs were empty. "Let's get something to eat," Nasser suggested, and we walked a short distance to a shop where we bought sandwiches made of eggs and fried eggplant. They were not very good, but I was so hungry I ate my sandwich quickly. I no longer felt like I might throw up.

In the restaurant bathroom, I took off my abaya and Kathrine's dress, which both smelled terrible from sweat, and swiped some wet towels underneath my armpits and across my neck. Then I changed into a pair of pants and a shirt from my bag. I was careful not to look in the mirror. I hadn't seen my reflection since that morning in Hamdaniya, and I was scared to see how I might look. Folding up Kathrine's dress, I carefully put it back inside. *I'll keep it until she is free, and then I'll give it back to her,* I thought. I got ready to throw my abaya into the garbage, but stopped at the last moment, deciding to keep it as evidence of what ISIS had done to me.

Outside, the streets started to fill with people on their way to work and school. Cars honked as the traffic thickened, and stores pulled up metal grates and opened their doors. Sunlight reflected off the sail-shaped skyscraper, which I could see now was covered in a bluish glass and had a round observatory on the top. Every bit of life made the city look more beautiful. No one looked at us, and I didn't fear anyone.

We called Sabah. "I'll come to Sulaymaniyah to get you," he offered, but Nasser and I said no. "There's no need," I said. "We'll come to you."

At first Nasser wanted me to go to Erbil alone. "You don't need me anymore," he said, but I argued with him until he agreed to come along. My old stubbornness was back, and I wasn't ready to say goodbye to him yet. "We will come to Erbil together," I told Sabah. "I want you to meet the man who helped me escape."

———

THE SULAYMANIYAH GARAGE was busy that morning while we waited for a taxi to take us to Erbil. Already four drivers had turned us down. They didn't tell us why, but we suspected it was because we had come from Mosul and because Nasser was an Arab. One by one the drivers would ask for our IDs and look them over, glancing at us, then back at the IDs, then back at us. "You want to go to Erbil?" they would ask, and we nodded.

"Why?" they wanted to know.

"To see family," we told them, but they just sighed and handed us our IDs back. "Sorry," they said. "I'm booked. Try someone else."

"They're scared because we are from Mosul," Nasser said.

"Who can blame them?" I said. "They are scared of Daesh."

"You still won't speak Kurdish?" Nasser asked, and I shook my head no. I wasn't ready to show them who I really was. We weren't in real trouble yet.

We sat there in silence as the sun got hotter, becoming more worried about finding a driver who would take us to Erbil. Finally a driver agreed, but since we were the first passengers, we would have to wait until he filled up his car. "Sit over there," he said, pointing to the sidewalk, where a large crowd had already gathered in small bits of shade, waiting for their drivers to tell them they were ready.

As the garage filled, I scanned the crowds. No one looked at us. I wasn't scared anymore, but I didn't have the feeling of relief I thought I would have. All I could think about was what life would be like when I finally made it to Zakho. So much of my family was dead or missing, and I wasn't going home, I was going back to all the holes left by the people I lost. I felt happy and empty at the same time, and I was grateful that Nasser was there to talk to.

"What if Daesh came into this garage right now?" I asked Nasser. "What do you think would happen?"

"Everyone would be frightened," he said. I imagined a militant dressed in all black, carrying an automatic rifle into this crowd of distracted, busy people.

"But who do you think he would try to get first?" I said. "Who would be worth more—me, the escaped sabiyya? Or you, a Sunni who left Mosul and who helped me escape?"

Nasser laughed. "It sounds like a riddle," he said.

"Well, I know the answer," I said. "He would get both of us. We would both be dead." And we laughed, just for a moment.

Chapter 7

KURDISTAN IS TECHNICALLY ONE TERRITORY CONSISTING OF distinct governorates. Until recently there were only three—Duhok, Erbil, and Sulaymaniyah—but in 2014 the KRG made Halabja, which was the biggest target during the Anfal campaign, a governorate as well.

In spite of all the talk about an independent Kurdistan and the emphasis on Kurdish identity, the provinces can feel very different from one another and very, very divided. The major political parties—Barzani's KDP, Talabani's PUK (Patriotic Union of Kurdistan), the newer Gorran Party, and a coalition of three Islamist parties—split the region's loyalty, and the division between the KDP and PUK is particularly noticeable. In the mid-1990s, people and peshmerga loyal to the two parties fought a civil war. Kurds don't like to talk about it because if they have any hope of becoming independent from Iraq, they have to be united, but it was a terrible war and left lasting scars. Some hoped that the fight against ISIS would unify Kurds, but when you travel through the region, you can still feel like you are moving between countries. Both parties have their own peshmerga and their own security and intelligence forces, called *asayish*.

Sulaymaniyah, which borders Iran, is the home of the PUK and the Talabani family. It's considered more liberal than Erbil, which is KDP territory. The PUK areas are influenced by Iran, while the KDP is in an alliance with Turkey. Kurdish politics are very complex. After I was freed and began doing human rights work, I started to see how something like the failure in Sinjar could have happened.

The first checkpoint on our way to Erbil was manned by peshmerga and asayish loyal to the PUK. After looking at our IDs, they told the taxi driver to pull over to the side and wait.

We were sharing the taxi with a young man and woman, who may have been a couple. The girl seemed startled when she heard Nasser and I speaking Arabic to each other. "Do you speak Kurdish, too?" she asked me, and when she was satisfied that I did, she seemed to relax. I sat in the back with them, and Nasser took the front. Both of the other passengers were from Kurdistan, and it was clear that we had been pulled over because Nasser and I had IDs from outside the region. The girl sighed impatiently when the officer told the driver to wait, flicking her ID against her hand and looking out the window, trying to see what was taking so long. I glared at her.

The peshmerga pointed to me and Nasser. "You two, come with us," he said. "You may as well go," he told the driver, and we grabbed our things before the taxi took off down the road. As we followed the soldier back to the offices, I suddenly felt scared again. I hadn't expected to encounter so much trouble once we were inside Kurdistan, but it was clear that, as long as I insisted on pretending to be Sousan from Kirkuk, traveling through Kurdistan was not going to be easy. If they suspected us of being Islamic State sympathizers, or if they simply doubted our connections in Erbil, they could easily turn us away.

Inside the office, the soldier started asking us questions. "Who are you?" he wanted to know. "Why are you going to Erbil when one ID says Mosul and the other says Kirkuk?" He was particularly suspicious of Nasser, who was the right age to be an Islamic State fighter.

We were exhausted. All I wanted was to make it to Erbil and see Sabah. I realized that the only way this was going to happen was if I stopped pretending and admitted who I really was. "Enough is enough," I told Nasser. "I'll tell them."

And then I addressed the soldier in Kurdish.

"I'm Nadia," I said. "I'm a Yazidi from Kocho. My ID is a fake. I got it in Mosul, where I was held captive by Daesh." I pointed to Nasser. "This man helped me escape."

The soldier was stunned. He stared at the two of us, and once he had recovered, he said, "You need to tell your story to the asayish. Follow me."

He made a phone call and then took us to a building nearby that served as the security headquarters for the asayish, where a group of officers waited for us in a large meeting room. Chairs were arranged for me and Nasser at the head of a large table, and a video camera, set up on the table, pointed to those two chairs. When Nasser saw the camera, he immediately shook his head. "No," he said to me in Arabic. "I can't be on film. No one can know what I look like."

I turned to the officers. "Nasser has taken a huge risk coming with me, and his whole family are still in Mosul," I told them. "If anyone knows who he is, he could be hurt, or his family could. Besides, why do you want to tape this? Who will see it?" I was also agitated that the PUK asayish wanted to film the interview—I wasn't ready to recall my experience in Mosul for an audience.

"It's just for our records, and we will blur Nasser's face anyway," they said. "We swear on the Koran no one will ever see this but us and our bosses."

When it became clear that they wouldn't let us pass until we told them our story we agreed. "Just as long as you swear that no one will be able to identify Nasser and that only the peshmerga and asayish will see this video," I said. "Of course, of course," they said, and we started. The interview lasted hours.

A high-ranking officer asked the questions. "You are a Yazidi from Kocho?" he asked.

"Yes," I said. "I am a Yazidi girl from the Kocho village in Sinjar. We were at the village when the peshmerga left. Daesh wrote on our school: 'This village belongs to Dawlat al-Islamiya.'" I explained how we had been forced into the school and the women and girls taken to Solagh and then to Mosul.

"How long were you in Mosul?" he asked.

"I'm not sure exactly," I told him. "We were held in dark rooms and it was hard to know how much time passed in each place." The asayish knew what had happened in Sinjar, that the Yazidi men had been killed and the girls taken to Mosul and after that distributed across Iraq. But they wanted to know the details of my story—in particular, what exactly had happened to me in captivity and how Nasser had helped me to escape. Nasser whispered to me, in Arabic, to be careful talking about both topics. When it came to his family, he told me, "Don't say that when you came to the home it was evening and we were sitting outside. Say it was midnight. Otherwise they will think that because we were sitting, just relaxing in our garden, we were with Daesh." I told him not to worry.

When it came to the rape, although the PUK officials pressed me for details, I refused to admit that it had happened. My family loved me, but until I saw them, I honestly didn't know how they, or the Yazidi community in general, would react when I returned if they knew that I was no longer a virgin. I remembered how Hajji Salman would whisper to me, just after he had raped me, that if I escaped, my family would kill me the moment they saw me. "You are ruined," he said. "No one will marry you, no one will love you. Your family doesn't want you anymore." Even Nasser worried about delivering me back to my family, and how they might react when they discovered that I had been raped. "Nadia, they are filming—I don't trust them," he whispered to me in the

PUK office. "You should wait to see how your family treats you. Maybe they will kill you if they find out." It was painful to have these doubts about the people who raised you, but Yazidis are conservative, sex before marriage is not allowed, and no one could have predicted this happening to so many Yazidi girls all at once. A situation like this would test any community, no matter how loving and no matter how strong.

One of the officers gave us a little water and some food. I was anxious to leave. "We are supposed to meet my family in Zakho," I said. "It's getting late."

"This is a very important case," they told me. "PUK officials will want to know the details of how you were taken and how you got out." They were particularly interested in hearing how the KDP peshmerga had left us. I told them about that and about how militants came to the slave market, choosing the most beautiful girls first, but when it came to my captivity I lied.

"Who took you?" the interviewer asked.

"One enormous guy chose me and said you are going to be mine," I said, shaking just thinking about Salwan. "I said no. I stayed in the center until one day I saw there were no guards and I was able to run away."

Then it was Nasser's turn to talk.

"It was around twelve-thirty or one o'clock in the morning when we heard knocking on the door," he said. He slouched a little in his seat and in his striped T-shirt looked younger than he was. "We were so afraid it was Daesh and they would have weapons." He described me, a scared girl, and how they made me an ID and he pretended to be my husband to get me out of Mosul.

The PUK peshmerga and asayish were very happy with Nasser. They thanked him and treated him like a hero, asking him what life was like under ISIS and declaring, "Our peshmerga will fight the terrorists until they are all gone from Iraq." They were proud that Kurdistan was a safe haven for people fleeing Mosul, and they were happy to remind us that it was not forces loyal to the PUK who had abandoned Sinjar.

"There are thousands of girls like Nadia in Mosul," Nasser told them. "Nadia was one of them and I brought her here." It was close to four in the afternoon by the time we finished the interview.

"Where are you planning to go now?" the officer asked.

"To the camp near Duhok," I said. "But first to see my nephew in Erbil."

"Who is in Duhok?" the officer asked. "We don't want to let you go into a dangerous situation."

I gave him the number of Walid, my half brother who had joined the peshmerga after the massacres, along with many other Yazidi men, eager to fight and desperate for a salary. I figured they would trust a fellow soldier, but it only made the PUK officer more wary. "Walid is a KDP peshmerga?" the officer asked, after he hung up the phone. "If he is, you shouldn't be going with him," he replied. "You know, they left you unprotected."

I didn't say anything. Already, even without knowing a lot about Kurdish politics, I sensed that it wouldn't be smart to take sides. "You should have talked about that more in the interview," the officer said. "The world should know that the KDP peshmerga left you to die.

"I can help you if you stay," he continued. "Do you even have enough money to go home?"

We argued for a moment, the officer insisting I would be safer in PUK territory and me telling him that I needed to go. Eventually he saw that there was no way to convince me. "I want to be with my family, KDP or not," I said. "I haven't seen them for weeks."

"Fine," he said at last, and handed Nasser a piece of paper. "Take this with you the rest of the way. Don't use your IDs at checkpoints—use this. They will let you pass."

They hired a taxi to take us the rest of the way to Erbil, paying him in advance, and thanked us for staying so long. Nasser and I didn't say anything when we got in the taxi, but I could tell he was just as relieved as I was to be past the checkpoint.

At every checkpoint after that, we showed the paper and were immediately let through. I slouched down into the seat, wanting to sleep a little bit before we met Sabah in Erbil. The landscape at this point was greener than before, and the farms and pastures were well kept because they hadn't been abandoned. Small farming villages, similar to Kocho with their mud brick homes and tractors, gave way to larger towns, which gave way to cities, some of which had grand-looking buildings and mosques, bigger than anything in Sinjar. It felt safe in the taxi. Even the air, when I opened the window, was cooler and more refreshing.

It wasn't long before Nasser's phone buzzed. "It's Sabah," he told me, and then he cursed. "He has seen our interview! They shared it after all."

Sabah called, and Nasser handed the phone to me. My nephew was furious. "Why did you do this interview?" he asked me. "You should have waited."

"They said they weren't going to share it," I told him. "They promised." I felt sick with anger, worrying that I had exposed Nasser and his family to ISIS and that right at that moment militants were knocking on Hisham and Mina's doors, ready to punish them. Nasser knew a lot of Islamic State militants, and they knew him as well. Even with his face blurred (at least the PUK asayish had kept that promise), they might be able to identify him. I couldn't believe that my story, which until that moment was something so private that only a few people I trusted knew, was now on the news. I was so afraid.

"This is the life of Nasser's family, and ours!" Sabah went on. "Why would they do that!"

I froze in my seat, close to sobbing. I didn't know what to

say. The video seemed like the ultimate betrayal of Nasser, and I hated the PUK asayish for giving it to the news, no doubt to make themselves look better than the KDP, who they insisted had abandoned the Yazidis. "I wish I was dead in Mosul rather than here with this video public," I told him, and I meant it. The PUK had used us.

That video haunted me for a long time. My brothers were angry that I had put my face out there and identified our family, and Nasser was worried about his safety. Hezni said, "How horrible it will be for us to have to call Hisham and tell him that because he helped you, his son is dead." They were angry that I had criticized the KDP peshmerga on camera. After all, the refugee camps for Yazidis were being set up in KDP territory; we were dependent on them again. I was quickly learning that my story, which I still thought of as a personal tragedy, could be someone else's political tool, particularly in a place like Iraq. I would have to be careful what I said, because words mean different things to different people, and your story can easily become a weapon to be turned on you.

Chapter 8

THE PUK PAPERS STOPPED WORKING AT THE CHECKPOINT outside Erbil. That checkpoint was big, with lines of cars separated by concrete blast walls in case of suicide bombers and decorated with photos of Masoud Barzani. This time neither of us was surprised when a peshmerga ordered us out of the taxi, and we followed him to his supervisor's office, which was just one small room. At the end of the room, the commander sat behind a wooden desk. There was no camera and no crowd, but before we started, I called Sabah, who had been texting asking what was taking so long, to give him directions to the checkpoint. We didn't know how long the interview would last.

The commander asked the same questions as the PUK security, and I answered them all, once again leaving out the rape and any details about Nasser's family. This time I was also careful not to say anything bad about the KDP peshmerga. He wrote down everything I said, and when we finished, he smiled and stood up.

"What you've done will not be forgotten," he told Nasser, kissing him on both cheeks. "Allah loves what you have done."

Nasser's expression never changed. "I didn't do this alone. My whole family risked their lives to get us to Kurdistan," he said. "Anyone who had a bit of human kindness in them would have done the same thing."

They confiscated my fake Mosul ID, but Nasser kept his. Then the door opened, and Sabah walked in.

So many of the men in my family were fighters—my father and the trail of heroic stories he left behind after his death; Jalo fighting alongside the Americans in Tal Afar; Saeed, who had been eager to prove his bravery since he was a little boy, dragging himself out of the mass grave with bullets in his legs and arm. Sabah, though, was a student and only two years older than me. He worked at the hotel in Erbil because he wanted to make enough money to one day go to university and get a good job and have a better life than as a farmer or a shepherd. Before ISIS came to Sinjar, that was how he fought.

The genocide changed everyone. Hezni dedicated his life to assisting smugglers in freeing sabaya. Saeed lived in the nightmare of the day he survived and became obsessed with fighting. Saoud passed his days in the monotony of the refugee camp, trying to cope with his survivor's guilt. Malik, poor Malik, who was just a young boy when the genocide started, had become a terrorist, sacrificing his whole life and even his love for his mother to ISIS.

Sabah, who never wanted to be a soldier or a police officer, left the hotel in Erbil and his school and went to Mount Sinjar to fight. He had always been shy and slow to show his feelings, but now that was coupled with a kind of manliness that hadn't been there before. When I hugged him at the checkpoint and started weeping, he told me to be calm. "There are officers here, Nadia. We shouldn't cry in front of them," he said. "You've seen so much, and you are safe now. You shouldn't cry." He had grown years in weeks; I supposed we all had.

I tried to collect myself. "Which one is Nasser?" Sabah asked, and I pointed to him. They shook hands. "We should go to the hotel," Sabah said. "There are some other Yazidis staying there.

Nasser, you'll stay with me, and Nadia, you can stay with some women in another room."

We drove a short distance from the checkpoint to the center of the city. Erbil is shaped like a big, uneven circle, with the roads and houses spreading out from an ancient citadel that some archaeologists say is the oldest continuously inhabited place in the world. Its high, sand-colored walls can be seen from much of the city, and they contrast with the rest of Erbil, which is new and modern. Erbil's roads are crowded with white SUVs, driving fast with few rules to slow them down, and malls and hotels line the streets, new ones always in the process of being built. When we arrived, a lot of those construction sites had been turned into makeshift refugee camps while the KRG figured out how to deal with the huge number of Iraqis and Syrians fleeing to the region.

We pulled up to the hotel, a small and nondescript place with some dark-colored couches. The windows were covered with gauzy curtains and the floors tiled with a shiny gray material. A few Yazidi men sat inside the lobby, and they said hello to me, but I wanted to sleep, and Sabah showed me to the room. Inside I found a family, an old woman with her son, who also worked in the hotel, and his wife. They were sitting together at a small table eating soup, rice, and vegetables from the hotel restaurant. When the woman saw me, she gestured to me. "Come sit," she said. "Eat with us."

She was about my mother's age and, like my mother, wore a flowing white dress and white headscarf. Seeing her, all the restraint I had tried to practice since leaving the Islamic State house in Mosul left me. I went crazy. I screamed with my entire body, and I could barely stand up. I cried for my mother, whose fate I didn't know yet. I cried for my brothers, whom I had seen being driven to their deaths, and for the ones who survived and who would have to live the rest of their lives trying to pick up the pieces of our family. I cried for Kathrine and Walaa and my sisters who were still in captivity. I cried because I had made it out and didn't think that I deserved to be so lucky; then again, I wasn't sure I was lucky at all.

The woman came to me and held me. Her body was soft like my mother's. When I had calmed down a little bit, I noticed that she was crying, too, and so were her son- and daughter-in-law. "Be patient," she told me. "Hopefully everyone you love will come back. Don't be so hard on yourself."

I sat down with them at the table. My body felt like it was made out of nothing, like I could float away at any moment. Just because they insisted, I ate a little bit of the soup. The woman looked very old, older than her age, and almost all her white hair had fallen out. Her skull, a delicate pink speckled with brown, was visible beneath what was left. She was from Tel Ezeir, and her recent life was a long tragedy. "I had three sons, all of them unmarried, die in 2007 in the bombings," she told me. "I told myself when they died that I wouldn't bathe until I saw their bodies. I wash my face and clean my hands. But I haven't taken a bath. I don't want to be clean until I can clean their bodies for burial."

She saw how tired I was. "Daughter," she said, "go to sleep." I lay down in her bed and closed my eyes, but I couldn't sleep. All I could think about were her three sons, their missing bodies, and my mother. "I left my mother in Solagh," I told her. "I don't know what happened to her." I began to cry again. The entire night, with her next to me in bed, we cried, and in the morning after I had put on Kathrine's dress, I kissed her on both cheeks.

"I used to think that what happened to my sons was the worst thing a mother could bear," she said. "I wished all the time for them to be alive again. But I am glad they didn't live to see what happened to us in Sinjar." She straightened her white scarf over what remained of her hair. "God willing, your mother will come back to you one day," she said. "Leave everything to God. We Yazidis don't have anyone or anything except God."

———

DOWNSTAIRS IN THE hotel lobby, I saw a familiar-looking boy and went over to him. It was the brother of a friend from Kocho. "Do you know what happened to her?" he asked.

The last time I saw his sister was in Mosul at the market where I first was taken by Hajji Salman. When Rojian and I left, she had not been selected by anyone yet, but I assumed she had been soon after. "One day, hopefully, she will be safe, too," I said. I was learning that for a lot of Yazidis in Kurdistan, I would be the messenger of bad news.

"She hasn't even made a phone call," he said.

"It's not easy to make phone calls," I told him. "They don't want us to have phones or to reach anyone. I didn't call Hezni until I escaped."

Sabah came into the lobby and told me that it was time for me to go to Zakho. "Nasser is in that room," he said, pointing to an open door down the hallway. "Go say goodbye to him."

I walked to the room and pushed open the door. Nasser was standing in the middle, and the moment I saw him, I began to cry. I felt pity for him. When I was with his family, I had felt like a stranger walking through someone else's life. My hope for my future began and ended with my escape, and here I was in Erbil, reunited with my nephew and other Yazidis. Nasser, though, had to retrace our terrifying journey and go back to the Islamic State. It was my turn to fear for him.

Nasser began to cry as well. Sabah was standing in the doorway watching us. "Sabah, could I talk to Nadia for two minutes?" he asked. "After that I will have to go." Sabah nodded and left.

Nasser turned to me, a serious expression on his face. "Nadia, you're with Sabah now, and you'll be going to join the rest of your family. There's no need for me to come. But I need to ask you something. Do you feel safe? If you are scared at all that something is going to happen to you or that they will do anything to you because you were a sabiyya, I'll stay with you."

"No, Nasser," I said. "You saw the way Sabah treated me. I'll be fine." In truth, I wasn't completely sure, but I wanted Nasser to find his own way. I still felt extremely guilty because of the PUK video, and I wasn't sure how much time he had before someone recognized him. "Don't believe anything Daesh said about Yazidis," I told him. "I'm crying for you, because you did this for me. You saved my life."

"It was my duty," he said. "That's all."

We left the room together. I couldn't find the words to tell him how grateful I was that he had helped me. For the past two days, we had shared every frightening and every sad moment, every worried glance and every terrifying question. When I felt sick, he had comforted me, and at every checkpoint, his calm had helped keep me from collapsing altogether from fear. I'll never forget what he and his family did for me.

I don't know why he was good and so many others in Mosul were so terrible. I think that if you are a good person, deep down, then you can be born and raised in Islamic State headquarters and still be good, just like you can be forced to convert to a religion you don't believe in and still be a Yazidi. It's inside you. "Be careful," I told him. "Take care of yourself, and stay as far away from those criminals as you can. Here, take Hezni's number." I handed him a slip of paper with Hezni's cell phone number, along with money for the taxi his family had paid for. "You can call Hezni anytime. I will never forget what you did for me. You saved my life."

"I wish you a happy life, Nadia," he said. "A good life from now on, going forward. My family will try to help others like you. If there are other girls in Mosul who want to escape, they can call us, and we'll try to help them.

"Maybe one day, after all the girls are freed and Daesh is gone from Iraq, we will meet again and talk about this," Nasser said. Then he laughed quietly. "How is everything, Nadia?" he said.

"It's hot," I replied, smiling a little bit.

"Never forget," Nasser said, teasing me. "It's very hot, Nasser, it's very hot."

Then, the smile leaving his face, he said, "God be with you, Nadia."

"God be with you, Nasser," I replied. And as he turned and walked toward the exit, I prayed to Tawusi Melek that he and his family would end up somewhere safe. Before I had finished my prayer, he was gone.

Chapter 9

AFTER NASSER LEFT ERBIL, I TRIED TO FOLLOW WHAT HAP-
pened to him and his family. I felt sick with shame when I
thought about the PUK video, and prayed that it wouldn't put
them in danger. He was just a kid from a poor neighborhood,
but Hezni and I worried that it was only a matter of time before he became entangled with the terrorists. For years ISIS had
been planting roots in the city, preying on the discontent among
Sunnis and the instability in the country. Men there had hoped
that the terrorists would be like the Baathists and give them their
power back. Even if they became disillusioned by ISIS, by the
time Nasser returned from Kurdistan, boys had grown into soldiers and, worse, into true believers. Had Mina's sons managed to
escape the battlefield? I still don't know.

Hezni was really worried about something happening to them.
"They helped you," he said. "How can we cope if they were punished because of it?" He took his responsibility as head of our family very seriously. Of course, there was nothing he could do from
Zakho or, later, from the refugee camp. Hezni spoke to Hisham
and Nasser a couple of times, and then one afternoon he called
and a voice on the line told him the number had been discon-
nected. After that, Hezni had to rely on secondhand information
about Nasser and his family. One day we got news that ISIS had,
in fact, found out that Nasser had helped me and arrested Basheer

and Hisham but that the men had convinced the militants that Nasser had acted alone.

The family was still in Mosul in 2017 when Iraqi forces began to liberate the city, and it became even harder to get information. Hezni heard through others that one of Nasser's brothers was killed in 2017 during the battle between ISIS and Iraqi forces for control of the road connecting Mosul and Wadi Hajar, but we don't know how or if it's true. The family lived in East Mosul, which was the first part of the city liberated that year, and they could have escaped or they could have died in the fight. I heard that ISIS was using people as human shields when the Iraqi forces came in, making sure that civilians were with them in the buildings that the Americans wanted to bomb. People fleeing Mosul described living in hell. All we could do was pray they were safe.

Before going to my aunt's house in Zakho, where Hezni had been staying since ISIS came to Sinjar, we stopped at the hospital in Duhok where Saeed and Khaled were still recovering from their wounds. The refugee camp wasn't finished yet, and the Yazidis who had fled to Iraqi Kurdistan were sleeping wherever they could. On the outskirts of the city, Yazidi families filled unfinished apartment buildings, pitching tents given to them by aid agencies on the concrete floors. The walls hadn't been finished yet on the high buildings, and I worried, passing them, about the safety of the families inside. A few times small children did fall out of the upper stories. But they had nowhere else to go. All of Sinjar had been packed into these bare buildings, and they had nothing of their own. When aid agencies brought food to distribute, people sprinted and pushed through the crowd to try to make sure they received a bag. Mothers ran as fast as their legs would carry them for just one can of milk.

Hezni, Saoud, Walid, and my aunt were waiting for me at the hospital. When we saw one another, we all burst into tears and hugged, asking question after question until the commotion died down and we were able to hear what people were saying. I told them briefly what had happened to me, leaving out the rape. My aunt wailed and started a funeral chant, one that mourners usually shout while walking in a circle around the body, slapping their chests hard to show their anguish, sometimes for hours and hours until your throat is in shreds and your legs and chest numb. My aunt didn't move while she chanted, but the volume of her shouts was big enough to fill the whole room, maybe all of Duhok.

Hezni was calmer. My normally emotional brother, who cried when any member of his family was sick and could have been the subject of a book of love poems while he courted Jilan, had become obsessed with the mystery of his own survival. "I don't know why God spared me," he said. "But I know I need to use my life for good." As soon as I saw his wide, friendly tan face and small mustache, I burst into tears. "Don't cry," Hezni said, hugging me. "This is our fate."

I walked over to Saeed's hospital bed. His wounds tormented him, but not as much as the memory of the massacre and the guilt of surviving when so many others had died. Even the people whom ISIS hadn't managed to kill had lost their lives—an entire generation of lost Yazidis like my brothers and me, walking around in the world with nothing in our hearts but the memory of our family and nothing in our heads but bringing ISIS to justice. Saeed had joined the Yazidi division of the peshmerga and was aching to fight.

"Where is my mother?" I cried, embracing him. "No one knows, Nadia," he said. "As soon as we can, we are going to liberate Solagh from Daesh and save her."

Khaled's wounds were worse than Saeed's, even though my half brother had been shot fewer times. Two bullets had shattered his elbow, and he needed an artificial joint, but nothing like that was available in the hospital in Duhok. To this day, his arm just hangs stiff from his body, useless, like a dead tree branch.

———

WHEN I FIRST arrived in Zakho, Hezni was still living near our aunt in the same half-built house he had escaped to from the mountain. My aunt and uncle had been in the process of building a small house for their son and his wife on their property, but they weren't rich, and so they had to build slowly, adding a bit here and there when they had a little extra money to spend. The war with ISIS stopped the construction altogether, and when I arrived, the house was just two bedrooms made of blank concrete, with windows that hadn't been covered and gaps in the seams between the concrete slabs letting in the wind and the dust. I had never been in that house without my mother, and I felt her absence like a missing limb.

I moved into the half-built house with my brothers Hezni and Saoud and my half brothers Walid and Nawaf. After they were released from the hospital, Saeed and Khaled joined us. We tried our best to make it a home. When the aid agency distributed tarps, we used them to cover up the windows, and when they handed out food, we rationed it out carefully and stockpiled what we could in the small room we used as a kitchen. Hezni ran long extension cords from the main house into our rooms and strung bulbs up to the ceilings so we could have light. We bought some caulk to fill in the gaps in the walls. Although we talked endlessly about the war, we rarely mentioned details that would upset one another.

Saeed and Nawaf were the only two unmarried men, and their loneliness was less palpable than my married brothers'. Hezni had not heard from Jilan yet; all we knew was that she was in Hamdaniya with Nisreen. We had no information about Saoud's wife, Shireen, or my half brothers' wives. I told them what I knew about ISIS and what I had seen in Mosul and Hamdaniya, but I was vague about what had happened to me in captivity. I didn't want to make my brothers suffer more by confirming their worst nightmares about what ISIS was doing to Yazidi girls. I didn't ask about the massacre in Kocho because I didn't want to remind Saeed and Khaled about what they had been through. No one wanted to add to another person's despair.

Although inhabited by survivors, the house was a place of misery. My brothers, who had once been so full of life, were like empty bodies, staying awake in the day only because it was impossible to sleep all the time. Because I was the only woman, I was expected to clean and cook, but there was a lot I didn't know how to do. Back home, my older sisters and sisters-in-law did the housework while I studied, and I felt useless and stupid fumbling around the makeshift kitchen and sloppily washing our clothes. My brothers were kind to me and knew that I hadn't learned how to do chores at home, so they helped, but it was still clear that once I learned, this would be my responsibility. My aunt knew that I didn't know how to make bread, and so she made extra to bring to us, but that skill, too, I was expected to pick up. School was a very distant memory.

I had escaped ISIS and was with my family, but still I felt like my life, when I recalled it, if I was lucky enough to grow old, would be just one long chain of miseries. In one misery, I am captured by ISIS, and in the next, I am living a life of total poverty, with nothing, no place to call my own, reliant on others for all our food, with no land and no sheep, no school and just a fraction of my big family, only waiting for the camp to be built and then waiting for the tents in that camp to be replaced with container homes. Then waiting for Kocho to be liberated, which I thought might never happen, and my sisters to be freed and my mother to be rescued in Solagh. I cried every day. Sometimes I cried with my aunt or with my brothers, and sometimes I cried alone in bed. When I dreamed, it was always about being returned to ISIS and having to escape again.

We learned how to make the most of what the aid agencies offered. Once a week big trucks came loaded with sacks of rice and lentils and pasta, as well as some cooking oil and canned tomatoes. We had no pantry or refrigerator, and so sometimes the food we saved would spoil or attract mice, and we had to throw away full sacks of sugar and bulgur until we found an empty oil barrel that we cleaned out and used to store our food. Throwing out the food was painful; without money to buy more, we would just have to eat less until the next truck came through Zakho. When the weather got colder, my aunt gave me some warm clothes, but I didn't have any underwear or bras or socks, and I didn't want to ask for anything, so I made do with what I had.

Hezni's phone rang often, and when it did, he would take the calls outside, away from the rest of us. I was desperate to know what kind of information he was getting, but he would only tell me a little bit, I think because he didn't want to upset me. One day he got a call from Adkee and went out into the yard to talk. When he returned, his eyes were red, as if he had been crying. "She's in Syria," he told us. Somehow she had managed to stay with our nephew, whom she had claimed was her son in Solagh, but she was worried that at any moment ISIS would discover she was lying and take the boy away from her. "I'm trying to find a smuggler in Syria," he told us. "But getting girls from there is even harder than in Iraq, and Adkee doesn't want to leave anyone behind." To make matters worse, the Syrian smuggling networks were developing separately from the Iraqi ones, making it even more difficult for Hezni to get Adkee out.

My aunt was the first person I told my entire story to, including the rape. She wept for me and held me close to her. It was a relief to tell someone, and I stopped worrying that Yazidis would reject me or blame me for what happened. So many of us had been killed or kidnapped by ISIS that those of us who survived, no matter what happened to us, had to come together and try to repair what was left. Still, most of the escaped sabaya were tight-lipped about their time with ISIS, as I had been at first, and I understood why. It was their tragedy and their right not to tell anyone.

Rojian was the first one after me to escape. She arrived at my aunt's house at two in the morning, still wearing the abaya given to her by ISIS. Before I could ask her any questions, she said, "What happened to everyone else?" and Hezni had to tell her the details. Telling was a burden. It was horrible to watch Rojian's face distort when she heard what had happened to our village and our family. The men were confirmed dead, we didn't know what happened to the older women, and most of the girls taken as sabaya were still with ISIS. After this, Rojian collapsed into such a state of sorrow I almost worried that she would take her own life right there at my aunt's house, as Hezni had tried to the month before after finding out about the massacre in Kocho. But she survived her own grief, just as we all had to, and the morning after she arrived, we moved into the refugee camp.

Chapter 10

THE ROAD LEADING TO THE CAMP WAS NARROW AND MADE of dirt. It reminded me of the road into Kocho before they paved it, and when we arrived there that morning, I tried to imagine that I was actually going home. But anything familiar only made it more clear how far away my old life was and just added to my sadness.

From a distance, you could see the camp's hundreds of white container homes spread across the low slopes of northern Iraq like bricks in a wall, each separated by a dirt path that was usually glutted with water from the rain, the showers, or the makeshift kitchens. Fences surrounded the camp—for our own safety, they said—but children had already bent holes where the metal met the ground so that they could more easily reach the outside fields to play soccer. At the camp entrance, larger containers were offices for aid and government workers, as well as a clinic and a classroom.

We moved in December, when it was beginning to get cold in northern Iraq, and even though the half-built house in Zakho offered more protection from the winter, I was looking forward to having a space that I could call my own. The containers were roomy enough, and we had a few next to one another, one that we used as a bedroom, another as a sitting room, and a third as a kitchen.

The camp didn't adapt well to northern Iraq's seasons. When winter came, the walkways between the caravans were sticky with mud, and we struggled not to track it inside. We had water for only one hour a day, and one heater that we shared to try to warm up the container homes. When there was no warmth, the cool air would condense on the walls and drip down onto our beds, so we fell asleep with our heads on damp pillows and woke up to the sharp smell of mildew.

Throughout the camp, people struggled to re-create the lives that were stolen from them. It's comforting to do the same thing you used to do at home, even if it's just going through the motions. In Duhok, in the camp, the routines were the same as they had been in Sinjar. Women cooked and cleaned obsessively, like if they did it well enough, they could be transported back to their villages, wake up their men from the mass graves, and return life to how it had been. Each day when their mops were stashed back in the corner and all the bread was baked, the fact that there was no home and no husband to go home to crashed down on them anew, and they cried, huge wails that shook the walls of our container home. Our houses in Kocho were always full of voices, children playing, and the camp was quiet by comparison. We even missed the sound of family members squabbling over things: those fights would play in our heads like the most beautiful music. We had no way to find work or go to school, so mourning the dead and the missing became our job.

For the men, life in the camp was even harder. There was no work, and they didn't have cars to go to the city for jobs. Their wives, sisters, and mothers were in captivity, and their brothers and fathers dead. Before my brothers joined the peshmerga or the police, we had no money coming in except for the stipends that the Iraqi government and some aid agencies, spearheaded by a Yazidi rights organization called Yazda, which was formed just after the Kocho massacre, were giving to survivors of the genocide. Yazda, which was being led by a group of Yazidis living all over the world who had dropped everything in their lives to help victims of the genocide (and to whom I would eventually devote my own life), was quickly becoming the main source of hope for Yazidis everywhere. We still ran for food when they came to deliver it, and sometimes we missed the trucks. One day they would stop on one side of the camp, and the next day on the other. Sometimes the food seemed rotten, and we would complain that the rice smelled like trash when you cooked it.

When summer came, I decided to take matters into my own hands. I went to work in a nearby field where the farmer, a Kurd, was employing refugees to harvest cantaloupe. "If you work all day, we will serve you dinner," he promised, in addition to the small wage, and so I stayed until the sun was nearly set, picking the heavy melons off their vines. When he served us the meal, though, I nearly gagged. It was the rancid rice from the camp, plain and stinking on our plates. I felt like crying because the farmer saw us this way—that he thought because we were so poor and we lived in the camps, he could feed us anything, and we would be grateful.

We are human! I wanted to tell him. *We had homes, we had a good life. We are not nothing.* But I stayed quiet and ate what I could of the disgusting food.

Back in the field, though, I grew angrier. *I'll finish my work today,* I thought. *But there is no way I'm coming back tomorrow to work for this person.* Some of the other workers started to talk about ISIS. To the refugees who had escaped their villages before the terrorists came, those of us who had been captured were a curiosity, and they were always asking us questions about what life was like under ISIS, as though following the plot of an action movie.

The farmer walked behind us. "Which of you came from Daesh?" he asked, and the others pointed at me. I paused my work. I thought he would say that he was sorry for the way he had treated us, that if he had known there were Islamic State survivors in the camp, he would have been nicer to us. Instead, he wanted to talk about how great the peshmerga were. "Oh, Daesh is going to be finished," he said. "You know how the peshmerga do it. They did a great job, and we lost a lot of people from the peshmerga to free a lot of Iraq."

"Do you know how much we lost?" I couldn't help saying back to him. "Thousands of our people died. They lost their lives because the peshmerga chose to withdraw." The farmer stopped talking and walked away, and a young Yazidi man turned to me, upset. "Please don't say anything like that," he told me. "Just work." When the day ended and I went to tell the Yazidi in charge that I didn't want to work for the farmer anymore, he looked at me angrily. "The farmer told us all not to come back," he said.

I felt so guilty that because of what I had said, everyone had lost their job. Soon, though, it became a funny story that spread throughout the camp. After I left and started telling my story outside Iraq, a friend of mine visited the camp and complained to some of my friends there that I was being too easy on the peshmerga. "Nadia should tell the world what they did to us!" he said, and one of the Yazidis started laughing. "She said that from the beginning, and we were all fired because of it!"

———

DIMAL MADE IT to the camp at four in the morning on January 1, 2015. She still teases me for being asleep when she arrived— "I can't believe you were able to fall asleep while I was running for my life!" she says—but I just hugged her tight. "I stayed up until four in the morning," I tell her. "You were late!" I did stay up as late as I could, until the moment that dizziness took over, and the next thing I knew my older sister was standing over my bed. She had run for hours along the border with Turkey and Syria, and her legs were bleeding where they had scraped the barbed wire on the border fence. It could have been worse, of course: she could have been discovered and shot by a border patrolman or stepped on a land mine.

Having Dimal back felt like a big wound had healed. But we weren't happy. We held on to each other and cried until ten in the morning, then she greeted the stream of guests who came to cry beside her. We didn't get to talk about anyone else until the next morning. That was the hardest moment of Dimal's homecoming—waking up that morning on mattresses next to each other and hearing her ask, her voice hoarse from crying, "Nadia, where is the rest of the family?"

Later that month Adkee also managed to escape. We were frantic with worry—we had received so little information about what had happened to her. Some weeks earlier a woman had escaped Syria and made it to the camp. She told us that she had been with Adkee in Syria. Eager for details, we begged her to tell us everything she knew. "They believed that Adkee was a mother," she told us, "so they would wait before they touched her." Keeping our nephew Miran safe was all Adkee cared about. "She told me that if I promised to take care of Miran, she would kill herself," the woman told us. "I told her to be patient, we will get out of there one day, but she was distraught."

After we heard that, we feared the worst for Adkee. We began to mourn her, my spirited sister who had yelled at the men who told her she couldn't learn to drive, and our sweet nephew. Then out of the blue, Adkee called Hezni's phone. "They are in Afrin!" my brother told us, ecstatic. Afrin is in Kurdish-held Syria and was not part of ISIS. It was being defended by the Kurds in Syria, and I thought since those fighters had helped Yazidis off the mountain, they would certainly help my sister.

Adkee and Miran had escaped Raqqa and been taken in by an Arab shepherd and his family. They stayed with them for a month and two days while they tried to figure out the safest way to get her out of Islamic State territory. The shepherd's daughter was engaged to a man in Afrin, and the family waited until the day of the wedding, when they would have a good explanation for why they were all going up north. Later Hezni told us that he had known Adkee had been with the shepherd's family, but he had kept it to himself because he didn't want to get our hopes up.

Two days after that first phone call from Afrin, Adkee arrived at the camp with Miran in tow. This time I waited up until six in the morning with Dimal. We dreaded having to tell Adkee what had happened to everyone else—those who we knew were dead and those who were missing—but we didn't have to. She figured it out on her own, somehow, and soon Adkee was living with us in our small, mournful world.

It was a miracle that my sisters got out. In the three years since ISIS first came to Sinjar, Yazidis have escaped slavery in extraordinary ways. Some have been helped by sympathetic locals, as I was, while others have had family members or the government pay money, sometimes huge sums, to smugglers or directly to the Islamic State member, buying the girl back from him. Each girl cost about five thousand dollars to get out, with a larger amount—what Hezni would describe as "the cost of a new car"—going to the head of the operation, who used his connections throughout Arab and Kurdish Iraq to coordinate the rescue. The money was spread among the many middlemen—drivers, smugglers, document forgers—that it would take to free one single girl.

Every story of escape is incredible. One girl from Kocho was taken to Raqqa, the Islamic State's capital in Syria, where she was held with a large group of women in a wedding hall to await distribution. Desperate, she tried to ignite a propane canister with a lighter and burn the hall down but was discovered before she could. Then she forced herself to vomit, and when an Islamic State militant told her to go outside, she and a group of girls ran into the dark fields surrounding the hall. Eventually they were turned in by a passing farmer, but she was lucky. Weeks later the wife of the man who had bought her helped coordinate her escape out of Syria. Soon after, the wife died of appendicitis; apparently there wasn't a surgeon in the Islamic State capable of saving her.

Jilan was in captivity for over two years before Hezni was able to get her out with the most elaborate and risky plan I've heard yet. Jilan's captor's wife had become weary of her husband's abuse of Yazidi girls, and she called Hezni, offering to help. Her husband was a high-ranking Islamic State member and a target for the anti-ISIS coalition that was bearing down on the caliphate. "You will have to get your husband killed," Hezni told her. "That's the only way." She agreed.

Hezni put the wife in touch with a Kurdish commander who was working with the Americans to strike Islamic State targets. "Tell him when your husband leaves the house," Hezni instructed her, and the next day the militant's car was hit in an air strike. At first, the wife didn't believe Hezni that her husband was dead. "Why isn't anyone talking about it, then?" she said. She was scared that her husband had escaped and would discover what she was doing. She wanted to see his body. "It's too destroyed," Hezni told her. "The car has basically melted away."

Now the women had to wait for further instruction, and they had only a small window in which to get Jilan to safety. After two or three days, it was confirmed that the militant was in fact dead, and other Islamic State members came to the house to get Jilan and take her to a new owner. When they knocked, the wife came to the door. "Our sabiyya was in the car with my husband," she told them, trying not to let her voice tremble. "She died, too." Satisfied, the militants left, and when they were out of sight, Jilan and the wife were smuggled to an Iraqi Army outpost and, eventually, to Kurdistan. A few hours after they left, their house was bombed as well. "As far as Daesh is concerned, they are all dead," Hezni told me.

Others were not so fortunate. I learned that they had found a

mass grave in Solagh in December 2015, a few months after I left
the refugee camp and moved to Germany with Dimal, part of a
German government program to help Yazidi victims of ISIS enslavement. Early in the morning I checked my phone. It was full
of messages from Adkee and Hezni. They called often to update
me on family who were still there, particularly Saeed, who had
gotten his wish and was fighting in Sinjar with a newly formed
Yazidi unit of the KDP peshmerga. "Saeed is close to Solagh,"
Adkee told me when I called her. "Soon we will know what happened there."

Dimal and I were supposed to go to a German lesson that day,
but we couldn't move. All day we sat in our apartment, waiting for
news. I got in touch with a Kurdish journalist who was covering
the fight to retake Solagh, and between him, Saeed, and Adkee,
my phone barely stopped ringing all day. Other than watch the
phone, Dimal and I prayed for our mother to be found alive.

Sometime in the afternoon, the journalist called. His voice was
low, and I knew right away he had bad news. "We found a mass
grave," he said. "It's near the institute, and it looks like there are
about eighty bodies, women." I listened to him and put down my
phone. I couldn't bear to be the one to tell Dimal or to call Adkee
or Hezni and say that our mother, who had survived so much for
so many years, was dead. My hands were shaking. Then Dimal's
phone buzzed; she had a message from our family. Everyone was
screaming.

I couldn't move. I called Saeed, and he cried as soon as he heard
my voice. "None of my work here has mattered," he said. "I've
been fighting for one year, and we have found nothing, no one."
I begged Hezni to let me come back to the camp for the funeral,
but he said no. "We don't have her body," he said. "The military is
still in Solagh. Even if you came, they wouldn't let you anywhere
near the grave. It's not safe for you," he said. I had already begun
my work as an activist, and ISIS threatened me every day.

After my mother's death was confirmed, I clung to the hope that Kathrine, my niece and my best friend, who was so kind and loved by everyone who met her, would be able to escape and we would be reunited. I needed her with me if I was going to survive the rest of my life without my mother. Hezni, who loved his brother's daughter like his own, had been struggling for months to find a way to get Kathrine to safety, and failing. Kathrine had tried to escape many times—from Hamdaniya and from Mosul—but she had always failed. Hezni kept a voicemail from her on his phone. In it, Kathrine begs my brother: "This time, please rescue me. Don't let them keep me—save me this time." Hezni would play it and cry, vowing to try.

In 2015, we had a breakthrough. Hezni got a phone call from a garbage collector in a small town outside Kirkuk that had been an Islamic State stronghold since the early days of the war. "I was collecting trash from a house belonging to Dr. Islam," he told my brother. "A girl named Kathrine came out. She asked me to call you to tell you she was alive." The garbage collector was scared that ISIS would find out he had made the call and told Hezni not to contact him again. "I won't go back to that house," he said.

Escaping would be very hard. The town is home to at least a hundred thousand Sunni Arabs, and Dr. Islam was now high-ranking within ISIS. But Hezni had a contact in the town and, using the messaging app Telegram, was able to reach Kathrine. The contact told Kathrine to go to a hospital. "There is a pharmacy nearby," he said. "I'll be inside holding a yellow file in my hands. When you see me, don't talk to me, just walk back to the house where you are being held, and I'll watch to see where you are going so I know where it is." Kathrine agreed. She was almost to the hospital when it was hit in an air strike, and she was so terrified, she immediately went back to the house without meeting the contact.

Next, Hezni tried going through some Arabs who didn't support ISIS and were trapped in the same town. They owned a house in a nearby village that they could reach without being stopped at major checkpoints and agreed to hide Kathrine there. Through them, Hezni was able to get messages to and from Kathrine, who said that after the air strike on the hospital, they had moved to a different house in the city. She described it to the new contact, who then took his wife to the neighborhood, knocking on doors, saying they were looking to rent a house nearby. When he knocked on the house where Kathrine was being held, another sabiyya opened the door. It was Almas, a nine-year-old girl from Kocho. Behind her he could see my niece and Lamia, my friend Walaa's sister. All three were being held captive by Dr. Islam. "Tomorrow morning, if there are no militants in the house, hang a blanket from the window," the contact whispered to Kathrine. "After nine-thirty a.m., if I see the blanket, I will know it is safe to come back." Kathrine was scared, but she agreed.

That morning he drove slowly by the house. A blanket hung out of the window, and he got out of his car and knocked on the door. The three Yazidi sabaya—Kathrine, Lamia, and Almas—ran out and got into his car. After the girls were safely in the nearby village, the man called Hezni, and he wired him some money.

Three days later Hezni found smugglers who, for ten thousand dollars, were willing to take the three girls, and the Arab family who had helped them, to safety. But without the right papers, they would have to walk across the Kurdish border at night. "We will take them as far as the river," the smugglers told Hezni. "After that another guy will take them to you." At midnight the first smuggler called Hezni and told him that he had made the handoff. My family prepared for Kathrine to come to the camp.

Hezni waited by his phone all night, expecting the call telling him that Kathrine had made it into Kurdish territory. He was desperate to see her. But the phone never rang that night. Instead, at about one-thirty in the afternoon the next day, a Kurdish man called and asked if Kathrine, Lamia, and Almas were our people. "Where are they?" Hezni asked.

"Lamia, she is badly wounded," the man told Hezni. They had stepped on an IED while trying to cross into Kurdistan, and it had exploded beneath them. Most of Lamia's body was covered with third-degree burns. "Bless the souls of the other two, they passed," he finished. Hezni dropped the phone. He felt as if someone had shot him.

I had already left Iraq by the time this happened. Hezni had called me after they made it to the first smuggler's house and told me that Kathrine was safe. I was ecstatic at the thought of seeing my niece again, but that night I had a terrible dream. I dreamed that I saw my cousin Sulaiman standing next to one of the generators that supplied Kocho with electricity. In the dream, I was walking with my brother Massoud and my mother, and when we got close to Sulaiman, we saw that he was dead and that animals were eating his body. I woke up in a sweat, and in the morning I called Hezni. "What happened?" I asked, and he told me.

This time Hezni agreed that I should come back to Iraq for the funeral. We arrived at four a.m. in the Erbil airport and went first to see Lamia in the hospital. She couldn't talk, her face was so badly burned. Next we went to Kirkuk to see the Arab family who had helped Kathrine and the others escape. We wanted to find Kathrine's body so that we could bury her properly, in the Yazidi tradition, but the family couldn't help us. "When they stepped on the bomb, she and Almas immediately died," they told us. "We carried Lamia to the hospital, but we couldn't take the bodies, too. They are with ISIS now."

Hezni was beyond consoling. He felt that he had failed his niece. He still listens to her pleading voicemail, torturing himself. "*Save me this time*," she says. I can picture Kathrine's hopeful face when I hear it and Hezni's face, too, covered in tears.

We drove to the refugee camp. It looked the same as when I had first moved there with my brothers, nearly two years before, although people had made their containers more like homes, hanging tarps to create shaded outdoor spaces and decorating the insides with family photos. Some people had jobs now, and there were more cars parked between the container homes.

As we got closer, I could see Adkee, my half sisters, and my aunts standing together outside. They were pulling at their hair and holding up their hands to the sky, praying and crying. Kathrine's mother, Asmar, had been crying so hard the doctor worried that she would go blind. I heard the sound of the funeral chant before we passed through the camp gates, and when we got to my family's container, I joined in, walking in a circle with my sisters, slapping my chest and wailing. I felt all the wounds of my captivity and escape open anew. I couldn't believe that I would never see Kathrine or my mother again. That was the moment I knew that my family was truly destroyed.

Chapter 11

YAZIDIS BELIEVE THAT TAWUSI MELEK FIRST CAME TO earth to connect human beings to God in a beautiful valley in northern Iraq called Lalish. As often as we can, we travel there to pray and reconnect with God and his Angel. Lalish is remote and tranquil; to get to it, you drive along a narrow road that winds through a green valley, past the conical roofs of smaller tombs and temples, and up a hill to the village. During important holidays, like our New Year, the road is filled with Yazidis making the pilgrimage, and the center is like a festival. At other times of year, it is quiet, with only a handful of Yazidis praying in the dimly lit temples.

Lalish has to be kept pristine. Visitors must take off their shoes and walk barefoot even through the streets, and every day a group of volunteers helps to maintain the temples and the temple grounds. They sweep the courtyards and trim the holy trees; they wash the walkways; and a few times a day they walk through the dim stone temples to light lamps fueled by a sweet-smelling oil made from Lalish's olive trees.

We kiss the door frames of temples before entering, careful not to step on the entranceway, which we also kiss, and inside we tie colorful silk into knots, each knot representing a wish and a prayer. On important religious occasions, the Baba Sheikh visits Lalish to wait for pilgrims in the main temple and prays alongside them and blesses them. That temple is the tomb of Sheikh Adi, a man who spread the Yazidi religion in the twelfth century and is one of our holiest figures. The White Spring runs through Lalish. We baptize ourselves outside where the spring pools into marble cisterns. And in the humid, dark caves beneath Sheikh Adi's tomb, where condensation drips off the rough walls, we splash ourselves with water in prayer at the site where the spring splits and ends.

The best time to go is in April, around the Yazidi New Year, when the seasons turn and new rain fills the holy White Spring. In April the stones are just cool enough underneath our feet to keep us moving, and the water is cool enough to wake us up. The valley is fresh and beautiful, becoming new again.

Lalish is a four-hour drive from Kocho, and traveling there—paying for gas and food and taking people away from their work in the fields, not to mention the animals many families sacrificed—was too expensive for us to go often, but I would often dream about making the trip. Our house was full of photos of Lalish, and on the TV you could watch programs about the valley and the holy sheikhs who lived there, and watch pilgrims dancing together. Unlike Kocho, Lalish is full of water, and that water feeds the trees and flowers that color the valley. The temples are made of ancient stone and decorated with symbols taken from our stories. Most important, it was in Lalish that Tawusi Melek first made contact with the world and gave human beings a purpose and a connection to God. Even though we can pray anywhere, prayer in the temples of Lalish is the most meaningful.

When I was sixteen years old, I went to Lalish to be baptized. I could hardly wait for the day to come, and in the weeks beforehand I listened to every word my mother said. She told us to be respectful of the other pilgrims and of every object in the valley, and that we were never to wear shoes or leave a mess. "Don't spit, don't curse, don't behave badly," she cautioned us. "Don't step on the entranceways to the temples. You kiss them."

Even Saeed, the mischievous one, listened carefully to her directions. "This is where you will be baptized," she told me, pointing to a picture of a stone cistern dug into the ground where a trickle of fresh water from the White Spring ran in ribbons down the main road. "And here is where you will pray for your family." I never felt like there was anything wrong with me because I wasn't yet baptized at sixteen; it didn't mean that I wasn't yet a "real" Yazidi. We were poor, so God wouldn't judge us for having to delay the trip. But I was delighted that it was finally happening.

I was baptized in the White Spring along with a few of my siblings, both boys and girls. A woman, one of the guardians of Lalish, dipped a small aluminum bowl into the stream and poured the cool water over my head, then left me to splash more onto my face and head while I prayed. Then the woman wrapped a piece of white cloth around my head, and I dropped a little bit of money, an offering, on a stone nearby. Kathrine was baptized at the same time. "I won't disappoint you," I whispered to God. "I won't go backward. I will go forward and stay on this path."

When ISIS came to Sinjar, we all worried about what would happen to Lalish. We worried that they would destroy our temples, as they had so many others. Yazidis fleeing ISIS took refuge in the holy city, guarded by the temple servants and the prayers of the Baba Sheikh and Baba Chawish. The Yazidis who fled their homes for the holy valley were on edge, mentally destroyed and physically exhausted by the massacres. They were certain that at any moment ISIS would storm the temples.

One day one of these fleeing Yazidis, a young father, was sitting in the entranceway to the temple courtyard with his son. He hadn't been sleeping: all he could think about was the people who died and the women who were kidnapped. The weight of these memories was tremendous. He took his gun out of his belt, and before anyone could stop him he shot himself, right there in the temple entrance beside his son. Hearing the shot and assuming it was ISIS, the Yazidis living there began fleeing into the Kurdistan region. Only the servants and the Baba Chawish stayed behind, to clean up the dead man's blood, perform the burial, and wait for whatever came next. They were prepared to die if ISIS came. "What do I have if this place is destroyed?" Baba Chawish said. But the terrorists never made it to the valley. God protected it.

After the massacres, as women were slowly escaping from Islamic State captivity, we wondered what our next trip to Lalish would be like. We needed the temples and the solace they offered, but at first no one was sure how the escaped sabaya would be treated by the holy men who lived there. We had converted to Islam, and most of us had lost our virginity. Maybe it didn't matter that both had been forced on us against our will. Growing up, we knew these to be sins worthy of expulsion from Yazidi society.

We shouldn't have underestimated our religious leaders. In late August, when the shock of the massacres was still new, they held meetings trying to determine the best response. Quickly they came to a decision. Former sabaya, they announced, would be welcomed back to society and not judged for what had happened to us. We were not to be considered Muslim because the religion had been forced upon us, and because we had been raped, we were victims, not ruined women. The Baba Sheikh met personally with escaped survivors, offering guidance and reassuring us that we could remain Yazidis, and then in September, our religious leaders wrote a dictum telling all Yazidis that what had happened to us was not our fault and that if they were faithful, they should welcome sabaya back to the community with open arms. I have never loved my community more than in that moment of compassion.

Still, nothing the Baba Sheikh said or did could make us feel completely normal again. We all felt broken. Women went to great lengths to try to purify themselves. Many survivors underwent "re-virginization" surgery, repairing the hymen in the hope of erasing the memory and the stigma of the rape. In the camp a couple of doctors treating survivors offered that service to us, saying casually to "come for the treatment," as though it were just a normal checkup. "It will only take twenty minutes," they told us.

I was curious, so I went with some of the girls to the clinic. "If you want to have your virginity back, it's just a simple procedure," the doctors said. Some of the girls I knew decided to do it, but I said no. How could a "simple procedure" erase the times Hajji Salman raped me, or when he had allowed his guards to rape me as punishment for trying to escape? The damage from those attacks wasn't to one body part, or even just to my body, and it was nothing a surgery could repair. Still, I understood why other girls would do it. We were desperate for any kind of solace, and if it helped them imagine a normal future in which they were married and had a family, then I was happy for them.

I had a difficult time thinking about my own future. When I was young in Kocho, my world was so small and so full of love. I had to worry only about my family, and everything told me that things were getting better for all of us. Now even if all of us girls survived and worked hard to recover, where were the Yazidi boys who would marry us? They were in mass graves in Sinjar. Our entire society had been nearly destroyed, and Yazidi girls were going to have very different lives from what we had imagined as children. We weren't looking for happiness, just to survive and, if we could, to do something meaningful with the lives we had been so randomly allowed to keep.

A few months into my stay at the refugee camp, I was approached by activists, one of whom asked me for my abaya. "I'm collecting evidence of the genocide," she said. "One day I want to open a museum." Another, after listening to my story, wondered if I would feel comfortable going to the U.K. to tell officials what had happened to me. I said yes, not knowing how much that one trip would change my life.

The last few months at the camp were spent preparing to go to Germany. Dimal and I were both emigrating, but Adkee refused. "I won't ever leave Iraq," she told us. She was always stubborn, and I envied her. Germany promised safety, school, a new life. But Iraq would always be home.

We had been through piles of paperwork to prepare for the move and had gone to Baghdad to get our passports made. It was the first time I had ever been to Iraq's capital and also my first time in an airplane. I stayed there for twelve days, every day going to a different office—to be fingerprinted, to have photos taken, to get vaccinated against various strange diseases. It seemed like an endless procedure, and then one day in September, we were told it was almost time to go.

They took us to Erbil and gave us each some money to buy clothes. Dimal and I wept saying goodbye to everyone in the camp, especially Adkee. I thought of Hezni, so many years ago, trying to sneak into Germany, thinking that if he made money— real money, the kind you can make in Europe—Jilan's family would have no choice but to let them marry. He had been sent back, and here I was with a ticket paid for by the government. And it was the hardest thing I had ever done.

Before leaving for Germany, we went to Lalish. Dozens of former sabaya flooded the streets of the holy village, crying and praying, dressed in mourning black. Dimal and I kissed the door frame of Sheikh Adi's temple and tied the colorful silk fabric into knots, each knot a prayer—for the safe return of everyone who was alive; for happiness in the afterlife to those, like our mother, who had died; for Kocho to be liberated; and for ISIS to have to answer for what they did to us. We splashed the cool water from the White Spring onto our faces and prayed to Tawusi Melek harder than we ever had.

Lalish was serene that day, and while we were there, the Baba Chawish came out to meet the group. The holy man is tall and thin, with a long beard and kind, inquisitive eyes that make people open up in his presence. As he sat with his legs folded underneath him in the courtyard of Sheikh Adi's tomb, his white robes fluttered in the breeze, and the thick smoke from the green tobacco he had packed into his wooden pipe floated over the large crowd of women who went to greet him.

We knelt in front of him, and he kissed our heads and asked us questions. "What happened to you?" he wanted to know, and we told him that we had been captured by ISIS but escaped and were now on our way to Germany. "Good," he said in a soft, sad voice. It was painful for him to see so many Yazidis leaving our homeland in Iraq. The community was dwindling before his eyes, but he knew we had to move on.

He asked us more questions. Where are you from? How long were you with ISIS? What was the camp like? And then at the end, when his pipe was nearly empty and the sun was lower in the sky, he turned to us and asked, simply, "Who have you lost?"

Then he sat and listened closely as each of the women, even the ones who had been too shy to speak before, recited the names of their family and friends, their neighbors and children and parents, the dead and the missing. Their answers seemed to go on for hours, as the air grew cooler and the stone on the temple walls darkened in the fading light, Yazidi names listed in an endless chorus, stretching out into the sky to where God could hear them, and when it was my turn I said: Jalo, Pise, Massoud, Khairy, and Elias, my brothers. Malik and Hani, my nephews. Mona, Jilan, and Smaher, my brother's wives. Kathrine and Nisreen, my nieces. Hajji, my half brother. So many who were taken and escaped. My father, who wasn't alive to save us. My mother, Shami, wherever she is.

Epilogue

I N NOVEMBER 2015, A YEAR AND THREE MONTHS AFTER ISIS came to Kocho, I left Germany for Switzerland to speak to a United Nations forum on minority issues. It was the first time I would tell my story in front of a large audience. I had been up most of the night before with Nisreen, the activist who had organized the trip, thinking about what to say. I wanted to talk about everything—the children who died of dehydration fleeing ISIS, the families still stranded on the mountain, the thousands of women and children who remained in captivity, and what my brothers saw at the site of the massacre. I was only one of hundreds of thousands of Yazidi victims. My community was scattered, living as refugees inside and outside of Iraq, and Kocho was still occupied by ISIS. There was so much the world needed to hear about what was happening to Yazidis.

The first part of the journey was by train through the dark German woods. The trees passed by in a blur close to my window. I was frightened by the forest, which is so different from the valleys and fields of Sinjar, and glad that I was riding by it, not wandering between the trees. Still, it was beautiful, and I was starting to like my new home. Germans had welcomed us to their country; I heard stories of ordinary citizens greeting the trains and airplanes carrying fleeing Syrians and Iraqis. In Germany we were hopeful that we could become a part of society and not just live on the edge of it. It was harder for Yazidis in other countries. Some refugees had arrived in places where it was clear they weren't wanted, no matter what kind of horrors they were escaping. Other Yazidis were trapped in Iraq, desperate for the opportunity to leave, and that waiting was another kind of suffering. Some countries decided to keep refugees out altogether, which made me furious. There was no good reason to deny innocent people a safe place to live. I wanted to say all this to the UN that day.

I wanted to tell them that so much more needed to be done. We needed to establish a safe zone for religious minorities in Iraq; to prosecute ISIS—from the leaders down to the citizens who had supported their atrocities—for genocide and crimes against humanity; and to liberate all of Sinjar. Women and girls who escaped from ISIS needed help to rejoin and rebuild society, and their abuse needed to be added to the list of Islamic State war crimes. Yazidism should be taught in schools from Iraq to the United States, so that people understood the value of preserving an ancient religion and protecting the people who follow it, no matter how small the community. Yazidis, along with other religious and ethnic minorities, are what once made Iraq a great country.

They had only given me three minutes to talk, though, and Nisreen urged me to keep it simple. "Tell your own story," she said, sipping tea in my apartment. That was a terrifying idea. I knew that if my story were to have any impact, I would have to be as honest as I could stand to be. I would have to tell the audience about Hajji Salman and the times he raped me, the terrifying night at the Mosul checkpoint, and all the abuse I witnessed. Deciding to be honest was one of the hardest decisions I have ever made, and also the most important.

I shook as I read my speech. As calmly as I could, I talked about how Kocho had been taken over and girls like me had been taken as sabaya. I told them about how I had been raped and beaten repeatedly and how I eventually escaped. I told them about my brothers who had been killed. They listened quietly, and afterward a Turkish woman came up to me. She was crying. "My brother Ali was killed," she told me. "Our whole family is in shock because of it. I don't know how someone can handle losing six brothers all at once."

"It is very hard," I said. "But there are families who lost even more than us."

When I returned to Germany I told Nisreen that any time they needed me, I would go anywhere and do anything I could to help. I had no idea that soon I would partner with the Yazidi activists running Yazda, and begin a new life. I know now that I was born in the heart of the crimes committed against me.

———

AT FIRST OUR new lives in Germany felt insignificant compared to those of the people living through war in Iraq. Dimal and I moved into a small two-bedroom apartment with two of our cousins, decorating it with photos of the people we had lost or left behind. At night I slept beneath large color photos of my mother and Kathrine. We wore necklaces that spelled out the names of the dead and each day came together to weep for them and to pray to Tawusi Melek for the safe return of the missing. Every night I dreamed about Kocho, and every morning I woke up and remembered that Kocho, as I knew it, no longer existed. It's a strange, hollow feeling. Longing for a lost place makes you feel like you have also disappeared. I have seen many beautiful countries in my travels as an activist, but nowhere I wanted to live more than Iraq.

We went to German classes and to the hospital to make sure we were healthy. Some of us tried the therapy sessions they offered, which were almost impossible to endure. We cooked our food and did the chores we had grown up doing, cleaning and baking bread, this time in a small portable metal oven that Dimal set up in the living room. But without the truly time-consuming tasks like milking sheep or farming, or the social lives that come with living in a small, tight-knit village or school, we had too many empty hours. When I first got to Germany, I begged Hezni all the time to let me come back, but he told me to give Germany a chance. He said I had to stay, that eventually I would have a life there, but I wasn't sure I believed him.

Soon enough, I met Murad Ismael. Along with a group of Yazidis living around the world—including Hadi Pir, Ahmed Khudida, Abid Shamdeen, and Haider Elias, the former translator for the U.S. military who had stayed on the phone with my brother, Jalo, almost until the moment of his death—Murad had cofounded Yazda, a group fighting tirelessly for Yazidis. When I first met him I was still uncertain about what my new life would be like. I wanted to help, and to feel useful, but I didn't know how. But when Murad told me about Yazda and the work they were doing—particularly helping to free and then advocate for women and girls who had been enslaved by ISIS—I could see my future more clearly.

As soon as these Yazidis heard that ISIS had come into Sinjar they left their normal lives to help us back in Iraq. Murad had been studying geophysics in Houston when the genocide started; others were teachers or social workers who dropped everything to help us. He told me about a sleepless two weeks spent in a small hotel room near Washington, D.C., where he and a group including Haider and Hadi spent every moment fielding calls from Yazidis in Iraq, trying to help them to safety. Often, they succeeded. Sometimes they didn't. They had tried to save Kocho, he told me. They had called everyone they could think of in Erbil and Baghdad. They made suggestions based on their time working with the American military (Murad and Hadi has also been translators during the occupation) and tracked ISIS on every road and through every village. When they failed to save us they vowed to do whatever they could to help anyone who survived and to get us justice. They wore their sorrows on their bodies—Haider's back aches constantly and Murad's face is lined with exhaustion—and in spite of that, I wanted to be just like them. After I met Murad, I started to become the person I am today. Although the mourning never stopped, our lives in Germany began to feel significant again.

When I was with ISIS, I felt powerless. If I had possessed any strength at all when my mother was torn from me, I would have protected her. If I could have stopped the terrorists from selling me or raping me, I would have. When I think back to my own escape—the unlocked door, the quiet yard, Nasser and his family in the neighborhood full of Islamic State sympathizers—I shiver at how easily it could have gone wrong. I think there was a reason God helped me escape, and a reason I met the activists with Yazda, and I don't take my freedom for granted. The terrorists didn't think that Yazidi girls would be able to leave them, or that we would have the courage to tell the world every detail of what they did to us. We defy them by not letting their crimes go unanswered. Every time I tell my story, I feel that I am taking some power away from the terrorists.

Since that first trip to Geneva, I have told my story to thousands of people—politicians and diplomats, filmmakers and journalists, and countless ordinary people who became interested in Iraq after ISIS took over. I have begged Sunni leaders to more strongly denounce ISIS publicly; they have so much power to stop the violence. I have worked alongside all the men and women with Yazda to help survivors like me who have to live every day with what we have been through, as well as to convince the world to recognize what happened to the Yazidis as a genocide and to bring ISIS to justice.

Other Yazidis have done the same with the same mission: to ease our suffering and keep what is left of our community alive.

Our stories, as hard as they are to hear, have made a difference. Over the past few years, Canada has decided to let in more Yazidi refugees; the UN officially recognized what ISIS did to the Yazidis as a genocide; governments have begun discussing whether to establish a safe zone for religious minorities in Iraq; and most important, we have lawyers determined to help us. Justice is all Yazidis have now, and every Yazidi is part of the struggle.

Back in Iraq, Adkee, Hezni, Saoud, and Saeed fight in their own ways. They stayed in the camp—Adkee refused to go to Germany with the other women—and when I talk to them, I miss them so much I can barely stand. Every day is a struggle for the Yazidis in the camps, and still they do whatever they can to help the whole community. They hold demonstrations against ISIS and petition the Kurds and Baghdad to do more. When a mass grave is uncovered or a girl dies trying to escape, it is the refugees in the camp who bear the burden of the news first and arrange the funeral. Each container home is full of people praying for loved ones to be returned to them.

Every Yazidi refugee tries to cope with the mental and physical trauma of what they have been through and works to keep our community intact. People who, just a few years ago, were farmers, students, merchants, and housewives have become religious scholars determined to spread knowledge about Yazidism, teachers working in the small container homes used as camp classrooms, and human rights activists like me. All we want is to keep our culture and religion alive and to bring ISIS to justice for their crimes. I am proud of all we have done as a community to fight back. I have always been proud to be Yazidi.

As lucky as I am to be safe in Germany, I can't help but envy those who stayed behind in Iraq. My siblings are closer to home, eating the Iraqi food I miss so much and living next to people they know, not strangers. If they go to town, they can speak to shopkeepers and minivan drivers in Kurdish. When the peshmerga allow us into Solagh, they will be able to visit my mother's grave. We call one another on the phone and leave messages all day. Hezni tells me about his work helping girls escape, and Adkee tells me about life in the camp. Most of the stories are bitter and sad, but sometimes my lively sister makes me laugh so hard that I roll off my couch. I ache for Iraq.

In late May 2017, I received news from the camp that Kocho had been liberated from ISIS. Saeed had been among the members of the Yazidi unit of the Hashd al-Shaabi, a group of Iraqi armed militias, who had gone in, and I was happy for him that he had gotten his wish and become a fighter. Kocho was not safe; there were still Islamic State militants there, fighting, and those who left had planted IEDs everywhere before they ran, but I was determined to go back. Hezni agreed, and I flew from Germany to Erbil and then traveled to the camp.

I didn't know what it would feel like to see Kocho, the place where we were separated and where my brothers were killed. I was with some family, including Dimal, and Murad (by now, he and others from Yazda were like family) and when it was safe enough to go, we traveled as a group, taking a long route to avoid the fighting. The village was empty. The windows in the school had been broken and, inside, we saw what was left of a dead body. My house had been looted—even the wood had been stripped off the roof—and anything left behind was burned. The album of bridal photos was a pile of ashes. We cried so hard we fell onto the floor. Still, in spite of the destruction, the moment I walked through my front door I knew it was my home. For a moment I felt the way I had before ISIS came, and when they told me it was time to leave I begged them to let me stay just an hour more. I vowed to myself that no matter what, when December comes and it is time for Yazidis to fast in order to draw closer to God and Tawusi Melek, who gave us all life, I will be in Kocho.

———

A LITTLE LESS than a year since giving that first speech in Geneva—and about a year before returning to Kocho—I went to New York with some members of Yazda, including Abid, Murad, Ahmed, Haider, Hadi, and Maher Ghanem, where the United Nations named me a Goodwill Ambassador for the Dignity of Survivors of Human Trafficking. Again, I would be expected to talk about what happened to me in front of a large group of people. It never gets easier to tell your story. Each time you speak it, you relive it. When I tell someone about the checkpoint where the men raped me, or the feeling of Hajji Salman's whip across the blanket as I lay under it, or the darkening Mosul sky while I searched the neighborhood for some sign of help, I am transported back to those moments and all their terror. Other Yazidis are pulled back into these memories, too. Sometimes even the Yazda members who have listened to my story countless times weep when I tell it; it's their story, too.

Still, I have become used to giving speeches, and large audiences no longer intimidate me. My story, told honestly and matter-of-factly, is the best weapon I have against terrorism, and I plan on using it until those terrorists are put on trial. There is still so much that needs to be done. World leaders and particularly Muslim religious leaders need to stand up and protect the oppressed.

I gave my brief address. When I finished telling my story, I continued to talk. I told them I wasn't raised to give speeches. I told them that every Yazidi wants ISIS prosecuted for genocide, and that it was in their power to help protect vulnerable people all over the world. I told them that I wanted to look the men who raped me in the eye and see them brought to justice. More than anything else, I said, I want to be the last girl in the world with a story like mine.